MIREILLE JOHNSTON

THE FRENCH FAMILY FEAST

Drawings by Rodica Prato

SIMON AND SCHUSTER

New York • *London* • *Toronto* • *Sydney* • *Tokyo*

SIMON AND SCHUSTER
Simon & Schuster Building
Rockefeller Center
1230 Avenue of the Americas
New York, New York 10020

10   9   8   7   6   5   4   3   2   1

Library of Congress Cataloging in Publication Data

Johnston, Mireille.
    The French family feast / Mireille Johnston.
        p.   cm.
    Includes index.
        1. Cookery, French.   I. Title.
TX719.J545   1988
641.5944—dc19
ISBN 0-671-64998-1   88-28333
                                      CIP

To Tom, Margaret-Brooke, Zabette, and all our friends who have shared so many heated conversations, gargantuan meals, and lazy siestas, I recall what Napoleon told his faithful Marshal MacMahon: "Let us continue."

I wish to thank my editor, Carole Lalli, wise, inspired, and always full of cheer. It has been a joy to work with her in the making of this book. And to Charles Pierce my thanks for his helpful rigor.

Et que vive la fête! to M. F. K. Fisher who knows one when she sees one.

CONTENTS

INTRODUCTION 15

APPETIZERS • 41

GREAT SUPERDISHES • 77

DESSERTS • 263

ACCOMPANIMENTS • 297

INDEX • 305

INTRODUCTION

It has been proven that only around a good table do people reconcile and push away the clouds of indifference dissipated by the sun of good food.

— GRIMOD DE LA REYNIÈRE

The true essentials of a Feast are only fun and food.
— OLIVER WENDELL HOLMES

WHEN one evokes the good life, there is nothing quite as heartwarming and reassuring as the thought of one's friends and relatives gathering around a full table. There is a communion of more than bodies when people share a meal. Indeed, if the destiny of nations depends on what and how they eat, the same is true of individuals.

What is potentially present in most people—love, humor, solidarity—can most of the time be exalted by a good meal shared with gusto. You address yourself to the sunny side of your friends and, trying to please eyes and palate, you may just reach the soul in the process. Inspiring food heightens inspired conversation and a heady blend of warmth and joy. It gives meaning and direction to the day, reality to the world.

We all have seen it again and again: As soon as a festive dish appears—a Thanksgiving turkey, a soupe au pistou, a Christmas pudding, a cassoulet—suddenly everything falls into place around the table. One rediscovers the simple joys of impatience and curiosity with the first bite of food, and then delight, passionate discussions, and soon a sense of well-being. The meal creates a bond, an exchange, an interaction of energies, a true connection. It is a truce when everybody around the table forgets hardships, evokes golden times, and moves toward new friendships. Among contented sighs, laughter, glowing eyes, and the clinking of crystal and plates, the generosity and the concentration of energy take everyone around the table back to the simple joys of childhood.

The French did not invent feasts shared around good food, but over the centuries they have turned them into a national art. With love, care, and intuition they have learned to make each guest feel like the child of the house, pampered, secure, and happy. Sunday meals in France are still very much a part of family ritual and are often a time one feels that food is the only thing agreed upon by impatient children, fragile grandparents, opinionated cousins, patronizing uncles, sophisticated gourmets, and good-natured gourmands. There have always been many reasons in France to come together to celebrate, from religious and secular feasts to special days for tradesmen and artisans: Saint Thomas for the cobblers, Saint Joseph for the carpenters, Saint Catherine for the spinsters, Saint Barbara for the firemen, Saint Anthony for the absent-minded—not to mention all of the births, weddings, and anniversaries shared. And should this abundance of festive opportunities in a family ever seem insufficient, one could always recall how Alice in Wonderland discovered we each have 364 unbirthdays a year, and we are free to celebrate them as well.

Cuisine started at home, of course. Eating out is a modern notion that began after the 1789 French revolution when the aristocracy emigrated and their chefs decided to open their own establishments. It was and still can be strange, wonderful, exotic, and exciting to eat out, but unfortunately one often visits a restaurant as if it were a museum, a library, or a cathedral. Even if today, at long last, inventiveness at all cost and minimal art in food seem no longer the rage, most restaurant menus are still virtuoso exercises where pedantic skills prevail.

So good entertaining in France means home cooking. Lusty "real food," no-nonsense *cuisine de mère* has taste and soul and meaning, and remains a civilizing force, the cement of our social lives. This is why it is no thin compliment to be invited to share a family meal and all the ritual it implies.

Sometimes, forgetting that the best might be the enemy of the good, inspired and challenged by a famous chef's repertory, a humble citizen takes a deep breath, invites a group of friends, and attempts single-handedly to prepare at home one of the chef's creations. The result is frequently a fussy, disheartening compromise because it is not realistic to think one can shop, trim, cut, cook, and serve a major extravaganza while remaining the lovely, witty friend that people came to visit in the first place. Without the chef's professional staff, equipment, and daily practice, this is an unequal battle that promises little real satisfaction for either the cook or her guests.

There are other ways to win the battle gracefully. In facing the challenges of cooking and entertaining at home today, most of us have come to understand that, just as in other realms as diverse as medicine, child-rearing, and city planning, the past, intelligently examined, holds many of the answers to what are very modern problems. After endless bouts with fickle culinary fads, it seems that *cuisine bourgeoise, cuisine de ménage, cuisine de femme, cuisine de mère*, and all their recipes sampled by so many generations remain the basis of serious, satisfying cooking. Nouvelle, Lean, Haute, and other exotic exercises may come and go; refined home cooking more than ever is the core of a successful family Feast.

We all know, of course, that nobody can expect every meal to be memorable. Most of the time one eats for sustenance and thinks no more of it. The road to the future may well be paved with fast-food eateries and convenience; industrialized products with fresh, frozen, or vacuum-bagged take-out food, all swallowed on the run for efficiency and instant gratification. No doubt also that chili dogs and stuffed croissants may come in handy for everyday fare, but none of these trendy creations is either truly satisfying, efficient, or economical. They cost two or three times the price of comparable homemade preparations, and often after one of those rather sleek meals, in and out of the oven, gulped down in a jiffy, one remains strangely hungry.

When the time comes for a special occasion that breaks with the daily routine, when the time comes to say something that cannot be expressed otherwise, modern French and American men and women may choose home cooking as their response to monotony and mechanization. The American man or woman who prepares a festive home-cooked meal today has much in common with his or her French counterpart. Neither has a professional entourage or an extraordinary amount of money to spend on food. Each has limited time for cooking, and as a result most meals must be pulled together quickly and relatively effortlessly. There is no reason to turn our backs on the high-tech kitchen gadgets that save us real time and effort; there is nothing wrong with using frozen spinach to prepare stuffed Pietsch, or with grating Swiss cheese and slicing potatoes with a food processor for a Gratin Savoyard, or with whipping Brandade in a blender.

These men and women are willing to devote time and energy to a family Feast as long as they remain confident the results are going to be truly satisfying. This is why I feel the glorious "one-dish meal"—le plat unique—the keystone to the French Feast, is the answer. It is a firm, decisive, totally reliable statement. Although often made with modest ingredients, since it is derived from peasant traditions, this ordinary food has been enhanced by centuries of editing into the most sophisticated of dishes. It represents the essence of a family tradition, the heritage of a region, and emerges from generations of shared experience.

Each of the thirty entrée recipes gathered in this book is an incantation to the memory of great simple, fresh, homemade meals shared by generations of congenial and convivial people. Curnonsky said that a great dish is the master achievement of many generations, and each in its way is just that—slow food as opposed to fast food. It is precisely this extra time and care, these real flavors mingled together naturally, that give each preparation its unique dimension.

These successful and exuberant dishes come principally from the French provinces, but a few foreign dishes such as Paella, Moussaka, and Couscous have been assimilated into French gastronomy in much the same way that painters such as Picasso, Chagall, and Zao Wouki are shared by France with their native lands.

Our cuisine, like the rest of our heritage, is rooted in a respect of the past, but as Goethe noted, true nostalgia should enhance, not limit, the quality of our experience. These traditional recipes must therefore fit the circumstances in which we enjoy them today. I offer you the fundamental classic recipes accompanied by the know-how, the *tour de main*, the *trucs*, the tips I have gathered along the way. We all enjoy hearty dishes, but they need not be "Christian chokers," the name given by the French in the past to well-intentioned but heavy versions of these classic dishes. My Blanquette de Veau is thickened with shallots rather than flour, and I add a bit more lemon than my grandmother did when she prepared hers for us. My Brandade has less olive oil than hers, and it is often served with endives or radishes rather than in a pastry shell. As you become familiar with these recipes, you too will want to alter them ever so slightly to suit your own preferences.

On the other hand, please remember that abundance—a touch of madness and excess—is essential in these meals. The platter of Jambon Persillé, the Gratin de Poulet au Fromage, the Potée, and all the others must be spectacular in size as well as appearance. They should bedazzle and communicate instantly a feeling of uninhibited generosity. Don't fret over the leftovers. After each recipe I give advice on how to use them, and I promise you they will bring you tomorrows that sing.

This is where the sensible, practical, unsentimental approach to cooking by French mothers and grandmothers has been so helpful and reliable for us. These women are neither casual, chichi, sentimental, nor vague. They have a knowing grasp of every problem, and they share all their serious, efficient knowledge with no frills as they transmit what they have gathered in their lives: cooking as a metaphor for the family life that nurtured them. Aside from personal interpretation, these dishes little by little will become a part of your life, for the taste for food comes from memory as well as imagination. As we contemplate the steaming tureen of spicy fish broth, our pleasure in anticipation of the rest of the Bouillabaisse mingles with reminiscences of Feasts past. How will it compare with the one we had last summer? Is the leek essential? Is lobster a distracting, ostentatious presence, or should one simply relax and enjoy it? Is the color of saffron more important than its taste? What did she ever do with that beautiful white silk blouse she stained that night?

I have selected thirty *plats uniques*, great dishes that are totally adaptable to the American kitchen and the American palate. To accompany them there are fifteen appetizers and fifteen desserts. Since the main dishes are generous, the beginning and the end of the meal should serve as light, relatively sober counterpoints to the heart of the matter—nothing elaborate, nothing heavy. Cooking, like music, is the art of mingling voices. The first course to awake the palate could be a vigorous tossed salad or a dish of crisp vegetables with a light sauce or a fragrant gratin, and the last course can be a satisfying cheese, a caramel custard, a light crêpe, or a bowl of fruit.

Organizing a Feast is a serious thing. It is a true demonstration of control where nothing of importance is left out. Preparing a meal is being able to face calmly a hundred little battles. Nothing happens by chance in such a party. Gratins, soups, stews are done ahead of time, reheated at the last moment, and served in the container in which they were cooked or the next best pot.

On the day of the Feast, being in perfect command of the situation, you will go through the meal effortlessly enjoying it as much as anyone else around the table, humming the old Charles Trenet refrain: "Why wait to join the fun? Why wait to join the Feast?"

Sensibly organized, with all the cooking done ahead of time, this sort of preparation is a pleasurable experience for the host and for the guests. If there are friends, children, or relatives at hand as you prepare your Feast, encourage them to shop, peel, chop, set the table, and fold napkins. They will feel involved in the Feast and share its success, and they may save you a little time and energy.

Give a little thought to your guest list. Guests do contribute to the quality of a meal. Tell them ahead of time about the menu so they can anticipate the occasion and the food. They may want to bring wine, a special cheese, a cake, or cookies to enhance it. There must be time to eat, speak, listen, and digest at a Feast. The luxury of having too much, the mindless abandon to idleness and small surprises leads to a *bonheur d'être*, a happiness of being that is truly contagious. For a few hours you join together with your guests to create a suspended moment in which food is the most agreeable of pretexts.

Medieval banquets often ended with the guests swearing on a golden pheasant their willingness to depart for the Crusades. Your family and friends will sit at your table exalted and firmly convinced that while the cloudy future may be in the laps of the gods, the glorious present is happily in their plates. And they will leave reassured by the knowledge that the energy and grace, the carefree laughter, and stimulating smells, the power of these great simple dishes—all of these miracles and more can be summoned up again at will.

A PRETTY TABLE

French family cuisine is the very opposite of *cuisine de spectacle*, so the decoration of your table should not be ostentatious, grand, or formal. There is no "theme dinner," no central motive; at best, a wink toward the regional dish you place at the center of the meal.

The setting should be consistently cheerful, warm, friendly, and above all truly express your personal response to the occasion, the guests, the menu, and the day.

With each dinner plan you will find a few suggestions for the table setting, but keep in mind at all times that it is the quality of the food and the quality of the friends sharing it, not a manicured, theatrical decor, that matters.

Your table should allow your guests to share the meal leisurely, to speak, to daydream, to enjoy the occasion fully. An attractive table does not need to be an extraordinary one, but it must be comfortable. As long as your accessories are functional and as long as you do not try to express too many things or display too many themes at once, the setting will be right. There is no need for a sugar-spun temple, ice figures, baroque marzipan objects, antique silver—nothing contrived, cute, overinspired, or fussy—in the decoration of your table. A confident superdish and a confident table setting will bring everyone together because the tone will be right and harmony will settle in the room.

A touch of insolence and insouciance, a rascal quality in the decoration as well as in the menu of your Feast will be welcome. Avoid anything pious, stiff, or overdone in either. Guests are intimidated by overly fancy or overly exotic settings. The priority in a family-type Feast is making sure that a consistent tone, a discreet charm, a quiet confidence prevail. It should all feel cozy and familiar. However, there is no need to "dress it down" either, in order to be reassuring.

Well done, a family Feast will bring intimations of a vegetable garden, a nearby fruit orchard, enjoying a long walk after the meal, gathering around a cozy fire later. There also may be memories of menus scribbled in purple, of lace-curtained windows, of jovial waiters in long black aprons, of all the pungent aromas, lusty stews, and warm laughter you find in a no-nonsense, traditional bistro, because that is precisely the food style and atmosphere here.

After the guests have been invited and the menu has been chosen, you may even find a reason to celebrate something or someone—perhaps the first day of snow, the reconciliation of Aunt Elizabeth and Cousin George, the arrival of a foreign friend, the last strawberry, the first totally sunny day. Or you may depend on more serious events—our culture is never at a loss for ceremonies, rituals, and anniversaries of all types. But it must be done tongue in cheek, and the thing never to lose sight of is the celebration of your family and friends gathered and sharing more than food around a pretty table.

Whatever the occasion, it will give you a good chance to display on your table lots of candles, sparklers, flowers, sweet wines, bright crockery, and pretty fabrics. This is the land of plenty, and generosity has to be your key word throughout the preparation of the Feast, especially when tablecloths, cuts of meat or fish, eggs or vegetables—all the elements you deal and work with in the following recipes—are reasonable in cost and easily available all year round throughout the country.

Use lighting to best effect. Carefully placed indirect lighting or spot lighting will transform the room. Place candles of different sizes around the table, but never too high and never scented, of course.

Use two glasses, for water and red wine or for white and red wines; this avoids getting up, and it is thoughtful. Use heavy silverware if you have any, instead of brittle, amusing, or exotic tools; a comfortable silverware is a pleasant thing to find at a dinner table.

For your centerpiece try two round vases full of flowers around a tiny terra-cotta object you particularly like, or choose pretty bowls or containers made of copper, pewter, silver, ceramic, china; or use an old wooden bowl or a glass bowl, or arrange a cake stand and several baskets. Fill your centerpiece with cut flowers, twigs, or small branches of greens, fruit, and vegetables.

Mix nuts in their shells with tiny tangerines and kumquats, or mangoes with a few twigs of ivy; mingle sweet peas and fresh fluffy roses in one or two birds' nests on each end of the table. Place a single flower in a bud vase in front of each guest, or scatter rose petals all over the table like the Romans used to do. You may like to fill a wide basket with tiny pots of fresh aromatic herbs, potted geraniums, or potted ivy. You may float candles and multicolored pansies in a wide, shallow crystal dish. Branches of tree shrubs, palmetto, and flowers both in full blossom and in bud will also look lovely in a wide bowl.

If you have them nearby, pick some honeysuckle, wisteria, jasmin, ivy, or any winding green vines you can find for your arrangement, intertwined or with their long stems stretching on the table two or three inches beyond the bottom of the container. Your centerpiece should have the casual grace of a country offering and feel as if it truly belongs there.

Ceramic, earthenware, and terra-cotta from France, Portugal, Italy, Greece, and Mexico have a simplicity and charm that will cheer any table if you make sure the pattern is plain enough and the colors enhance one another. Avoid pristine white in favor of fresh blues, bold yellows, deep reds, and muted greens.

Whether you prepare a *dîner fin* around Marmite Dieppoise or a dinner *à la bonne franquette* around Aioli Monstre, it is a fresh, unpretentious, and easy feeling that must inspire your table so everybody wants to belong to this spirited group, participate in its magic, and merge into its energy. As you start to dress your table, think once more of a Renoir *Fête Champêtre*, a Bonnard table set in a garden, a country wedding in a cheerful inn, or a crowded good-natured bistro brimming with life.

The aim of your efforts is to give pleasure to your guests, not to show off. The meal, the decoration of the table, and the feeling must mingle and harmonize so that everybody feels comfortable and elated. In a meal you have organized and orchestrated to the last detail there is still plenty of room for this gusto, this burst of happiness, this impromptu quality that transforms and transcends a fine meal into a genuine Fête.

Here are some things to have on hand for decorating your table for a Feast:

1. A few wide kitchen towels or napkins to wrap casually around the soup kettle, casserole, or gratin dish when you take it from the oven or stove to put on the table.

2. Many pretty baskets, some in natural wicker, some sprayed with a can of spray paint (from any dime store) in pretty shades of dark red, ivory, white, bright blue, to serve breads (using at least three bread baskets when you have more than six guests), raw vegetables, boiled potatoes, cookies, fruit, or to use for the centerpiece. The little crates that berries come in from the market also can be charming and useful.

3. Two or three sets of solid-colored, large, preferably cotton napkins to match your various tablecloths. Use dark red with different shades of brown in your napkins and accessories *or* dark red and various shades of greens for your winter or fall Feasts. Use salmon, pale blue, and ivory *or* all shades of yellow or pale green and pale pink in spring and summer. Avoid white—it may make your guests feel intimidated as sauces and bowls are gingerly passed from animated guest to eloquent guest down the table. There is nothing more pleasant and luxurious than wide, all-cotton napkins. Fold them and place them between the flatware at each place instead of the plate, which is kept warm in the kitchen.

4. A few tablecloths: You may buy fabric by the yard for a very moderate price in all department stores or at a discount mill sale. Measure your table for an ample tablecloth that will reach the floor. If the fabric is not wide enough, sew a seam in the center. Make a little hem all around the edges or else simply cut the fabric with pinking shears. Choose colored fabric to avoid the pretentious, stiff look of a white table. If you can avoid it, do not choose either a fragile fabric or one hundred percent polyester.

You may select a piece of quilted cotton for a Provençal effect and a pretty flowery or patterned cloth to make one, two, or three tablecloths that will be inexpensive and truly interesting, and will last for years. But if you don't want to sew at all, buy two printed king-size sheets; if you place one slightly overlapping the other, they will cover your table and go down to the floor. You may also look for a simple pink-and-brown or green-and-blue patched Indian bedspread as big as you can find to cover the table generously. You may be tempted by a bright blue or dark red piece of oilcloth; in solid colors, oil cloth with its wet look can be very dashing and also eminently practical. Over a tablecloth that touches the floor you may like a smaller square or round cloth in a contrasting color. The main thing is to have plenty of fabric for a feeling of comfort and abundance.

5. A round wooden tabletop larger than your table can be placed over it to increase your seating capacity, but within limits; certainly a round table for eight can become large enough for twelve.

6. Place a pad of felt, fabric, or polyester foam under your tablecloth. It makes for a quiet and cozy table.

7. Colored candles, beeswax candles, and plain white votive candles in glass, wood, tin, brass, terra-cotta, silver, or crockery holders. You may like to use a loaf of bread or a large cake as a candleholder (not too fresh, not too hard, just a bit stale), and of course you may use vegetables or fruit as candleholders. Cauliflowers, artichokes, and squash seem to be the safest vegetables, and apples are perfect.

8. Pretty silver, wood, china, or straw napkin rings. Or you may want to wrap each napkin with a bright piece of ribbon or a long piece of grass and leaves, or tuck in a sprig of herbs. Napkin rings are truly not necessary at a Feast, but they do give a feeling of homeliness. I often slip a place card in each napkin ring.

9. Dry eucalyptus leaves or small white or colored place cards, 2 inches by 1 inch. If you use only the first name of your guest, it remains informal but is so very useful to plan your table arrangement ahead of time, to avoid last minute decisions while the dish is on the table ready to be served and to prevent any awkward waiting. Just as you choose the menu and the decoration of your table, you must place your guests yourself so they enhance one another and are ready to participate in the easiest and most convivial of exchanges during the meal.

10. A collection of small and very large shells can be a very easy and effective centerpiece for certain meals, or try a collection of very small and large pebbles and stones in different shades if you can find them.

11. A wooden bucket, a copper bowl, a china tureen, a tin antique, or an earthenware utensil can be filled with flowers as a centerpiece.

12. As many pretty salt and pepper shakers and grinders in wood, terra-cotta, crockery, or silver as possible.

13. Three or four wine decanters or wine jugs (for eight to ten guests you need at least three wine bottles to avoid getting up, passing too much, and stretching across the table).

14. Water pitchers.

15. Pots of delicate ferns, baby's breath, beige and rose plump roses, geraniums, and amaryllis to use as a centerpiece.

Keep your table in mind when you are in antique shops or at thrift sales. Some little object might be just the thing to add charm or amusement to your table.

THIS IS NO TIME FOR MAYBES

A FEW WORDS ON STRATEGY

Escoffier said that "like music, the structure of gastronomy is built upon the harmony and sequence of its elements." It is this graceful flow that the successful host masters; the point is to be decisive and efficient. To that end, the Feasts that follow are executed according to a strategy. Much of the organization and actual preparation of food is accomplished a day in advance of the party. On the day, you will be able to deliver gracefully a perfectly synchronized meal.

When all is said and done, the cornerstone of a good festive meal is probably that sensible, deliberate, and attentive strategy. A meal is a delicate spider's web when both organization and patience are required. Success in cooking is basically the sum of a lot of small things correctly done.

Two days before the Feast, a cook must turn into a field marshal, making lists and keeping ahead of all the details so that on D-Day serenity will prevail and she can become, as the saying goes, a guest at her own party.

Most people don't have time or energy to cook a big meal very often, but when nothing else will do, when only a festive meal can give meaning and shape to a special day, that is the time to jump with confidence and gusto into the kitchen and prepare a Feast.

One day ahead, fully armed to face all challenges, the Feast is prepared and—noblesse oblige—on the day of the party, you will even be able to display the touch of abandon and spontaneity that spells happiness.

Although the truth is that a well-organized, calmly prepared festive meal is easy to cook, it is not the whole truth. In spite of organization and good sense, preparing an interesting meal is not a small pastime.

Cooking is no picnic, and one may just as well acknowledge it before one starts in order to avoid surprises later. When we entertain we must display a lot of energy and heart, a little imagination, and a great amount of attentive care. All simple dishes rely on details; in good family-type food, one does not hope for "the sauce to cover up the fish"; things are not disguised here.

With processed food, frozen food, and canned food we have gotten used to marching "without fear and without hope" to the kitchen, as the troops of Napoleon did to Waterloo. Cooking has turned into a painless, disembodied activity. For a Feast we embark on a different path.

There are shortcuts to everything, yet the long way of preparing a rich family dish is not only the best and the surest but also the easiest. Last-minute, little whipped-up creations are never totally foolproof, and they take more time than you can spare while your guests are waiting. It is far better to prepare calmly ahead of time and be confident throughout. And now to the strategy.

Well in advance, the guests are invited, the menu is chosen, all the silver, linen, glasses, and chairs are checked. Make clear notes to yourself about wine, flowers, bread, and accessories; be sure to have the right dishes and serving pieces for the menu in hand. Select serving baskets, napkins, and tablecloths.

Keep in mind when you prepare your lists, that although one does not actually EAT one's guests, they are truly an essential part of a meal. So, as you invite your guests, avoid too many people who tend to talk shop and avoid too varied a group in age and professions. At the same time, people should be compatible on some ground and yet surprise and amuse one another. Generally, a good meal and a round table make for the most congenial of dinner partners. Up to ten or even twelve at a round table is truly best for a general conversation, but eight is the most you should have at a rectangular one.

One or two days before your party, carefully read the recipes you have chosen for your Fête. Take time to understand and even to visualize the different steps involved so it is a clear process, not a mysterious exercise involving technical virtuosity.

Make a detailed shopping list with different sections for meat, vegetables, and such things as candles and flowers; in this way things will go quickly when you set out to market.

Once you have gathered all that is needed, the actual preparation of the meal can begin. Peel and trim all the vegetables over a large piece of plastic or newspaper so the refuse can be discarded easily. For most of the Feasts that follow, the main dish, the sauces, and the vegetables can be prepared and set aside a day ahead. You can even grate cheese and crush bread crumbs. You will not forget to sit down as often as you can during the process so you don't end up exhausted.

If you follow your schedule, by the end of the day most of your meal will be ready in the refrigerator and the silver, linen, glasses, and tablecloths will be out and ready. Keep the flowers in large containers so you have only to arrange vases in the morning. Have the wine ready to be opened or chilled. You should not have to purchase anything on the day of your party, and you should have a minimum of things to do, mostly reheat and serve.

On D-Day, set the table with the flowers, seating cards, and wine. The bread can be cut and wrapped in a napkin, then placed in a large plastic bag until the last minute when it goes into its basket. As the time draws near, all the prepared or almost prepared dishes are taken out of the refrigerator. Dessert plates and cheese tray are set out.

Although it is not included in the Feast menus that follow, a cheese course may be added, if you like, to dessert or as a substitute.

Line a tray—the woven basket type, if possible—with fresh or dried leaves, vines, straw, or a plain paper doily. Choose one large ripe Brie or one perfect big piece of Roquefort or two goat cheeses—a fresh one and a dry one—and a mellow Couloumiers, and arrange them, along with a bowl of walnuts, a few ripe pears, and a bottle of old port if you have some. Cover the cheese with a glass bell or a napkin.

At formal affairs in France, host and hostess sit across from each other with their most important guests on their right. The other guests are then seated in order of dwindling importance. The "bouts de table"—the ends of table—are generally occupied by young, unclassified free spirits who lack authority and social credits but compensate with their wit. For family Feasts no stiff protocol needs to be followed, yet there should be no last-minute improvisation in the seating arrangement. Place cards—plain white—are best and save lots of time and confusion when the guests go to the table and your meal is piping hot, ready to be served. Seat your guests according to what you hope will be the best chemistry, the best *faire-valoir*, the most interesting counterpoints.

You must be dressed and totally ready one hour before your guests are expected, so when the time comes to welcome them, you will be fresh and full of zest as well as attentive to the safe and steady progress of your meal. Whether the Potée is simmering or the Pietsch and the Gougère are baking in the oven, all is under control.

Serve the appetizers with the drinks if you possibly can; then when you sit down for the main dish you'll need only one change of plates for dessert. Make sure that all your guests have time to come to the table and find their places and are sitting before you actually bring the main dish. A good dish needs people waiting for its arrival, not the opposite. Select one or two friends to assist you with removing the plates. The next course will arrive gracefully, and the meal will not be interrupted. A smooth, uninterrupted flow and your presence at the table are what you aim for.

Avoid running water, the clatter of dishes, and the sound of the dishwasher operating from the kitchen. The process of changing plates should be simple, quiet, and unobtrusive. A rolling table is ideal for this. If you are fortunate to have one, pile on it the soiled dishes, cover them with a cloth, and place the flatware in a basket so it doesn't rattle or fall off.

After the main dish, especially if it is a very fragrant one such as a Fondue, Aioli Monstre, Bouillabaisse Royale, or Paella, you might like to open the windows briefly to make the room fresh and light for the dessert.

Bring coffee and tea to the table along with cups. Don't waste time asking your guests in advance what they want to drink, just bring all the pots at once. Later, offer one or two brandies—a cognac, an Armagnac, and aged Calvados—some white fruit alcohol (eau-de-vie) such as Mirabelle (plum brandy) or Framboise (from raspberry). These are wonderful after such a meal. Eau-de-vie means water of life. They come from the fruits and are redolent with their tastes. And even if they do not aid the digestion as much as we like to think, they represent a delightfully superfluous touch that Voltaire, for one, thought so necessary to happiness.

Sometime after the coffee, pass a tray of cold water, chilly fruit juices, or mineral water with thin slices of lemon.

In the days following a Feast, leftovers will be welcome in your house. Suggestions on how to use them best follow each recipe. Keep bread crumbs (preferably homemade), fresh herbs, a good Swiss cheese or a piece of Parmesan, and some wine in your kitchen, and your leftovers will easily turn into "Singing glorious tomorrows."

We also have some suggestions for simple dishes for when friends stay and linger after a midday feast and seem never ready to part. Soupe au Pistou prepared a day ahead or Gratinée Lyonnaise reheated at the last moment and served with a bowl of fruit or a plateau of cheese will save you from last-minute decisions and make the day longer. Keep almonds, olives, cookies, and fruit compote in your refrigerator; they may be helpful for this *après-fête*, this improvised second meal you never expected to serve. This is also a good scheme if you have weekend guests and the time of their departure is not quite clear.

Keep a book with the dates, the menus, the wines served, the names of the guests, the table setting used, and note your impressions of the evening. This will guide you throughout the years and prevent you from making the same mistake twice. It will also keep you from serving the same dish over and over to the same people and become a Johnny one note, a Madame Blanquette to some, a Monsieur Daube to others.

And always remember Napoleon's advice to "divide and conquer." Clear strategy relies on a detailed list of the steps to be taken that will help solve them separately without fuss or angst. Let's not speak of grace under pressure—who needs it?—but you can be assured that at the end of the day you will win the battle. And now, *que la fête commence*. On with the feast! Let it be glorious and contagious for all.

A Word About Wines

Although rich, subtle, expensive wines are always an addition to a meal, they may not be the most appropriate choice with the regional family-type food served at festive gatherings. Enjoyable *vins du pays*, light, fresh white wines, or simple robust red wines, reasonably priced, would be enjoyable. They are unpretentious and promote conviviality. Of course, this is to say nothing against the *crus classés*, the classified varieties, *petits châteaux*, or glamorous American wines. But with the dishes we offer, an honest, serious wine, one that you find appropriate, is truly the only rule to follow. In any case, don't forget that if you have a superior wine, always offer it *after* the plainer one.

A robust, hearty wine can overpower a light and delicate dish, while a strong cheese or a highly spiced preparation needs a vigorous wine. In this kind of meal, trust your taste, since classical rules and traditional combinations of wine and food are not always to be followed blindly.

Here are a few suggestions you will accept or discard according to your mood:

Dry champagne is best served before the meal as an apéritif; sweeter varieties are perfect with dessert.

Sweet wines generally are best with Flan au Caramel, Mousse au Chocolat Glacée, Panier de Frivolités, and Tarte Tatin. Muscat wine, a heady sweet wine, is perfect with most sweet dishes; it has appeared in all happy gatherings in France for centuries. This delicate and festive wine is seldom served here, but there are good California muscat wines and good Rhône valley muscats exported by Paul Jaboulet Aîné and Prosper Maufoux.

Light, dry white wines such as Muscadet, Alsatian Riesling, and Chablis, and local varieties are good with shellfish, fish, cold meats, and omelets. Or try Fumé blanc or Sauvignon blanc from California.

Heavier dry white wines, such as Côtes du Rhône, Burgundy, Graves, and some of the richer California chardonnays, will do well with Gratin de Poulet au Fromage, Poulet Fricassée Provençale, and Blanquette de Veau. The lighter reds can also be served with such dishes.

Good rosés, which are now more available here, such as the lovely Bandol wines of Tempier, are light, pleasant, and unpretentious, and go with almost any dish.

Simple, hearty, regional red wines go well with Bouillabaisse Royale, Daube de Boeuf en Gelée, Boeuf à l'Orange Niçoise, and most rich strong cheese.

IS THAT A MAN I SEE IN THE KITCHEN?

Yes, Virginia, there *is* a man in your kitchen. See Harold. He is peeling and chopping vegetables *and* meticulously discarding the peels. Oui, Marie France, this is Jean Pierre officiating above the kitchen sink, scrubbing mussels *and* discarding the shells.

Let's take a closer look at this species. Homo faber? Homo sensualis? Homo ludens? Homo sapiens? As Nietzsche noted, the truly big events in our lives usually land in our midst with the lightness of a dove. No one can pinpoint the beginning of this mutation, but men in the kitchen are today a permanent part of the landscape in France where I was born as well as in America where I have lived much of my life. They are here to stay.

In fact, just last year the Future Homemakers of America elected their first male president. This 185-pound football player summarized his platform soberly: "My definition of a homemaker is someone who contributes to the well-being of the family." In primitive times such an attitude would not have provoked comment or paved the way to high elective office. Once upon a time men were contributing to the well-being of the family by hunting elephants and buffalo, building fires, and roasting deer as a matter of course, while women picked roots and greens. With civilization's advance, masculine participation took a different turn, and in the eighteenth century we find such individuals as the king of France cooking stews in his solid silver pans and brewing robust coffee every morning for his entourage.

But then a new Dark Age fell upon the home. Men forgot everything including their way to the kitchen. Selecting, cooking, cleaning, and serving became women's undisputed turf. Man went to war, raised skyscrapers, built Wall Street, destroyed it, and walked on the moon. Everyone seemed to agree that this was indeed a biologyis-destiny sort of certitude. Roles were clearly defined; one had only to play his or hers. Cuisine was woman's comforting response to man's frantic crusades and trivial pursuits. The rich culinary heritage and precious tips from the past were not strictly for her eyes only. Man did while woman . . . cooked.

Of course men—at work, at play, traveling—liked to reminisce about their mother's Pot-au-Feu, their wife's Mouclade, and when eating out, they favored bistros run by a mom-and-pop team that felt just the way they thought home should feel. Men offered judicious advice and measured praise, grading various culinary efforts of the women in their lives, keeping up the good fight for high standards on the dining table. Yet, left to their own devices, face to face with hunger, they would walk to the kitchen reluctantly to survive mostly on cookies, candy bars, beer, and strong coffee, and occasionally gobbling canned soups or frozen dinners when inspired.

Their sense of not quite fitting in a kitchen was so clear they could not even try. In movies and novels men were described as perpetual outsiders. Men identified with Dustin Hoffman's frustration preparing breakfast for his child, Jack Lemmon straining his cooked spaghetti through a tennis racket, and Bill Cosby's outrage: "Why should I prepare breakfast now? It's bad for the children's stomachs—they ate just twelve hours ago!" They sympathized with Russell Baker describing his cooking exploits with an ungreased frying pan over maximum heat, holding slices of bologna until the entire house filled with smoke, and then serving it with "air-filled white bread and thick slashings of mayonnaise." Men were clumsy, nervous, and out of place in a kitchen. And when it was not considered off limits, since "a man never knew where anything was anyway," it was clear to all that he needed lots of help, lots of helpers. Hence the almost military operation run by great Chefs in restaurants, the assumption that to be a cook a male needs brigades and brigades of apprentices.

Once or twice a year, however, for a special occasion inspiration did strike in some homes, and a thrust for challenge might send an adventurous man into the kitchen. Eager to attend and to elaborate, remarkable, bewildering creations, he would enter the arena with gusto in a mood of "anything she can do I can do better." Such deeds were always noted and highly praised before, during, and after by all the friends and relatives. Of course, peeling, chopping, trimming, and cleaning were never part of such exercises; men had other things in mind.

I remember my father's flamboyant tours de force. He would appear in his double-breasted suit, cuff links and all, tie flying to one side, a hare or a lobster in hand — Lievre à la Royale and Homard à l'Armoricaine were his specialties. He walked in, we tiptoed out, but we were not far and could reappear in a jiffy. Was the Chef looking for butter, salt, forks, chopped onions, an old cognac, a young Beaujolais? In a minute we became disciplined apprentices, "petites mains" trying to help in this vertiginous creative process in which his demands seemed so urgent, his aims so clearly defined, the elements in all the dishes so noble. He did upgrade our daily fare. The hare and lobster dishes were indeed fit for a king. Paul Bocuse could not have done any better.

The ritualistic importance of my father in the kitchen left strong memories in all of us. We were stunned, dazzled, and a little exhausted. I remember the sink full of pots and pans, the blackened silver spoons used to stir his sauces ("silver is a noble metal; therefore . . ."). I remember feathers and vegetable peels, piles of kitchen towels scattered here and there. Unused eggs would roll on the table, sticks of butter would melt by the stove. I remember a Pollock-like ceiling once when, neglecting to place a lid on top, he used the blender for a tomato sauce. Creators don't linger over such trivia.

A few years later my husband, full of nostalgia for his sweet Kentucky home, prepared ribs, fried chicken, and corn pudding for a group of French friends. He came, selected his tools, inspected the assembled ingredients, created. My daughters and I stood in the pantry puzzled, awed, breathless. A thick smoke, the crackling of roasted pork — or was it the crackling of chicken crust? Our kitchen walls and ceiling would never be the same. But it was a perfectly wonderful meal. Prudhomme could not have matched it. We were stunned, dazzled, and a little exhausted. Creators' manners did not seem to change very much from one generation to the next.

Then came the era of gadgets galore, a time of great splendor in gastronomical paraphernalia. Whenever men chose to enter the kitchen, they did it in full attire: large chef's hats, huge aprons decorated with humorous slogans and deep pockets, elbow-high oven mittens. They would beat the veal cutlets with shiny mallets, ponder and pontificate over the olive oil (Lord, may it be extra-virgin) for their Caesar salad, ignite chicken breasts, sweetbreads, and shrimp with the finest Calvados and the oldest Armagnacs. Expectations were high and preparations were always conducted in the heroic mode; and whether the chef flew into a rage or kept his cool, the meal never appeared on the table before 11 P.M. The wives, children, and friends would display loud admiration for the *grand artiste*, but faced with sleepy guests, a topsy-turvy kitchen, and serving and cleaning still ahead of them, some of the female species present would secretly hope for the barbecue grill to melt, the lobster to escape, and the Cuisinart to crumble. The Thurber drawing in which an exasperated lady tells her dog, "For heaven's sake, why don't you go outdoors and *track* something?" repeatedly came to mind at such moments.

But times have changed. The Amazon woman is tired, and so is Supermom. The flamboyant Rambos, the absentminded hubbies, are ready to go back to their huts. And a discreet mutant, a new breed of man appears on the scene and seems willing to save the day and carry the flame. He now tends the kitchen as if it were his own garden, sensitively and efficiently. Somehow anatomy and destiny are no longer at odds. He belongs.

"Elegance is the art of not astonishing," said Cocteau, and today man's concerns in a kitchen are no longer to set criteria, to display panache, but rather to get into the game through legitimate means. No razzle-dazzle, no mad inventions. The new man is not transgressing, challenging, defying; he is following Margaret Mead's observation: A man's burden and glory lies in building a civilized home. And so he shops and chops and keeps the whole process under control. No longer an intruder, a fair-weather artist, an ineffectual virtuoso, he does not try to be stubbornly inventive. Lucid in front of exotic technology and rare ingredients, he respects the slow elaboration of plain ingredients into fine dishes.

And yet the mystery of man, his love for challenges, speed, sport, and gambles, seems far from the gentle, patient art of women's cuisine. What draws him into the kitchen? Is cooking an escape, a solution, a means? If it is self-expression, what is he trying to express? Is it a need to control part of the universe? Does man finally discover the charm in small things? Is cooking a quest for authenticity or one more existential adventure in which he wants to measure his self and define his authentic values?

Can he cook by instinct as women are supposed to? Does he

integrate the whole philosophy that comes with this type of traditional cooking? Is he anything other than a woman clone? Or is he
cooking because no one else wants to be in the kitchen? Perhaps
instead of asking questions such as these we should simply say,
"You've come a long way, buddy! Welcome to the kitchen."

Virginia, Marie France, and others like them who have gone
through various degrees of suspicion, fear, amused tolerance, exhaustion, exasperation, or "forced liberal responses" to this new-
man-in-the-kitchen situation have begun to sit back and enjoy the
results. Male cooks no longer seem sweet and touching to their
family; they are not fussed about but are judged instead on the
quality of their onion soup or stuffed cabbage. There is a weekly
television program in Paris called "Darling Man, What Are You
Cooking Today?" and it is in those terms that man's odyssey in the
kitchen will be measured from now on.

The old Manichaean views seem silly and dated. We used to ask
why a woman couldn't be more like a man and vice-versa, but now
we see men and women becoming more alike in many ways that
matter. *Cuisine de mères, cuisine de pères*, who cares? The future of food
activists is henceforth conjugated in the male as well as the female
tense, and the gender of the Kitchen Vestal irrelevant. Although men
seem less sturdy in the kitchen than the epic women of the past, they
bring good will and a special zest and freshness to their new turf.

The war of the sexes may not have ended, but there is at least a
happy truce in the kitchen, a buffer zone across the butcher block.
Some even go as far as to whisper that the couple that cooks together
might stay together.

I look into the year 2000 and see my daughter leaning over her
husband's heady Cassoulet and murmuring softly, "Darling, this
looks delicious, but when my daddy back in the eighties used to
make it, he always added some fresh mint at the last minute. You
might want to give that a try." I see many such scenes in the future
framed by a Dantesque arch declaring, "Enter, brave souls, into this,
the bravest of new worlds." And next to it I see a small sign on which
someone has scribbled, "Relax and enjoy it."

KITCHEN EQUIPMENT

A few labor-saving devices and a few tools worth having in your kitchen are as follows:

1. A large soup kettle for Bouillabaisse Royale, Marmite Dieppoise, Mouclade, and other dishes.

2. A large, heavy iron skillet, still the best for sautéing.

3. A 9-by-12-by-4-inch-high oval casserole, enameled cast-iron or earthenware, with a tight lid; not used to sauté but to simmer. It can go in the oven and on the stove.

4. A 14-by-9-inch or two 8-by-12-by-2 inch-deep (approximately) oven-proof dishes made of porcelain, Pyrex, or earthenware for gratins and for reheating food. They can go straight from the oven to the table.

5. Two 7-inch crêpe pans.

6. A pair of large kitchen shears to cut fresh herbs and also to get rid of gristle, cartilage, and for easy cutting of fruit tarts.

7. A long-handled wooden spoon.

8. Two wide, flexible metal spatulas for sliding items onto plates.

9. A big roasting pan and a rack for leg of lamb and other large roasts.

10. A wooden board the size of your terrine top so that as the ingredients cool under the board loaded with heavy cans, their texture becomes homogeneous. You will also use this wooden board when slicing. You may replace the board with a piece of cardboard wrapped with aluminum foil.

11. A citrus zester, the small, flat type with tiny holes so precise it grates only the tasty, thin, colored part of the peel.

12. A double-decker steamer, which is wonderful to prepare Pot-au-Feu and vegetables. It also keeps things warm when your meal

has to wait. The model I favor is of a capacious oval design with an enameled surface made by Terraillon. Other models can be found in good cookware shops and through mail-order catalogs.

13. A plate warmer. Plates for some dishes, such as Blanquette de Veau, Marmite Dieppoise, Brandade, and Coq au Vin, should arrive, if at all possible, very warm on the table so the sauce does not congeal.

14. An eight-cup charlotte mold, $7\frac{1}{2}$-inch diameter by 4-inch deep can be used for Moussaka, Poulet en Gelée, and Daube de Boeuf en Gelée. You may also use a soufflé dish (but it has no handles) or a 10-inch-wide glass bowl to make a dome.

15. Ten individual porcelain soufflé dishes to be used for onion soup, Cassoulets, caramel custards, and leftovers.

16. A pretty, large glass bowl for Oeufs à la Neige, Granité au Vin, Cervelle de Canut, and other dishes, and also as a centerpiece on the table, filled with floating candles and cut flowers.

17. A rolling table or side table. This is so useful when you have a large gathering. Present the wonderful dish to your guests to admire, then settle it on the rolling or side table and serve each plate. Everyone can follow the process while the main table remains pretty and tidy. You can keep a cheese tray, some dessert plates, a bowl of compote, and a set of plates on a lower shelf. A good two- or three-level rolling table is an absolute blessing.

APPETIZERS

CAVIAR D'AUBERGINES

An eggplant purée seasoned with parsley, garlic, lemon juice, and olive oil, and served with slivers of fennel, endives, cucumbers, radishes, and thin warm slices of bread.

This fresh, delicious purée can be passed around the table or served with drinks before the meal. It is accompanied by slivers of raw vegetables, large potato chips, grissini bread sticks, and thin warm slices of oven-dried country bread. It is presented in either scooped-out raw fennel bulbs or half-scooped-out raw eggplants, or it is piled as a dome in a wide, shallow dish decorated with very thin slices of lemon. The combination of cold Caviar with cool, crisp vegetables and warm toast is irresistible. In France, where general conversation is the national pastime, this light and pungent appetizer with its rich offering of vegetables is the best kickoff to a warm and festive meal.

FOR *8* PEOPLE

UTENSILS

Food processor *or* blender *or* Mouli mill
Brightly colored bowl
1 or 2 platters

PURÉE

4 large eggplants, unpeeled, with stems removed and cut in half lengthwise
5 garlic cloves, peeled and crushed
Juice of 2 lemons
½ cup olive oil
Salt
Freshly ground pepper
1 tablespoon chopped onions or shallots
2 tablespoons chopped flat parsley or basil
1 lemon, peeled or unpeeled, cut into very thin slices

VEGETABLES	*1 fennel bulb, trimmed and cut lengthwise into very thin slices, then again* *in half if too wide* *3 endives, trimmed, each leaf not wider than 1½ inches* *Handful of radishes, cleaned and trimmed, with a little stem left on* *2 cucumbers, peeled and cut into sticks* *1 celeriac, peeled and cut into very thin slices, then into 1-inch slivers*
BREAD	*4 slices whole wheat bread, toasted and cut in half* *10 grissini bread sticks*

Make a few gashes on the flat part of the eggplants, and rub a little oil on them. Broil, cut side up, in a medium oven for about 30 minutes, until soft.

Meanwhile, prepare the vegetables. Arrange on a platter, cover with plastic wrap, and refrigerate.

When the eggplants are soft, place them, skin and flesh, into a food processor or blender along with the garlic cloves, lemon juice, and olive oil; beat for a few seconds. When the purée is smooth, pour into a bowl, season with salt and pepper, and add the chopped onions. Cover with plastic wrap and refrigerate. It should be served very cold.

A few minutes before you are ready to serve the Caviar, heat the slices of bread in a warm oven, then take the vegetables and Caviar out of the refrigerator. Stir the parsley or basil into the Caviar bowl, correct the seasoning with salt, pepper, or more lemon juice, and pour into a pretty bowl (or a scooped-out fennel or eggplant). Place very thin slices of lemon all over the surface of the dome and offer 2 baskets: 1 with warm crisp rounds or triangles of country bread and a few grissini bread sticks, and 1 with fennel, endives, radishes, cucumbers, and celeriac slivers, along with a bowl of large, good-quality potato chips.

CRUDITÉS EN PANIER

A basket of trimmed raw vegetables served with five pungent sauces.

A wonderful way to begin a Feast and linger over apéritifs without a worry in the world, knowing you will be ready for the main course whenever you choose.

This type of pretty, healthy, varied finger food, with its assortment of lively sauces displayed on a side or coffee table, eliminates the passing of hors d'oeuvres and does not stop the flow of conversation. It truly is a perfect introduction for a convivial dinner.

You may like to present your Crudités in an antique footed dish, in a long, shallow basket or a plump, round one, on a wooden platter, in tiny or big Chinese bamboo steamers, in an antique ice bucket, on a white china cake stand, or in a bright ceramic bowl. If you choose to eat the Crudités seated at the table, they will be the most edible and engaging of still lifes.

Three sauces are generally enough, but the variety of vegetables has to be rather ample.

FOR *8* PEOPLE

UTENSILS   Basket, china bowl, footed dish, wooden platter, Chinese bamboo steamers, ice bucket, ceramic bowl, or cake stand
3 or 4 pretty bowls for the sauces

VEGETABLES   You may use a selection of:
tiny artichokes, trimmed
romaine and endive leaves
sprigs of watercress
cauliflower florets
scallions with green stems
cucumbers, peeled and cut into thin sticks
tiny mushrooms, cleaned and dried, with their stems
carrot sticks or tiny carrots, peeled and washed, with their green stems on
tiny cherry tomatoes
broccoli, washed and trimmed, in tiny bunches
fresh fava beans, shelled, if you can find them

celery and fennel bundles, trimmed, cut vertically into very thin slices with some ferny green left on
zucchini, unpeeled and sliced, or peeled zucchini sticks
asparagus spears
red peppers, cut into thin slivers
radishes, trimmed, with a little green stem on
bunch of bread sticks wrapped with thin strips of Virginia or prosciutto ham

Wash and trim all the vegetables ahead of time. Arrange them in their chosen container, sprinkle them with a little cold water, and cover with plastic wrap or foil as well as you can; chill until ready to use.

Puncture your elaborate pyramid of vegetables with shiny pea pods, thin scallions, sprigs of flat parsley, or some long stems of mint and basil twigs stuck between the Crudités for a fluffy, rich, and lively display.

For a more delicate offering, place a choice of thinly sliced turnips, cauliflower, mushrooms, green and red peppers, and radishes in clumps over a glass bowl filled with crushed ice.

Prepare the sauces, cover with plastic wrap, and refrigerate.

SAUCES

THOIONNADE
1 egg yolk
One 6½-ounce can tuna packed in olive oil; use the tuna and the oil
2 garlic cloves, peeled and crushed
Juice of 2 lemons
1 tablespoon Dijon-style mustard
Freshly ground pepper
Salt, if needed
Tabasco to taste
4 ounces firm black or green olives, pitted and coarsely chopped (½ cup)
2 tablespoons coarsely chopped capers

Put all the ingredients, except the olives and capers, in a blender or food processor; blend for a few seconds until you have a smooth paste. Chill and correct the seasoning with a little Tabasco. For added texture, add the chopped olives and capers just before serving. The sauce must be smooth but thick enough to stick to the vegetables as you dip them. Add a little oil if you find the sauce too thick; add a little crushed tuna if you find it too runny. Cover with plastic wrap and refrigerate.

BAGNA CAUDA

4 garlic cloves, peeled, crushed, and finely chopped
2 tablespoons butter
1 tablespoon olive oil
8 anchovy fillets, chopped and crushed, or 1 tablespoon anchovy paste
1 cup heavy cream
1 cup sour cream
Freshly ground pepper

Sauté the garlic in the butter and oil until soft but not browned. Add the chopped anchovies, lower the flame, and stir for 1 minute. Add the heavy cream and sour cream, and sprinkle with pepper. Serve from a chafing dish. If you want to use it later, cover with plastic wrap and refrigerate. Reheat over a low flame before serving.

BAGNA CAUDA 2

(A more pungent and spirited version)
20 anchovy fillets, crushed
2 slices of bread moistened in 2 tablespoons water, then squeezed
2 garlic cloves, peeled and crushed
1 cup olive oil
4 tablespoons red wine vinegar
Freshly ground pepper
1 tablespoon butter, softened

Place the anchovy fillets, bread, and garlic in a blender or food processor. Add the olive oil to make a smooth mixture. Put the mixture on a very low flame, add the wine vinegar, pepper, and softened butter, and when it is barely warm, pour into a crockery pot or chafing dish.

Note: The sauce must be only barely warm so as not to scorch the lips, since vegetables are different with it. If the sauce is not used immediately, cover, set aside, and reheat gently over a very low flame.

PISTOU SAUCE

5 garlic cloves, peeled and crushed
1 teaspoon coarse salt
2 cups basil leaves, washed, trimmed, and cut up with scissors a few hours
   ahead so they lose their extra moisture

½ *cup olive oil*
½ *cup grated Parmesan, Romano, or Swiss cheese*
Freshly ground pepper to taste
Salt to taste

Crush garlic and coarse salt in a mortar to make a paste or, alternatively, use the back of a fork and a small mixing bowl. Pour into a blender or food processor with the basil leaves and olive oil and mix on a high speed. Cover and refrigerate. Just before serving, add the grated cheese, pepper, and a little salt if needed. If too thick, add a peeled, seeded, and puréed tomato.

SAUSSOUN

(A sauce I love but it might be an acquired taste, so try it first)
3 tablespoons olive oil
1 cup chopped almonds
12 anchovy fillets, crushed
2 large fennel bulbs, coarsely chopped
Drop of Tabasco
3 tablespoons sour cream
Salt, if needed
3 tablespoons basil or fennel (fine leaves), cut with a scissor

Put everything except the basil in a food processor or blender. It should be smooth; if you feel it is too dry for a dip, add a little more olive oil. Stir in the basil, pour into a bowl, cover with plastic wrap, and refrigerate until ready to serve.

This sauce is also delicious served with warm or cold pasta.

TAPENADE

(Which means *capers* in Provençal)
1 cup Nice black olives or black Italian, Greek, or Spanish oil-cured
  olives, pitted
6 anchovy fillets, crushed
2 tablespoons capers
1 garlic clove, peeled and crushed
1 tablespoon Dijon-style mustard
Juice of 1 lemon
4 tablespoons (or more) olive oil
Freshly ground pepper
1 tablespoon cognac (optional)
2 tablespoons chopped fresh basil

Place everything in a blender or food processor except the basil leaves. Mix at a high speed for a second, then pour into a bowl; correct the seasoning, adding more oil if the sauce is too thick. It should be smooth and soft. Sprinkle basil on top. Cover with plastic wrap and refrigerate.

ANCHOYADE

20 anchovy fillets, crushed
5 tablespoons olive oil
1 tablespoon wine vinegar
2 garlic cloves, peeled and crushed

Pour everything into a food processor; mix at a high speed for 1–2 seconds. Correct the seasoning. Pour into a bowl, cover with plastic wrap, and refrigerate. Stir well before serving.

Note: Make a large quantity of this sauce—it is spectacular. The leftover sauce can be used as a spread on warm toast or, if there is enough, tossed on pasta.

Take everything out of the refrigerator just before your first guests arrive. Remove the plastic and foil and place all on the living room table along with the drinks. You may also add a small basket of potato chips and thin prosciutto slivers wrapped around the bread sticks along with the Crudités.

You may like to pass a bowl of coarse sea salt or kosher salt and a bowl of Aioli Monstre (page 84) or a bowl of Rouille (page 114) to your tray where you have displayed your sauce assortment.

GOUGÈRE

A cheese delight.

In most wine cellars of Burgundy, Gougère is served during the traditional tastings because it is the favorite counterpoint to a rich wine.

It is a lovely appetizer to offer at home. It looks, smells, and tastes delicious, and it wonderfully enhances drinks. Quickly and easily prepared, it is placed in the oven one hour before your guests are due. It will be fluffy and golden on its white doily with the drinks before you sit down at the table for the main dish.

Make sure you don't open the oven door for forty-five minutes while Gougère is cooking, in spite of the tantalizing aroma. The following recipe makes for a very big Gougère, but as you will see firsthand, "less is more" does not apply to this dish.

Pass the platter of Gougère with the drinks. It is a time for shared memories, silly information heard as if it were essential, lively exchanges, gossip, and spats. With the lovely cheese pastry and the fresh Kir drink, it all makes for a truly happy hour.

FOR *8* PEOPLE

INGREDIENTS
1½ cups milk
8 tablespoons butter
1⅓ cups flour
Salt
Tabasco
Freshly ground nutmeg
6 eggs
2 cups coarsely grated or finely diced Swiss cheese (with additional cubes for garnish)
1 tablespoon Dijon-style mustard

Preheat the oven to 400°.

Bring the milk to a boil and add the butter. Remove from the heat and vigorously stir in the flour all at once. Use a wooden spoon or a whisk in a steady motion until the mixture comes away from the side of the pan and forms a ball. Add salt, Tabasco, nutmeg, and eggs, vigorously beating the mixture after the addition of each egg. Stir in the cheese and mustard. The mixture should be smooth, shiny, and highly seasoned, so add a little Tabasco or salt if needed.

Butter a cookie sheet and pile the dough on it by tablespoonfuls, forming a wide circle with a 2-inch hole in the center. You may place a little round mold in the middle of the crown to form a perfect center hole. Smooth the top with a little milk using a brush or a piece of cheesecloth, then sprinkle a tablespoon of tiny cubes of Parmesan or

Swiss cheese on top. Bake for 15 minutes, lower the temperature to 350°, and bake 30 minutes more. *Do not* open the oven door, no matter how fierce your curiosity, no matter how seductive the smell.

After 45 minutes, open the oven and leave the door ajar for 5 minutes while you place a paper doily or clean napkin on your platter and prepare the stack of paper napkins.

Using 2 wide spatulas, place the Gougère on the platter. Take it to where the guests are so that everyone can marvel at the sight, then cut it into 2-inch slices. Pass the platter around. It can be eaten piping hot or lukewarm.

WINE

Kir, the apéritif made from white wine and black currant liqueur, served chilled, or a good red wine, a dry white wine, or a cool rosé is usually offered with Gougère, but you will discover that it is compatible with almost any drink, even Perrier with lemon.

GRATIN D'AUBERGINES

A light and easy dish to prepare. You may serve it as a first course or as a garnish.

Make sure your eggplants are truly firm and shiny, and use a pretty oven-proof dish.

FOR *8* PEOPLE

UTENSILS

Skillet
Porcelain oven-proof gratin dish, 14 by 9 by 2 inches deep

INGREDIENTS

7 plump (5-inch) eggplants (about 4 pounds), unpeeled, stem removed, and sliced lengthwise
Salt
4 tablespoons (or more) olive oil
4 large tomatoes (about 2 pounds), peeled, seeded, and sliced
6 garlic cloves, peeled and thinly sliced

2 teaspoons dry thyme
1 cup chopped flat parsley
1 tablespoon freshly cracked peppercorns
1 cup freshly grated Parmesan, pecorino, Romano, or Swiss cheese
6 tablespoons bread crumbs (preferably homemade)
1 teaspoon olive oil

Sprinkle the eggplants with a little salt. (*Note:* Peel them *only* if they are not truly fresh and smooth.) Pile them on top of each other and place a heavy lid or board on top.

After an hour, dry the eggplant slices with a kitchen towel and cook them in hot olive oil until golden and tender on both sides. You will have to make several batches, so let the cooked eggplants drain on paper towels as you proceed. Add olive oil as you need it. (Remember that although eggplants absorb oil, they exude it when they are cooked.)

Add the tomatoes to the skillet and cook for a few minutes, then stir in the garlic, thyme, and parsley. Cook 2 minutes more, then turn off the flame.

Line the baking dish with a layer of cooked eggplant. Sprinkle with cracked peppercorns, salt, and a little grated cheese, and then pour on some of the cooked tomatoes. Add another layer of eggplants, peppercorns, salt, and cheese. Cover with plastic wrap and refrigerate.

An hour before the meal, take the gratin out of the refrigerator. Sprinkle with a little Parmesan and all of the bread crumbs, and dot with olive oil.

Preheat the oven to 400° and bake for 10 minutes. Lower the temperature to 375° and bake 20 minutes more. Wrap a pretty towel around the dish, place on a small tray, and bring to the table. This may be served lukewarm or cold.

LEFTOVERS   Add a little cooked rice, or two tablespoons of moistened bread, and an egg. Fill halves of parboiled zucchini or cucumbers. Sprinkle with bread crumbs and bake until warm and golden.

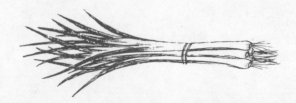

GRATIN DAUPHINOIS

A gratin of potatoes, milk, onions, and cheese.

A succulent accompaniment to Agneau au Pistou (page 79), Daube de Boeuf en Gelée (page 160), Poulet en Gelée (page 250), Hachis Parmentier (page 186), Pietsch (page 212), or Jambon en Saupiquet (page 191). It has defied all trends and remains its glorious lusty self no matter when or with what you serve it. It is one of those dishes that never go out of date and are never out of place. Splendid to start a light meal.

If your guests are late or if you want to put the Gratin in the oven earlier, cover it with a piece of oiled foil and lower the temperature. The foil will be discarded during the last ten minutes for a crisp top.

FOR *8* PEOPLE

UTENSIL   Porcelain or earthenware gratin dish, 14 by 9 inches, or 2 small ones, 12 by 8 inches

INGREDIENTS   *10 large potatoes (3–4 pounds), peeled, thinly sliced, and well dried*
4 shallots, peeled and minced
2 cups milk or light cream or evaporated milk
2 garlic cloves, peeled and crushed
2 tablespoons butter
Salt
Freshly ground white pepper
Freshly ground nutmeg
1½ cups grated cheese, half Swiss and half Parmesan
2 eggs, beaten

You may do the following ahead of time: Peel the potatoes and place them in a large bowl of water. Prepare the shallots. Refrigerate everything a few hours before you cook the Gratin.

An hour and a half before you are ready to serve the Gratin, preheat the oven to 350°.

Bring the milk to a boil. Slice and dry the potatoes. Rub 1 large or 2 smaller oven-proof dishes with the crushed garlic clove. Coat with butter and add the potatoes, salt, pepper, nutmeg, and shallots. Mix with your hands to make sure all the slices are evenly seasoned. Add $\frac{1}{2}$ cup of cheese and the beaten eggs, making sure they are distributed evenly throughout the dish. Pour the lukewarm milk over the potatoes. Cover with the remaining cheese, dot with butter, and bake for 1 hour covered with a piece of foil. (Spread with a few drops of oil so it will not stick to the cheese.) Remove the foil for the last 30 minutes. This should be creamy, crisp, and utterly delicious.

Wrap a pretty kitchen towel around the Gratin and bring it to the table along with a long-handled serving spoon.

JAMBON PERSILLÉ

A dome of fragrant ham aspic cooked in a tasty broth and seasoned with parsley, garlic, and pepper.

A glistening dome of green and pink Jambon Persillé is a memorable sight. First created in Burgundy and served during Easter, it was often molded in an old-fashioned washbowl for huge Feasts. For a lighter, more pungent appetizer, we have increased the quantity of herbs and seasoning and removed most of the fat from the ham.

You can offer this as a first course in an alfresco summer meal or as part of a buffet. You can serve it with toasted country bread, butter, fresh scallions, and tiny gherkins, or with a light herb Mayonnaise. But no matter where or how you offer it, its heady taste and mellow texture are always welcome at a festive table.

Jambon Persillé is best prepared at least one day ahead so all the flavors mingle, and then you have only to take it out of the refrigerator and place it on the table at the last moment.

It is an uncomplicated dish, but, as always, choose the ingredients carefully and make the effort to secure the best. It will keep a week in the refrigerator, so make a generous bowl of Jambon Persillé and offer your guests a spectacular appetizer.

FOR *8* OR MORE PEOPLE

UTENSILS   8-quart kettle (approximately; big enough to cook the ham in its liquid)

3-quart glass bowl or round crockery dish
Piece of clean wood, heavy cardboard wrapped in foil, *or* a plate
   or a lid to cover the top of the bowl
Long knife
Wide platter

BROTH

(to make 3 cups)
1 veal knuckle, trimmed and cracked (optional)
1 pound veal bones, trimmed of fat (optional)
1 celery stalk, cut into 2-inch pieces
1 carrot, peeled and cut into large pieces
2 bay leaves, crumpled
10 peppercorns
2 onions, quartered

HAM

2 onions studded with 5 cloves each, cut in half
4-pound ham butt, shank, or picnic ham, fully cooked (Check the label
   carefully to be sure you are getting a correctly prepared one.)
10 peppercorns
3 tablespoons dry thyme
2 tablespoons dry tarragon or 1 tablespoon chopped fresh tarragon
3 bay leaves
4 whole garlic cloves, peeled and crushed
1 medium carrot, peeled and cut into 1-inch pieces
1 piece of orange rind, about 5 inches long
3 cups (or more) dry white wine
1 package unflavored gelatin (about 1 tablespoon)
3 cups chopped flat parsley
1 cup minced chives or scallions, green part only
3 garlic cloves, peeled and crushed
3 tablespoons minced fresh tarragon leaves (optional)
2 tablespoons red wine vinegar
Salt and coarsely ground pepper
Sprigs of parsley as garnish

ACCOMPANIMENTS

Gherkins
Toasted whole wheat or country bread
Sweet butter
1 cup Mayonnaise (page 168), with 2 tablespoons heavy cream stirred
   into it and flavored with 2 tablespoons minced fresh herbs

Prepare the broth: Combine all broth ingredients in a large stock pot and cover with cold water. Bring to a boil, lower the heat, and simmer for about 2 hours. Skim often.

Cut the onions studded with cloves in half and place them in a skillet, cut side down. Brown over medium-high heat. These will give an amber quality to the broth.

Place 5 cups of broth (degreased), cooked ham, browned onion studded with cloves, peppercorns, thyme, tarragon, bay leaves, garlic, carrot, and orange rind in a big kettle with enough wine to cover. Bring slowly to a boil. Skim. Simmer for about 2 hours, until tender enough to mash with a fork.

Remove the pot from the heat and let the ham cool to room temperature in the broth.

Remove the ham and set aside. Discard the rind, bones, and veal bones. Reduce the cooking liquid to 5 cups. Discard the herbs, orange peel, and vegetables. Strain the liquid through a sieve lined with a double piece of cheesecloth. Cool the liquid and then carefully degrease it. Sprinkle the unflavored gelatin over the liquid. Leave to dissolve for 5 minutes. Stir into the liquid (aspic).

Coarsely shred the cooked ham with 2 forks into rather large chunks, about 1 by $\frac{1}{2}$ inch or so, discarding fat and gristle. Stir in the parsley, chives, garlic, tarragon, red wine vinegar, salt, pepper, and the 5 cups of aspic.

Chill the 3-quart serving bowl in the refrigerator for a few minutes, then fill it with the ham, herbs, and aspic. When full, cover with the plate, a piece of wood or foil-covered cardboard the size of the bowl top. Place a few cans on top to weigh it down for about 2 hours. Remove the cans and leave the bowl of Jambon Persillé in the refrigerator for 1 or more days. Unmold on a large platter.

Just before serving, place a parsley stem on top and surround the dome with tiny sprigs of parsley. Sprinkle a little red wine vinegar on the surface. Serve with warm toasts, gherkins, and fresh butter. Cut in slices or scoop out. Pass around a bowl of Mayonnaise enriched with a little cream.

If you'd rather serve this dish unmolded, sprinkle vinegar and minced herbs on top and scoop out each serving with a long-handled spoon.

WINES   White Burgundy Aligoté or a dry white wine

LENTILLE OU POIS CHICHES EN SALADE

A lukewarm lentil or chick-pea salad seasoned with fresh herbs, onions, oil, and vinegar.

Whether served as an appetizer or as an accompaniment, this salad is always a treat. It is truly foolproof and can be served cold when needed. But the vegetables must be warm when the sauce is poured on them, so if you cook them ahead, reheat them gently before seasoning them.

Surround the lentils or chick-peas with lamb's lettuce leaves.

FOR *8* PEOPLE

VEGETABLES
4 cups dry lentils or chick-peas
2 onions studded with 2 cloves each
1 garlic clove, peeled and crushed
3 bay leaves
Twig of thyme
Salt
Freshly ground pepper

DRESSING
9 tablespoons olive oil
Salt
3 tablespoons red wine vinegar
Tabasco
2 teaspoons chopped thyme
1 tablespoon coarsely crushed peppercorns
3 shallots, peeled and chopped, or 2 onions, peeled and thinly sliced
2–3 scallions, trimmed and minced

GARNISH
3 tablespoons chopped parsley or chervil
Handful of small lettuce leaves

Soak the lentils in cold water, then drain into a pan and cover with cold water. Add the onions, garlic, bay leaves, and thyme. Cook the lentils following the directions on the package.

Meanwhile, prepare the dressing. Put the oil and salt in a bowl and beat with a fork or a whisk. Add the vinegar, Tabasco, thyme, peppercorns, shallots, and scallions. Beat until well blended.

When the lentils or chick-peas are tender, discard the onions, garlic, and herbs, and pour into a large bowl. Pour the dressing over and toss carefully. Pour into a clean bowl, sprinkle with fresh herbs (parsley or chervil), and tuck a few lettuce leaves all around before you bring it to the table.

If you have cooked the lentils or chick-peas ahead of time, reheat them gently so the vegetables are warm when you season them. Serve at room temperature. As long as it was seasoned with warm vegetables, this salad will be fragrant.

LEFTOVERS

1. Soup: By adding a little broth, a crushed garlic clove, and a twig of thyme, you will turn the leftovers into a lovely soup. Season it with a drop of raw olive oil and a little grated cheese just before serving.

2. Side dish: Serve as part of Aioli Monstre (page 84) or Couscous (page 150), but such a salad can also be served on a platter of cold appetizers or become the side dish for Fondue Bourguignonne (page 166), Pot-au-Feu (page 228), or a Poule Verte (page 256).

MOUCLADE

A spirited mussel stew prepared with cream and seasoned with curry.

The word mussel comes from the latin word *musculus* (little muscle); hence, the name of this mussel soup. Mussels are prehistoric animals that, as far as history records, have always been eaten by man. In Charente where Mouclade was created, the culture of mussels started in the thirteenth century and has been prosperous ever since. Wild mussels are gathered in the rocks, or they are cultivated flat in parks or on wooden posts (*bouchots*) stuck in the sea or clinging in clusters on ropes. They are removed at low tide in flat boats.

This recipe comes from the Atlantic coast around La Rochelle which, during the reign of Louis XIV, provided the king with this mussel soup every week. Given a chance, of course, most of the kingdom would have loved the same treat. Mouclade is truly a metaphor for all the good things the sea brings us. The traditional flavoring of curry powder goes back to the days when the spice trade was a seafaring endeavor and sailors unloaded their spices at the port of La Rochelle.

This is a glorious soup, an easy one to prepare, and quite an inexpensive one.

Note: When you prepare mussels, remember they must always be closed. Open or broken ones should be discarded. The shell should be black or brownish black. New varieties are appearing here, such as green mussels from New Zealand; they are supposed to be very fine, but I am not familiar with them yet. Taste differs: Orange or yellow mussels are stronger in flavor, and white or pale yellow ones are more delicate. By adding a pinch of soda in the cooking pot, one can never be poisoned by a bad mussel. By inserting a silver spoon into the cooking broth, one can check whether the mussels are truly fresh; the spoon turns black if they are not.

Around Christmas time mussels have the most nutritional qualities, and new mothers are given mussels to improve the quality of their milk. Mouclade is a wonderful first course for a Thanksgiving or Christmas family dinner.

Mouclade is prepared ahead of time, and you can serve it in a small amount as a first course or as a rich main course by leaving half of the shells in the plates and adding yolks to the sauce for a richer broth.

FOR *8* PEOPLE

UTENSILS   Large soup kettle
              Piece of cheesecloth

INGREDIENTS   *5 quarts mussels*
              4 cups white wine
              2 bay leaves
              1 large onion, chopped
              3 tablespoons butter (softened or kneaded with 6 tablespoons flour)
              3 garlic cloves, peeled and crushed

6 shallots (approximately), peeled and chopped ($\frac{1}{2}$ cup)
1 teaspoon curry powder
1 cup heavy cream
Salt
Freshly ground pepper
Pinch of cayenne pepper
Juice of 2 lemons
3 egg yolks (optional)
3 tablespoons finely cut parsley

Immerse the mussels in a sink filled with cold salty water for about 30 minutes. Scrub them and remove their beards.

Meanwhile, heat the wine, bay leaves, and onion in a large saucepan or kettle. Add the mussels and shake the pan once or twice, until they open. They should not cook through. Remove the mussels with a slotted spoon and shell them (you should have about 4 cups). Discard all shells except for about 16 and remove the onion. Place them with the shelled mussels, cover with plastic wrap, and place in the refrigerator.

Pour the broth into a saucepan through several layers of cheesecloth folded over a sieve. Stir the butter and flour for 2 minutes, then add the hot broth while stirring. Add the garlic, shallots, and curry powder, and reduce for a few minutes over a high flame. You should have 4 cups of liquid. Add the cream to the broth. Simmer, stirring. Cool. Cover with plastic wrap and place in the refrigerator.

Thirty minutes before the meal, pour the broth into a saucepan and reheat slowly, without reaching the boiling point, stirring once. After 20 minutes add the cooked mussels and the empty mussel shells. Add salt, pepper, cayenne, and lemon juice. Check the seasoning. (If this is your main course, stir 3 egg yolks with a little of the warm broth in a bowl, then quickly pour into the broth. Simmer and stir for a few minutes.) Do not let the soup get near the boiling point. Wrap a kitchen towel around the cooking pot and bring it to the table piping hot with warm soup plates and a bowl of chopped parsley.

Place a few mussels, a ladleful of broth, and a few shells in each plate. Sprinkle with fresh parsley and pass to your guests.

WINE   A dry white wine

OLIVES SAUTÉES, OLIVES FARCIES

A lively appetizer of stuffed olives and olives sprinkled with herbs and sautéed.

In the terraced olive groves of Provence, the dark, twisted olive trees with their disheveled silvery foliage evoke enduring civilization. All along the Mediterranean Sea, a handful of olives and a slice of bread make the healthiest and best of meals. Thomas Jefferson was fascinated by olive trees and planted many in Monticello. The olive seems not to have gained its full social status in American menus, yet this peppery, fresh-spirited fruit is better than a "poor man's truffle," as the saying goes. When you buy olives in the U.S., make sure to choose carefully. You may choose from Greek black and purple olives, small black Nice olives, Gaeta dark purple Italian olives; all are very good. These types are routinely available in most fine food stores and also in Italian, Spanish, and Greek neighborhood stores. Never buy pitted olives or water-packed olives; they are soggy and tasteless. Wonderful olives are grown in California, but the commercial canning process leaves much to be desired. The exceptions, if you are fortunate enough to find them, are the home-cured olives sometimes sold at farm stands around Fresno, where the big crop is grown.

Serve Olives Sautées and Olives Farcies together (or only Olives Sautées if you are in a hurry) on a wide platter with thin slivers of oven-dried bread spread with a little sweet butter, a few trimmed new onions with a two-inch stem or trimmed radishes with a two-inch stem, and a stack of paper napkins. If time is running short, you may want to serve only Olives Sautées, with or without warm almonds.

This is a pungent, unusual appetizer that is easy to serve with drinks before sitting down at the table for your *plat de résistance.*

FOR *8* PEOPLE

UTENSIL   Wide skillet

OLIVES SAUTÉES   *1½ pounds firm green, purple, or black olives*
                 Thyme and savory

3 bay leaves
Pinch of coarsely ground black pepper
2 tablespoons (approximately) olive oil

OLIVES FARCIES

12 ounces large, firm green olives
2 shallots, peeled and finely minced
2 tablespoons olive oil
¾ cup roughly chopped good country ham or *cooked chicken* (¾ *cup equals* ½
    lb. of meat)
2 tablespoons chopped flat parsley
1 tablespoon grated Swiss cheese
1 egg
Freshly ground pepper
Flour
Dry thyme or *savory*
Juice of 1 lemon

To make Olives Sautées: Sprinkle the olives with the herbs and pepper. Sauté in warm olive oil, tossing them with a wooden spoon for about 5 minutes.

Note: The sautéed olives are nice accompanied by warm almonds. Bake some whole, shelled, and skinned almonds in a 300° oven for a few minutes until lightly colored, then sprinkle with a little kosher salt.

To make Olives Farcies: Pit the olives. Sauté the shallots in the olive oil until soft. Add the ham, parsley, grated cheese, egg, and pepper. Stir and remove from the heat. Pour into a food processor and process for a few seconds.

Stuff the olives with the mixture, then roll them in flour and the thyme. Fry briefly, turning them with a wooden spoon on all sides.

Sprinkle with lemon and serve warm.

PISSALADIÈRE

A crisp and mellow onion tart seasoned with herbs, anchovies, and black olives.

This wonderful tart comes from Nice where it is sold in the streets, in the marketplace, and in bakeries; it is also prepared at home and is part of all the summer Feasts. Mediocre pizzalike tarts prepared with a few onions and some tomatoes are called Pissaladière, but the real article is quite unique and very distinctive. It has a crumbly, tasty dough and a thick filling of puréed sweet onions punctuated with spirited herbs, garlic, anchovies, and olives. The result of this marriage of contraries offers an interesting counterpoint in texture and taste that makes for a traditional Pissaladière.

Light, crisp, sweet, and highly seasoned, it is a perfect appetizer to serve with drinks before sitting down for the main dish at the dining table.

It can be baked on a rectangular cookie sheet and cut into 2-inch squares for easy bite-size appetizers or cooked in a round mold and cut into wedges. You will plan your decoration with anchovy fillets and olives according to the shape you choose.

You can make this ahead and reheat it for a few minutes just before your guests arrive.

FOR *8* PEOPLE

UTENSILS   Baking pan or cookie sheet, 11 by 7 inches (approximately), *or* 2 round tart molds
Large skillet

FILLING   *5 tablespoons olive oil*
16 (about 4 pounds) large yellow onions, peeled and sliced or coarsely chopped
2 garlic cloves
3 bay leaves
2 teaspoons thyme
Salt

Freshly ground pepper
8 anchovy fillets
1 tablespoon dry thyme, oregano, or *marjoram*
Freshly ground pepper
20 (or more) tiny whole, unpitted Niçoise black olives or *good oil-cured*
  olives from Italy or Greece, pitted and cut in half

CRUST

⅓ teaspoon dry yeast
⅓ cup lukewarm water
1⅓ cups flour
2 tablespoons (approximately) cooking liquid from the onion purée
1 tablespoon olive oil
1 teaspoon salt

To make the filling: Heat 3 tablespoons of olive oil in a large skillet and cook the onions, garlic, bay leaves, and thyme over a low flame, stirring with a wooden spoon from time to time. Add salt and pepper to taste. Cover and simmer for about 2 hours over very low heat. The onions should turn into a pale amber color at the end of the 2 hours and never turn brown. You may want to make 2 batches for easier cooking if your skillet is too small.

Remove the onions from the skillet and pour all the cooking liquid into a bowl. You will use it for the crust. Set the onions aside while you prepare the dough.

To make the dough: Dissolve the yeast in the lukewarm water and let it rest for a few minutes, according to the directions on the package.

Preheat the oven to 200° for about 5 minutes, then turn it off.

Pour the yeast mixture into a large bowl. Add the flour, cooking juices, remaining olive oil, and salt, and knead for about 15 minutes with both hands. Your dough should become supple and very smooth. Add a little more oil and make a ball. Place in a clean, greased bowl, cover with a thick damp towel, and allow to rest in the warmed oven for 1 hour.

Check after 1 hour: The dough should have doubled in bulk. Remove the dough from the bowl and punch it with your finger. Sprinkle a little olive oil on top, knead the dough for a minute, replace it in the bowl, cover with the damp towel, and place it back in the oven for about 15 minutes.

Oil a big baking pan, about 11 by 17 inches, or 2 fluted round French tart pans. Take the dough out of the oven and heat the oven to 375°.

Pat down the dough and press it into the pan, spreading it to three-fourths or one-third up the sides.

Spoon the puréed onions onto the crust. Arrange the anchovy fillets in a lattice pattern on the rectangular pan or like the spokes of a wheel on the round one. Sprinkle with thyme, pepper, and olive oil, and bake for about 30 minutes. Add the olives and lower the temperature to 350°. When the dough separates a bit from the sides, remove from the oven. Take care not to overcook Pissaladière, especially if you plan to reheat it before serving.

Reheat for about 10 minutes in a 350° oven. Cut in squares or wedges, sprinkle with a bit of cold olive oil, and serve. You may wish to put a few twigs of basil as garnish on your Pissaladière platter.

WINES   Spirited rosé or a light, strong red wine.

PISSENLITS AUX LARDONS (GREENS)

A tossed salad of dandelions or chicory with crisp nuggets of bacon and a warm vinegar and oil dressing.

Gathering snails and dandelions is an exercise practiced by the very young and the very old in France. As soon as the snow melts, dandelions show their pale tender shoots and their tiny buds, and each spring they are picked by eager gourmands and docile children. In the U.S. the larger white dandelions are available in vegetable markets during the summer. Chicory, escarole, and arugula are even easier to find and can successfully replace dandelions in this recipe.

This robust, invigorating salad is prepared differently in each province: In Burgundy, herbs and verjuice are added; in Provence, garlicky croutons; in Lyon, a soft-boiled egg is put on top of each individual plate. Sometimes a chopped hard-boiled egg is sprinkled on top of the salad, and sometimes a tablespoon of local brandy is stirred into the dressing.

FOR *8* PEOPLE

UTENSILS   Skillet
                  Large salad bowl

INGREDIENTS   *2 cups green (about 8 handfuls)—either dandelions or chicory or escarole,*
                  or arugula cut into 2-inch bits
                  2 tablespoons olive oil
                  8 ounces lean bacon or lean salt pork (about ⅔ cup when cut into ½-inch
                  dices or 1- by-½-inch strips
                  4 tablespoons red wine vinegar
                  1 tablespoon Dijon-style mustard
                  Freshly ground pepper
                  Salt to taste
                  4 slices of bread, each cut into 4 triangles and oven-dried (optional)
                  2 garlic cloves, peeled (optional)

Wash, trim, and cut the greens. Keep them wrapped in a kitchen towel and refrigerate until ready to use.

Pour the oil into a thick-bottomed skillet and fry the pieces of bacon until crisp.

Meanwhile, fill a large salad bowl with warm water so it is thoroughly warm. Empty the bowl, dry it, fill it with the greens, and pour the crisp bacon and warm cooking oil on top. Add the vinegar to the warm skillet and bring to a boil. Stir in the mustard and then pour the whole mixture over the greens. Sprinkle with pepper and a little salt. Toss and serve.

You may also want to oven-dry the bread triangles, rub them with garlic, sprinkle them with a little oil, and toss them in the salad just before serving.

POIREAUX TIÈDES VINAIGRETTE

Lukewarm leeks seasoned with a spirited vinaigrette.

Nicknamed the "poor man's asparagus," it is only recently, with the nouvelle and lean cusine, that leeks have acquired their *titres de noblesse*, but they always were a favorite in my home cooking repertory.

A fresh and delicate dish, Poireaux Tièdes Vinaigrette is a traditional appetizer in family meals and on bistro menus. This is one of those dishes that at once gives the tone of a Feast and is wonderful when you plan a heavy main course.

FOR *8* PEOPLE

INGREDIENTS
24 thin to medium-size leeks (about 4 pounds)
2 teaspoons Dijon-style mustard
Salt
Coarsely ground pepper
2 tablespoons red wine vinegar
3 hard-boiled eggs, peeled and yolks separated from whites
1 cup olive oil
3 tablespoons coarsely chopped parsley

Prepare the leeks: Trim off the roots, remove all withered or bruised leaves, and cut off the dark green tops. Slice lengthwise. All the leeks should be the same length, about 6 inches. Plunge in a pan of cold water to remove all grit, spreading the leaves slightly apart. Tie them with string into 5 little bundles, as you would asparagus. Cook them in boiling water for about 10 minutes. They should not be too soft.

Meanwhile, prepare the dressing: Mix the mustard, salt, pepper, and vinegar. Mash and stir with a fork. Add the egg yolks, then stir in the oil until blended.

Drain the cooked leeks. Place them on a thick kitchen towel to absorb the excess moisture; remove and discard the strings, and place another thick towel on top. Slide the leeks into a warm serving dish and pour the vinaigrette over them. Sprinkle with finely chopped egg whites and chopped parsley. Sprinkle a little oil on top. Serve with a spatula and a serving spoon. Pass around with the lukewarm leeks a basket of warm, toasted whole wheat bread.

Note: If your leeks have been prepared ahead of time, cover the dish of leeks with a piece of foil and place it in a 325° oven for a few minutes to take the chill off. Add the vinaigrette, egg whites, parsley, and a little olive oil just before serving.

RATATOUILLE

A vegetable and herb stew.

The secret of this superstar summer dish is to simmer the vegetables separately and gently so they don't turn into a purée and to cook them, uncovered, in a wide skillet so they are not too watery. In other words, forget shortcuts; they never seem to work with this dish. Made carefully, this is a reliable dish that never has been touched by the dictatorship of the fickle, the inventive, or the improved but remains truly popular. Expectations are always raised when one mentions Ratatouille, and fairly so. It can be served as an accompaniment with Agneau au Pistou (page 79), Canard Farci (page 122), Hachis Parmentier (page 186), Pietsch (page 212), Poulet en Gelée (page 250), and Porc aux Herbes (page 222), or as an appetizer. Whether served warm, lukewarm, at room temperature, or even cold, it is delicious and gets even better when prepared a day ahead.

FOR *8* PEOPLE

UTENSILS   Skillet
              Casserole or thick-bottomed pan

INGREDIENTS   *3 large eggplants, peeled only if very large*
              Coarse kosher or plain salt
              8 zucchini, unpeeled, trimmed, and cut into 1-inch slices

3 large, fleshy, red or *yellow peppers, seeded and cut into 1-inch strips*
9 tomatoes
10 tablespoons olive and *peanut oil (half of each)*
5 onions, peeled and sliced
6 garlic cloves, peeled and crushed
3 bay leaves
2 large twigs of thyme or *3 teaspoons dry thyme*
Freshly ground pepper or *Tabasco*
Salt
¾ cup dry white wine
2 cups basil leaves or *flat parsley, cut with a scissors*
Juice of 1 large lemon (optional)

Trim stem end of eggplants and cut into 1-inch dice. Sprinkle with salt and leave to drain in a large colander while you prepare the rest of the vegetables.

Trim and cut the zucchini and peppers. Dip the tomatoes in boiling water for a few seconds and then remove their skins; cut them in half crosswise gently, and squeeze out the seeds. Prepare the onions and garlic.

Heat 1 tablespoon of oil in a large skillet. Add the onions and sauté for a few minutes, stirring from time to time, until soft. Add the crushed garlic, stir, then add the tomatoes, bay leaves, and thyme. Simmer, uncovered, for about 10 minutes. Pour into a side dish and set aside.

Blot the eggplants and zucchini with paper towels and clean the skillet with a paper towel. Add 3 tablespoons of oil in the skillet and cook the eggplants for 5 minutes. Sprinkle a little pepper and pour into the side dish. Clean the skillet again with a paper towel, add 3 tablespoons of oil, and cook the peppers for 5 minutes. Sprinkle with salt and pepper, and pour into the bowl with the rest of the cooked vegetables.

Clean the skillet with a paper towel and heat 3 tablespoons of oil. Add the zucchini and cook, uncovered, for 5 minutes. Pour, along with the rest of the vegetables, into a casserole or large thick-bottomed pan. Add the wine and basil, stir gently with a wooden spoon, and simmer, uncovered, for 1 hour.

Cool, cover with plastic wrap, and refrigerate.

Thirty minutes before the meal, remove the herbs and pour off the top oil and excess juices. You should have a moist mixture but not a runny one. Correct the seasoning with salt, pepper, and thyme. Pour into a pretty dish, sprinkle with basil, and serve.

If you serve Ratatouille cold or at room temperature, sprinkle with the juice of 1 lemon and surround the edges of the dish with very thin lemon slices. If you reheat it gently to serve it warm, sprinkle a little basil or parsley on top and dribble with olive oil.

LEFTOVERS

1. Soup: Add a little broth or water, a twig of thyme, and a crushed garlic clove. Bring to a boil and dribble a little olive oil on top just before serving.

2. Gratin: Discard the excess juices, pour into a baking dish, sprinkle with grated cheese, chopped parsley, bread crumbs, and a little olive oil, and bake.

If you don't have quite enough leftovers for a gratin, add a few slices of boiled potatoes.

3. Omelet: Prepare an omelet, then pour the leftover lukewarm Ratatouille in the center. Fold the omelet over and slide it onto a warm platter. Serve sprinkled with chopped basil and a little olive oil on top.

SOUPE AU PISTOU

A vegetable soup seasoned with garlic, basil, cheese, and olive oil.

Although it is a known fact that whoever pretends to please everybody and his father must be mad, I would venture to say that Soupe au Pistou can succeed where most other dishes might fail. I can testify that in my house it has pleased everyone and his father over and over.

The apotheosis of a vegetable extravaganza, this pungent and cleansing dish has been called *potage de santé*, health soup, and when the heady mixture of basil and garlic is stirred into the warm broth, the wonderful scent rising from the tureen is so potent, so exquisite, so invigorating that it could give heart to the meekest—and to his father.

Soupe au Pistou is also the perfect answer when, after having shared one of your festive luncheons, no one seems in a hurry to go home. You have taken your guests for a long walk, they have played cards, and now they are lingering and chatting and time seems suspended. Everybody is happy, no one is leaving, and you know you must come up with a glorious solution.

A large pot of Soupe au Pistou prepared the previous day is exactly what you want. A light, fragrant, highly digestible dish, it is a whole meal in itself and will be the perfect ending to a perfect day.

It is better in the summer and fall, of course, when there is a wide choice of fresh white beans, tiny carrots, and good basil. But if you crave it off-season, keep a jar of frozen basil, cheese, and oil paste, and add fresh garlic, a handful of fresh flat parsley, and a little raw olive oil at the last moment. Prepare your soup with the best vegetables available, adding squash, pumpkin, leeks, or whatever fresh vegetable your market is offering. Soupe au Pistou may be served warm, lukewarm, or cold.

FOR 8 PEOPLE

UTENSILS

Skillet
Large soup kettle

VEGETABLES

1 pound green beans, trimmed and cut into 1-inch pieces
6 large or 8 small carrots, peeled and diced
6 onions, peeled and sliced
3 turnips, peeled and diced
6 zucchini, unpeeled and diced
6 potatoes, peeled and diced
1 head of celery, trimmed and diced
2 leeks, white part only, trimmed and diced
1½ pounds white Great Northern beans, preferably fresh in summertime, or
    dry precooked
8 ounces fresh or frozen small lima beans
Olive oil
½ cup (about 3 ounces) diced lean salt pork or country ham or bacon
3 bay leaves
Twig of thyme
Pinch of sage
Salt
Freshly ground pepper

PISTOU

4 cups shredded fresh basil leaves
8 garlic cloves, peeled
1 cup grated Parmesan or Swiss cheese
¾ cup olive oil (approximately)
Salt
Freshly ground pepper

GARNISH

Bowl of grated Parmesan or Romano or Swiss cheese
Basket of sliced oven-dried bread
Basket of sliced fresh bread

Wash, trim, and cut all the vegetables. Shell and blanch the white beans and lima beans.

Heat 3 tablespoons of olive oil in a large skillet. Sauté the sliced onions until golden. Add the salt pork and cook for a few minutes. Slide the contents of the skillet into a large bowl with the white beans and lima beans.

Add a little oil to the skillet, then sauté the rest of the vegetables in batches for a few minutes.

Note: If you are in a hurry, the vegetables need not be sautéed before being added to the soup.

Bring a large pot of water to a boil. Add the bay leaves, thyme, sage, all the vegetables, salt, and pepper. Simmer, uncovered, for 30 minutes. Add the salt pork and beans. Correct the seasoning. Cool, cover the bowl with plastic wrap, and then place the bowl in the refrigerator.

Meanwhile, prepare the Pistou sauce: Place the basil leaves, garlic, and cheese in a food processor and blend for a few seconds. Add a little olive oil, stir with a spoon, run again for a minute, and add more oil. You should have a smooth mixture. Correct the seasoning with salt and pepper, and pour into a bowl. Cover with plastic wrap and place in the refrigerator until ready to use.

Thirty minutes before the meal, grate some cheese and put it into 2 pretty bowls. Reheat the soup on a low flame and pour into a large tureen.

Bring the soup and the bowl of Pistou to the table. Stir the Pistou into the soup tureen when all your guests are seated—the stunning aroma is intoxicating. Serve and pass the plates around the table along with the bowls of cheese, the basket of oven-dried bread, and a basket of fresh bread.

TERRINE AUX HERBES

A country pâté of veal, ham, chicken livers, herbs, garlic, and wine.

This is a creation made with beautifully interrelated things: meat, herbs, spices, and wine. All you need when you prepare it are love, confidence, and of course quality ingredients.

Technically, a pâté is a mixture of meats enclosed in pastry (*en croûte*). When it is not en croûte but simply cooked in crockery, it is a terrine. A good terrine must have a variety of meats and a diversity of textures and flavors. This terrine is a bright, reliable, rich star in the firmament of terrines. It will keep—and improve—for about a week and be prettier and safer if you serve it with a spatula out of its own porcelain or earthenware cooking dish, rather than sliced on a plate. Serve with a crisp, bitter dandelion, chicory, or arugula green salad, fresh butter, gherkins, and toasted whole wheat bread.

ABOUT *10* PEOPLE

UTENSILS
Skillet, 9 by 3 inches deep
2-quart terrine with a lid pierced with a hole for the escape of steam during cooling, made either of enameled cast iron or oven-proof porcelain

INGREDIENTS
8 ounces chicken livers, clean and as lightly colored as you can find
Flour
1 tablespoon butter
2 tablespoons vegetable oil
1½ pounds lean veal, lean pork, and boiled ham, coarsely chopped separately by hand (about 4 cups altogether)
1 tablespoon dry thyme or savory
4 garlic cloves, peeled and crushed
2 onions, peeled and chopped by hand
1 tablespoon red, green, and black peppercorns
3 eggs
1 tablespoon juniper berries
1 cup dry white wine
2 tablespoons port

½ cup chopped parsley

A few strips of fatback, ⅛ inch thick, or 4 thick slices bacon, enough to
   line your mold

2 by ½-inch slices of cured ham, Virginia, country, or prosciutto, each cut
   into 4 strips

4 bay leaves

GARNISH   Gherkins
               Bitter tossed salad
               Whole wheat bread, toasted and sliced
               French-type loaf bread
               Sweet butter

Trim the chicken livers; rinse and pat them dry. Dredge with 1
tablespoon of flour. Heat the butter and oil in a skillet and sauté the
chicken livers on all sides for 2 minutes. Remove from the heat and
set aside.

Mix the coarsely chopped veal, pork, and ham with a wooden
spoon. Add the herbs, garlic, onions, peppercorns, eggs, and juniper
berries. Stir in the wine, port, and parsley, and cook for a few
minutes.

Note: Don't use a food processor to chop and combine the ingredients, or the terrine will turn pasty and dry. You should have a
smooth, grainy texture, not a baby food purée.

Preheat the oven to 350°.

Line the bottom and sides of the terrine with half of the slices of
fatback. Put one-third of the stuffing in the bottom of the terrine.
Cover with the strips of cured ham and pat down gently with the
palms of your hands. Spread half of the remaining stuffing, the
remaining strips of cured ham, and the rest of the stuffing. Place 4
bay leaves on top and cover with thin slices of fatback.

Place a piece of foil on top of the fat, place the lid on, and set in
a baking pan. Add enough hot water to come halfway up. Set in the
preheated oven and bake for 2 hours. Remove the foil and lid, and
bake 15 minutes more, uncovered, to allow the top to brown.

The Terrine should shrink from the sides and the juices should run
yellow. Take the terrine out of the oven and cover it with a wooden
board or piece of cardboard (the shape and size of the inside of the
top) wrapped in a piece of foil. It should fit as snugly as possible.
Place 2 or 3 cans on top to weigh down the terrine as it cools. When

cool, refrigerate the terrine, still weighted down, and keep it 1 or 2 days before serving. In this way all the flavors will blend, and the dish will have a nice, firm texture.

When you are ready to serve the Terrine, remove the weighted top. Slice it lengthwise with a long, sharp knife (so each slice is then easier to cut and take out), then place a knife and a narrow spatula in the mold and let each guest cut his slices directly. It will be pinkish, moist, and quite homogeneous. A Terrine presented in its mold and wrapped with a white napkin is more generous and fresher looking than when it is already sliced on a platter.

Pass the Terrine from guest to guest with a thin spatula and a sharp knife for serving, along with a bowl of gherkins, a bitter tossed salad, and a basket of sliced toasted whole wheat bread as well as a basket of sliced French-type loaf bread. There will be plenty of sweet butter on the table.

WINES   A dry white wine, a rosé, or a light red wine, such as Beaujolais or a domestic wine

GREAT SUPERDISHES

AGNEAU AU PISTOU

Marinated roasted leg of lamb served with a warm pureed garlic sauce and a cold Pistou sauce

SUGGESTED MENU

Caviar d'Aubergines
Crudités en Panier

Agneau au Pistou
Gratin Dauphinois
Easter Salad

Granité au Vin
Panier de Frivolités

Beaujolais

This is the traditional spring meal to celebrate Easter. In Latin countries this festivity is more important than Christmas. It is a time of rejoicing with family and friends, a challenge, a revenge on long, lonely winter. After such a meal, where lamb, ham, and eggs all speak of resurrection, the bleak cold days are forgotten, and everyone leaves the table confident in the renewal powers of spring.

Genuine spring lamb, *agneau pascal,* is on sale in April, but a leg of such a lamb is only about four pounds. In winter it is twice the size, and although the taste is not as delicate, it is still called lamb until one year old. Always choose lamb with dark pink meat (not red), tight flesh, light, thin bones, and very white—never yellow—fat. If you are on very good terms with your butcher, have him detach the bone. Place some sliced garlic cloves in the cavity, and then slide the bone back while it cooks. You will remove it only when it is cooked and you are ready to slice it. For eight people, choose a seven-pound leg of lamb, which means the lamb should be a little under a year and will absorb the marinade without losing its fresh quality.

This could be served along with Gratin Dauphinois (page 53), a warm Ratatouille (page 68), a dish of Great Northern beans, fresh green beans, or diced celeriac blanched for twenty minutes and then sautéed with butter, lemon juice, and parsley.

Make sure your accompaniment is prepared ahead of time and

reheated along with the lamb, so both arrive together piping hot at the table.

FOR *8* PEOPLE

UTENSILS   Large roasting pan with a rack
Carving board with a well for collecting the juices or a platter with a rim

MARINADE   *8 heads of garlic (about 48 cloves)*
3 teaspoons thyme or a few twigs of fresh thyme
2 onions, peeled and thinly sliced
2 bay leaves, crushed
Salt
Freshly ground pepper
3 cups dry white wine such as Muscadet or white Burgundy
2 tablespoons olive oil
½ cup Dijon-style mustard
A bowl of chopped fresh herbs: basil, parsley, thyme, fresh coriander

LAMB   *One 6–7-pound leg of lamb, with bone in but separated, if possible (see*
*   above), and trimmed of excess fat*
2 tablespoons dry rosemary or thyme or savory
Olive oil

COLD SAUCE   *Pistou sauce, page 47, or Aioli Sauce, page 87*

ACCOMPANIMENTS   Choose from:
Gratin Dauphinois, page 53
Ratatouille, page 68
Blanched Great Northern white beans with butter
Boiled green beans
Easter salad: watercress or endives with vinaigrette (page 302) and 2
*   hard-boiled eggs*

Prepare the marinade: Set aside 8 raw garlic cloves to insert in the meat. Blanch the rest of the garlic cloves in salted water for 10 minutes. Drain. Mix together the remaining marinade ingredients and add the blanched garlic cloves.

Put the lamb in a large dish. Add the marinade, cover, and leave overnight on the lower shelf of the refrigerator, turning the lamb a few times.

Note: Such an enormous quantity of garlic will not be overwhelming once it is blanched. The strong taste when raw will be replaced by a sweet, delicate, and nutty flavor.

Prepare your accompaniment. Cover and keep it refrigerated. Cook 2 hard-boiled eggs. Cool, peel, and pass them through a sieve into a small bowl. Cover with plastic wrap and refrigerate.

On the morning of the dinner, peel the potatoes for the gratin and leave in a bowl of cold water until ready to cook. Peel the shallots and garlic, and keep tightly wrapped in a piece of foil.

Two hours before the dinner, take the lamb and gratin (or other dish) out of the refrigerator. Dry the surface of the leg of lamb with a paper towel, then add dry rosemary or thyme or savory herbs. Cut the remaining 8 cloves of garlic into slivers. If you have the bone detached, insert the slivers into the cavity, then replace the bone. If you have not had the bone detached, gashes should be cut into the flesh and the slivers inserted.

Preheat the oven to 400°.

Rub the lamb with a little olive oil. Pour a little marinade in the bottom of the cooking pan, put the rack in place, and set the leg of lamb on it. Set aside the rest of the marinade.

Don't use any marinade on the meat while the lamb is cooking. A very hot oven is necessary initially to dry the lamb, which is still a little moist from its marinade no matter how carefully it has been patted. A strong, dry heat will lock in the juices and produce a crisp skin. After 10 minutes of cooking, baste the surface of the lamb with a little olive oil, then lower the heat to 375°. Turn the lamb on the other side and bake 1 hour more, turning it once again. As your lamb cooks, baste it with a brush dipped in olive oil (and not with the marinade, which would make the lamb soggy). When the skin is crisp enough, stop adding fat (it would turn brown or black).

Meanwhile, dry the peeled potatoes, slice them, heat the milk, and prepare the gratin. Bake the gratin for 1 hour. Reheat whatever other accompanying dish you have chosen according to its recipe.

Prepare the tossed green salad: Pour the dressing into the bottom of a large bowl, cross a spoon and fork over the top, then place the green leaves and minced hard-boiled eggs on top, ready to be tossed later for a perfect Easter salad.

The lamb should cook for about 9 minutes per pound, uncovered.

When it is done, remove it from the oven and let it rest for 15 minutes before you slice it.

Skim off the fat from the roasting pan. Also discard the herbs from the marinade. Crush the cooked garlic cloves with a fork and return them to the warm pan juices of the roasting pan. Boil briskly on top of the stove for 5 to 10 minutes, scraping the coagulated juices with a fork. Transfer all the juices into a small saucepan and reheat on a low flame.

Bring the warm plates, bowl of salad greens, gratin, and side dish to the table wrapped in a kitchen towel.

Also bring a bowl of chopped fresh herbs — basil, parsley — warm sauce, cold sauce, and leg of lamb on a platter with the carving knife and fork.

Make sure everybody has a chance to see the whole display. Remove the bone and start carving the lamb in thin slices, cutting parallel to the bone so the juices won't run outside. Give each guest some gratin, and 2 small slices of lamb. Pour a little warm sauce, sprinkle fresh herbs over the meat, and pass each warm plate.

When you have served everyone, place the bowls of warm sauce and cold sauce on a little tray and pass them around for each person to help himself. Place the bowl of tossed greens on the table and let your guests help themselves.

WINE   A rather strong red wine, such as a Bordeaux Graves, a Beaujolais, a Bourgogne Beaune, or a dry white wine, such as Muscadet, Pouilly sur Loire, Bordeaux Graves, or Bourgogne Meursault

What to Serve Before and After Agneau au Pistou

APPETIZERS TO BE SERVED WITH THE DRINKS

1. Caviar d'Aubergines, page 43, with Crudités en Panier, page 45
2. Olives Sautées with warm almonds, page 61
3. Gougère, page 49
4. Jambon Persillé, page 54, for a traditional Burgundian Easter meal

DESSERTS

1. Granité au Vin, page 278
2. Panier de Frivolités (page 286) with a fruit salad
3. Tarte Tatin aux Poires et aux Pommes, page 290
4. Oeufs à la Neige et aux Fruits, page 284

Decoration of the Table

This is a joyful time and the inspiration here is spring, so you may want to choose an ivory, white, or pale yellow tablecloth because these colors evoke Easter and induce joy.

Place one or two cake stands on the table, and pile on all the fresh, exotic, rustic, or antique eggs you can find. Arrange all the daffodils, lilies, daisies—all the white and yellow flowers you can find—in a white enameled basket, a white porcelain tureen, or a glass bowl, and place them in the center of the table surrounded by white or yellow candles.

It should be a cheerful, festive, beautiful table but not an overly elegant, glitzy one. Be careful not to go wild with accessories or be excessive.

In France it is believed that the bells of cathedrals, chapels, and all the churches of the land fly to Rome to be blessed and that on Easter morning they come back full of goodies which they pour on lawns, around trees, and on dining tables wherever the fancy hits them.

For dessert, platters of chocolate beasts are passed around to the guests (chocolate—bitter dark, milk, and white—in the shape of tiny chickens, bells, fish, and eggs; in the U.S. one can add rabbits to this chocolate bestiary).

Strategy for the Suggested Menu

- Guests invited for 7:30 P.M.
- Meal served at 8:30 P.M.

- One day before the Feast: Marinate the lamb; prepare the chopped shallots, greens, or salad and dressing; prepare the hard-boiled eggs and Granité au Vin.

- On the morning of the Feast: Peel the potatoes and leave them in a large bowl filled with cold water.
  Wash the greens for the salad and prepare the dressing.
- 7:00—Preheat the oven and oven-dry the bread for 30 minutes. Take the lamb, shallots, peeled potatoes, and greens out of the refrigerator. Slice the potatoes and heat the milk.
- 7:25—Bake the Gratin in the oven. Bake the lamb in the oven. They take about the same time.
- 7:30—Your first guests arrive. Bring the Caviar, Crudités, and warm toasted bread to the living room.

· 8:15 — Remove the lamb from the oven and finish the sauce according to the recipe. Take the cold sauce out of the refrigerator.
· 8:30 — Light the candles. Ask your guests to sit down to the table. Bring the warm plates, Gratin, lamb, sauces, and salad to the table.
· 9:00 — Serve the Granité au Vin either with a platter of cookies or with a basket of Frivolités and, of course, a platter of tiny chocolate fish, chicken, bells, and rabbits.

· Later — Coffees and teas.
· Later — Cold water, fruit juices, or Perrier.

LEFTOVERS

1. A fresh spring mixture: Diced leftover lamb with diced turnips, carrots, and potatoes are sautéed in olive oil and then sprinkled with chopped parsley or basil.

2. Moussaka Provençale, (page 201).

3. Curried lamb: Sauté onions; add tomatoes, curry powder, and diced leftover lamb. Cook for a few minutes. Correct the seasoning. Serve with rice.

4. Hachis Parmentier (page 186), replacing beef leftover lamb.

AIOLI MONSTRE

Aioli — ai for garlic, oli for oil — is the heady sauce that is the soul of one of the most loved and celebrated superdishes of Provence.

Garlic was introduced to France after the Crusades from the Middle East and adopted at once in the south of France as a sacred herb. It was and still is rubbed on babies' lips, given to athletes and soldiers, used

SUGGESTED MENU

Roasted Hazelnuts and Almonds

Aioli Monstre

Granité au Vin
Panier de Frivolités

Full-bodied dry Rosé

against evil spirits, rhumatism, plague, diabetes, and dull temperaments. "It is not an exaggeration to say that peace and happiness begin geographically when garlic is used in cooking," said a famous French gourmet. And Aioli, the marriage of garlic and olive oil, is more of a philosophy than a dish. As Proust's Madeleine vividly evoked and brought back with full intensity the charm of long lost afternoons, a mere dot of Aioli opens all the bright fragrant world of Provence. Mistral, the Provençal poet, wrote: "Aioli intoxicates gently, it fills the body with warmth and the soul with enthusiasm. In its essence it concentrates the strength, the gaiety of the Provençal sunshine." This fabled dish requires a true passion for garlic, and timid gourmands fulfilled with the elusive whiff of that vegetable should either fasten their belt and enjoy it or abstain.

In Provence, Aioli is traditionally served with dry codfish on Fridays, which were once Catholic fast days and from that habit continue often to be meatless days in Latin countries. The dish also appears on Ash Wednesday and for Christmas Eve supper, along with snails, before midnight Mass. But Aioli is in full great attire as *Aioli Monstre* throughout Provence every summer when it concludes the three-day festivals that celebrate each village's patron saint.

Seated side by side at long tables set out in village squares, tourists, farmers, children, local dignitaries, shopkeepers, and cousins gather to share the huge platters of fish, vegetables, and meats. Through a long afternoon they visit, gossip, joke, and digress, and the bowl of Aioli passes from hand to hand, spreading a good-natured communion among all. Aioli fills the soul and pleases all the senses with its fiery, satiny sauce; with its blissful embarrassment of offerings as rich and diverse as a Provençal market, it makes for a memorable Feast.

It is difficult to describe fairly a Feast organized around Aioli. Some claim it is not unlike a trip to paradise: To understand it fully, you must have been there. Others — myself among them — claim that although Provence is the cradle of Aioli, Aioli cannot stay eternally in its cradle and, unlike local wines, travels well.

This is not a dish for timid souls; it is not the sort of dish one can eat or prepare — so to speak — on tiptoe. Aioli is exhilarating and overwhelming, and one must prepare properly for it. All the principals are now easy to obtain: Squid, mussels, and dry or salt codfish are widely available; if snails are not, they can easily be done without.

The preparation is done the day before, and it needs very little in the way of additional accompaniments. The wonderful display of dishes on the table is spectacular in colors, flavors, and textures, and its diversity enables every guest to choose according to his taste and appetite. Each one creates his own meal—a bit of this, a touch of that. The heady sauce enhances the bland vegetables and meats, and challenges the spirited dry codfish and the firm squid.

So, fortified against evil spirits and diseases of all kinds, your guests will leave the table contented, drowsy, and in a blissful state of well-being, ready for a little siesta or a peaceful chat. And that's the way it's meant to be.

Since there is no general agreement on what an Aioli Monstre should include, I give here the exhaustive list of possibilities. Even the most extravagant Aioli Monstre would not include all of this, so choose according to the season and what your market offers, the size of your party, and what you feel like spending. Snails, squid, octopus and, certainly, lobster are not of the essence, but the essential ingredients are dry codfish, hard-boiled eggs, and a wide variety of vegetables including boiled potatoes. Snails, squid, octopus, and certainly lobster are optional.

For each guest plan on two or three raw, and two or three cooked vegetables, one hard-boiled egg, some tuna fish, some fresh fish and, if possible, some dry codfish and a slice of meat. Always choose the smallest, freshest vegetables. The lavish meal, Aioli Monstre, with its staggering variety of ingredients, is wonderful for an out-of-doors meal, but you can serve Aioli, the sauce itself, in any way and in any season you like. Even simply spread on a warm slice of country bread, it is a delightful treat.

UTENSILS   Marble mortar and a pestle, and/or a food processor
2 large kettles
2 or 3 ample platters

Generally, Aioli sauce is served from the mortar in which it traditionally is made, but of course it can also be served in bowls. There are many truly "authentic" recipes, but I will give you the version I find most delectable—and the most overwhelming!

FOR 8 PEOPLE

FISH   Choose 1 or more of the following:

2–3 pounds dry codfish

4 bay leaves

3 pounds squid, cleaned, trimmed, and sliced into ½-inch strips

2 pounds octopus, trimmed and sliced into ½-inch strips

Salt

Freshly ground pepper

Bowl of mussels, thoroughly cleaned, in their shells (about a quart)

Wine for broth

2 pounds snails or periwinkles (tiny sea snails found on the Atlantic coast)

1 can of tuna

1 uncooked lobster (or 2, if you feel extravagant)

3 pounds fillets of lean fresh fish such as codfish, striped bass, halibut, whiting, swordfishd

MEATS   Choose 1 of the following:

One 4-pound bottom roast beef, sliced

One 4–5-pound chicken, cut into 6 or 8 pieces

One 4-pound boned leg of lam

RAW VEGETABLES   Choose 2 or 3 of the following:

4 endives, trimmed and halved lengthwise

4 tomatoes, cut in half, or 8 whole if small

1 cauliflower, cut into florets

4 very small artichokes, cut in half lengthwise

1 pound lima beans, shelled, or fresh favas

1 bunch of celery, trimmed and cut into sticks

2 pounds very thin green asparagus, trimmedb

SAUCE   *14–16 garlic cloves*

Pinch of salt

1 cup vegetable oil

2 egg yolks

1 teaspoon Dijon-style mustard

1 cup olive oil

Juice of 2 lemons

2 teaspoons lukewarm water

Pinch of freshly ground white pepper

Pinch of crushed saffron

COOKED
VEGETABLES

Choose 3 or 4 of the following:

1 pound dry or already cooked chick-peas (in a can), well rinsed
8 thin carrots, whole and peeled
8 beets
4 turnips
8 fennel bulbs, trimmed, or 4 halved if they are big
1 cauliflower, trimmed
4 big round artichokes, trimmed
8 potatoes, unpeeled if they are new
2 pounds flat, wide green beans, trimmed
2 pounds purple-tipped asparagus, trimmed
8 zucchini, whole if small, otherwise cut lengthwise
4 sweet potatoes, peele

GARNISH

4 hard-boiled eggs, peeled and halved
A little watercress
2 lemons, sliced
Bunch of parsley, washed and trimmed
A few lettuce leaves

The day before, place the pieces of dry codfish, skin upward, on a plate and place the plate in a large bowl or kettle so the salt can fall to the bottom, or place the cod in a colander inside a deep bowl of water. Cover with cold water and soak for 24 hours, changing the water 5 or 6 times. Place the codfish in a saucepan and cover with fresh cold water. Add a bay leaf and bring the water to a boil. Turn off the flame and let the fish cool in the water. Drain. Keep covered in the refrigerator.

Wash and trim the squid and octopus, and slice into $\frac{1}{2}$-inch strips. Heat a pan of water with 2 bay leaves, salt, and pepper, and simmer for 30 minutes. Drain and keep in the refrigerator until ready to use.

Cook the cleaned mussels in a little wine for a few minutes, until the shells open. Keep in the refrigerator until ready to use. Do not remove the mussels from their shells.

Cook the snails in a pan of salty water for 10 minutes, drain, and keep in the refrigerator until ready to use. Serve in their shells.

If using the chick-peas, cook according to the directions on the package, drain, and pour into a bowl. Keep for later use.

Note: Canned chick-peas can be substituted for dried. Rinse them under cold water and keep in a bowl until ready to use.

Roast or boil the piece of beef or chicken, or roast the lamb. Let the meat cool to room temperature, then slice it, wrap it in plastic wrap, and keep in the refrigerator. Add a few twigs of watercress to the center of the dish before serving.

A day ahead or on the day of the party, trim, wash, and cut the raw vegetables. Place them in a pretty basket or dish, sprinkle with a little cold water, cover with plastic wrap, and leave in the refrigerator until ready to use.

For the garnish, slice the lemons and wash the parsley, and cover with plastic wrap until ready to use. Everything will be prepared ahead of time (trim the vegetables and fish, which will be cooked at the last moment), covered with plastic wrap, and refrigerated.

Some hints before preparing the sauce: Boiled garlic cloves instead of raw garlic will make a highly digestible but milder Aioli. A boiled potato can be added to the raw garlic cloves for a smoother, lighter Aioli. A slice of toasted bread soaked in vinegar may be added to the garlic and egg yolk base.

To prepare the sauce using the mortar and pestle method: Have all the sauce ingredients at room temperature, away from drafts, as you prepare this sauce. Peel the garlic cloves and remove the green germ in the center, if any, to make it more digestible. Place the garlic in a large mortar. Add a pinch of salt and a tablespoon of oil and crush with the pestle. Continue to pound the mixture until it is a paste. Add the egg yolks and the mustard and mix in thoroughly.

Note: The experienced Aioli maker merely holds a finger over the opening of the oil bottle to control the flow, estimating the quantities by eye and feel. Combine the oils and then slowly dribble in, stirring all the while, until the sauce thickens to a custard-like texture.

Note: Aioli like mayonnaise, is an emulsion that can occur only if the oil is incorporated into the yolks very slowly, especially at the beginning.

Beat in the lemon juice and the water. Check the seasoning and add salt and pepper to taste. Your sauce should be satiny and silvery gold. Place half of the Aioli in a bowl and cover with plastic wrap. Add a pinch of crushed saffron to the other half and stir well. Cover both bowls with plastic wrap and place on a low shelf of the refrigerator until ready to use.

To prepare the sauce using the food processor method: Force the garlic through a press to make it into a paste. Put the garlic paste into the processor bowl with the yolks and mustard, and whirl together for a few seconds to combine. Add the oil as described above, slowly, through the feed tube while the machine is running. When the sauce is firm, add the lemon, water, salt, and pepper. Whirl again briefly to combine. Complete as in the method using a mortar and pestle above.

Note: If your Aioli sauce separates, add a teaspoon of hot wine vinegar and stir until it becomes firm again, or start with a fresh egg yolk in a clean bowl and beat in the sauce slowly until firm and smooth.

On the day of the Feast:

Half an hour before the beginning of the meal take all the raw vegetables, squid, octopus, mussels, dry codfish, snails, sliced meats, and chick-peas from the refrigerator. Arrange them on platters and decorate with lemon slices and lettuce leaves, watercress, and parsley. Place the platters on the dining room table.

Open the can of tuna fish, drain it, and place the tuna on a plate with a few lettuce leaves tucked around it.

Boil or broil your fish according to its size and quality, about 30 minutes. Place it on a platter, add a small bunch of parsley and a few lemon slices around the dish, cover it with a piece of foil to keep it lukewarm, and place it on the table with the rest of the dishes.

If you are including lobster, boil it in a large pot of salty water for about 12 minutes per pound. Drain, break it in large hunks, and place it on a platter.

If you have a double-decker steamer, proceed as follows:

Fill the bottom part of the steamer with hot water. In the first compartment place your choices among carrots, beets, turnips, fennel, cauliflower, and small artichokes, cover, and cook for 10 minutes. Then add the second compartment on top and fill it with potatoes, green beans, asparagus, zucchini, eggs, and sweet potatoes, cover, and cook 10 minutes more. Turn off the flame. The vegetables will still be lukewarm when they are served with the Aioli.

A few minutes before serving the meal, place the cooked codfish on a piece of foil placed on top of the vegetables in the steamer compartment or in the lid placed over the top of the vegetable compartment. Codfish is fluffier and tastier when it is lukewarm.

If you don't own a double-decker steamer, cook your choices among carrots, beets, turnips, fennel, cauliflower, and artichokes, in a large pan of boiling salty water for about 30 minutes, or until they are just cooked. Remove vegetables as they finish. In the other pan cook your choices among potatoes, green beans, asparagus, zucchini, and sweet potatoes for 15 to 20 minutes.

Peel the eggs, cut them in half, and serve them around the lukewarm codfish. Serve the lukewarm vegetables from a large platter and the raw vegetables from a basket. The selection of meats, raw vegetables, snails, mussels, squid, cold tuna, and chick-peas are already on the table. Check to see if every bowl and dish is decorated with either lemon slices, watercress, or parsley. Take the Aioli bowls from the refrigerator. If you have a pretty marble or wood mortar, serve one of the Aioli sauces in it. It is traditional, and if it is marble, the mortar will help keep the sauce pretty and cool.

Have your guests pass the platters and bowls around to one another and then leave everything on the table because it is beautiful, and because everyone will have second and third helpings. You should not have to get up until dessert.

WINE   There are no special rules on the wine you should serve with Aioli. Some people think only cool water is appropriate, some think you should serve a strong red wine, some a white or rosé very dry wine. I suggest two pitchers of water and a full-bodied red, white, or rosé wine, as long as it is dry.

WHAT TO SERVE BEFORE AND AFTER AIOLI MONSTRE

This is an abundant dish, so the appetizer and dessert should be mere counterpoints.

APPETIZERS   You may start the meal with a glass of dry white wine with a drop of black currant or raspberry liquor for a light "Kir apéritif," or a glass of sweet vermouth or anise-flavored *pastis*, and before you sit down offer:

1. Roasted almonds and hazelnuts warmed for a few minutes in the oven for extra crunchiness
2. Olives Sautées, page 61
3. Pissaladière, page 63
4. A thin slice of Terrine, page 73, with gherkins and thinly sliced country bread

DESSERTS   1. Cold Mélange de Fruits, page 281
              2. Granité au Vin, page 278
              3. Panier de Frivolités, page 286
              4. Poires, Pruneaux, Oranges au Vin Rouge, page 289
              5. Tarte au Citron, page 291

DECORATION OF THE TABLE

A printed tablecloth in warm tones of blue, peach, yellow, and all the shades of ochre is perfect for a Mediterranean feeling.

Use as many straw or lacquered baskets as you can find and pretty crockery platters. Wide cotton napkins are essential, and finger bowls, wet paper towels, or paper napkins as well are a good idea.

Place a bowl filled with flowers and fruit dotted with perhaps a few shiny peapods or asparagus spears in the center of your table. This is a very crowded table with all the platters of raw and cooked vegetables, fish, meat, bowls of sauce, so food is truly the heart of the matter here — and your centerpiece must be attractive but small.

STRATEGY FOR THE SUGGESTED MENU

- Guests invited for 7:30 P.M.
- Meal served at 8:30 P.M.
- One day before the Feast: Prepare the Frivolités, Granité, Aioli sauce, meats, codfish, and chick-peas. Refrigerate.

- On the day of the Feast:
- 6:30 — Arrange platters of cold vegetables, hard-boiled eggs, codfish, and cold tuna fish. Cook the fish and vegetables.
- 7:30 — Guests arrive. Serve hazelnuts and almonds with drinks.
- 8:30 — Aioli and platters of cooked vegetables, eggs, codfish, meat, and fish are set out on the dining room table. Give a final check to the table. Light the candles. Call the guests to the table.
- 9:30 — Change plates. Serve the Frivolités. Unmold the Granité au Vin and serve it as well.

- Later: After the meal offer strong coffee and a very pungent herb tea such as Mint or Anise Tisane. And *to help the breath* offer mints or parsley, a few coffee beans, or a piece of lemon peel or bitter chocolate to nibble, or glasses of cold water with lemon juice.
- Later: Cold water, fruit juices, or Perrier.

In a family Feast nothing is lost, all is transformed, and this alchemy of glorified leftovers shows a genuine French gift of leaving nothing to waste and doing wonders in the process. All the ingredients of an Aioli Monstre always provide singing tomorrows with such delicious dishes as:

1. A light lunch, a true "bistro" dish: Cook some hard-boiled eggs. Remove the shells and cut in half lengthwise. Add an additional pinch of saffron and a little lemon juice to the leftover Aioli sauce and spread it on the hard-boiled eggs. Serve the eggs on a bed of watercress or leaf lettuce.

2. Sprinkle some chopped fresh basil into your leftover Aioli sauce and serve it as a dip. Place it in the center of a flat basket surrounded by endive leaves, slivers of young zucchini, celery sticks, and very thin bread sticks.

3. Prepare a big bowl of steamed mussels. Strain, shell, and let cool. Add diced celery. Stir the juice of one lemon into the Aioli sauce and then stir it into the celery and mussels. Check the seasoning and serve as a lunch dish or as a first course sprinkled with chopped parsley.

4. For a tureen of Bourride soup serving eight people: Stir eight tablespoons of Aioli sauce into two egg yolks, then add about two quarts of warm fish broth, stirring all the while. Check and correct the taste, adding salt, pepper, or more Aioli. Place over a low flame while continuing to stir for a few minutes. The soup will thicken, but don't let it come to a boil or the eggs will curdle.

Pour the creamy soup into a tureen and serve with crisp slices of toasted French bread. This is usually a first course followed by the fish used in making the broth and served with a bowl of Aioli. Genuine Bourride is prepared with white-fleshed fish, but you may use any light fish soup with your leftover Aioli sauce and enjoy a substantial and delicious soup.

5. With the leftover vegetables: Cut them into slivers or dice and pour warm vinaigrette (one-third cup wine vinegar, two-thirds cup olive oil, salt, and pepper) over them. Serve as a first course sprinkled with fresh herbs.

6. With leftover fish: Peel and slice two onions and sauté them in

one tablespoon of butter and one tablespoon of oil until golden. Add the fish, codfish, and squid, and lower the flame, stirring once. Sprinkle on three tablespoons of wine vinegar, fresh ground pepper, and chopped basil or chives. Serve warm as a lunch course with either toast points or warm boiled potatoes, thickly sliced

BLANQUETTE DE VEAU

A veal stew with onions, mushrooms, and capers in a lemony sauce.

SUGGESTED MENU

Gougère

Blanquette de Veau
Rice
Snow Peas

Poires, Pruneaux,
Oranges au vin Rouge
et aux Épices

Fumé blanc

This is a real jewel of the family repertory. However, like all living things, it has changed and evolved a little over the past decades. For instance, there tends to be less flour, more vegetables, and more lemon in my version than in my grandmother's.

This delicate and elegant dish can be prepared entirely a day ahead, and it is not difficult to execute but, as always, organization is essential. Our sensible strategy will have us fresh and ready to enjoy our guests on D-Day and share with them a memorable meal. Whether you honor a friend's arrival, commemorate an anniversary, or celebrate your favorite cousin's plan for a summer in Patagonia, Blanquette de Veau will turn your meal into a coherent and exciting Feast.

Always choose a very white, mother-of-pearl-colored veal, and try to select different cuts. You should have lean meat for the most part, but also some bones and cartilages for texture, body, and flavor. Choose firm, creamy-colored mushrooms and small pearl onions. Cook them separately and add them at the last moment to the Blanquette so they retain texture and flavor. By adding leeks and celery to the broth, and lemon peel, lemon juice, capers, and nutmeg to the sauce, Blanquette de Veau becomes a truly festive dish.

Choose a large earthenware, enameled ironware, or stainless-steel casserole, pretty enough to bring to the table. Avoid a black iron pot, which would turn the veal gray.

In springtime, Blanquette de Veau served with new boiled potatoes and asparagus is a wonderful treat. But you may serve the Blanquette with a dish of plain rice cooked with bay leaves, a dish of buttered pasta, or boiled artichoke hearts, as it is often served in Brittany. You may also offer tiny lima beans or pea pods or braised sliced endives or blanched celery halves as a second accompaniment. Both accompaniments will be brought to the table along with the warm plates and the Blanquette.

FOR *8* PEOPLE

UTENSILS

1 or 2 casserole dishes, 8 by 12 inches, in enameled cast iron (so it does not discolor meat) or earthenware with a tight lid

INGREDIENTS

2 pounds mushrooms, cleaned and trimmed into roughly the same size
1 teaspoon lemon juice
24 small pearl onions, peeled
2 large carrots, peeled and sliced
2 leeks, washed and sliced lengthwise
2 celery stalks, chopped
5 garlic cloves, peeled
4 tablespoons freshly chopped chervil or flat parsley
4 pounds veal breast, shoulder, or round, cut into 2-inch pieces; at least
  30 pieces of firm, lean meat with all the fat trimmed off
1 (or more) cracked veal bones (optional)
1 quart water (approximately)
1 quart dry white wine
2 onions, peeled and studded with 2 cloves each
Handful of parsley stems, washed
2 bay leaves
A few thyme twigs or 2 teaspoons thyme
2 1½-inch pieces lemon peel (yellow only)
Salt
Freshly ground pepper
8 tablespoons butter
Juice of 1 large lemon, or more to taste
5 tablespoons flour

4 egg yolks
1 cup heavy cream
Zest of 1 lemon, grated
Pinch of freshly grated nutmeg
4 tablespoons capers
Salt to taste
Pepper to taste

ACCOMPANIMENTS   *Rice (see recipe on page 303)*
2 pounds snow peas

Wash and trim the mushrooms, and sprinkle a teaspoon of lemon juice on them to prevent discoloration. Submerge the pearl onions in boiling water for a minute so they are easier to peel. With the tip of a knife, pierce a cross in the root end of each onion. Prepare the carrots, leeks, celery, garlic cloves, and chervil. Set chervil aside for garnish.

Place the meat and bones in a very large pot and cover with cold water. Bring slowly to the boiling point. As it simmers, a grayish white scum rises to the surface. Remove it with a large slotted spoon and discard. Stir once or twice with a long-handled spoon and skim the top carefully. After 30 minutes all of the scum should be removed.

Add the white wine, onions with cloves, parsley, bay leaves, thyme, lemon peel, carrots, leeks, celery, and garlic. Sprinkle with salt and pepper, cover partly, and simmer for $1\frac{1}{2}$ hours. Pierce a piece of veal with a fork; it should be tender but not overcooked.

Remove the meat and bones from the pot. Pour the broth into a colander placed over a large pan. Discard the bay leaves and thyme, and press the rest of the vegetables with the back of a spoon through the colander into the pan.

Place the cleaned mushrooms in a large saucepan. Add 2 tablespoons of butter, the juice of 1 lemon, and $\frac{3}{4}$ cup of the meat broth. Cover and cook over medium heat, stirring occasionally. Remove the mushrooms with a slotted spoon, and keep in a bowl to cool and for later use. Add the pearl onions to the liquid in the pan, cover, and bring to a boil. Simmer for about 25 minutes, until tender. Pour into the bowl of mushrooms and cool completely. Cover with plastic wrap and place in the refrigerator for later use.

Bring the large pan of meat broth to a boil and allow it to reduce until you have about 5 cups of broth left.

Meanwhile, prepare the meat: Discard the bones and, with a pair of kitchen shears, carefully remove all the gristle and gelatinous parts from the meat and discard. Cover the meat with a piece of plastic wrap and set aside.

If you choose rice as an accompaniment (you may prefer plain noodles), cook it in accordance with the directions given in the recipe.

For the vegetable accompaniment, cook the snow peas for a minute or so, cool them, and then cover with plastic wrap and keep in the refrigerator.

Melt the remaining 4 tablespoons of butter in a large, heavy-bottomed saucepan. Add the flour, stirring until it foams. Beat in the hot broth, little by little, stirring vigorously with a whip. As it reaches the boiling point, lower the heat and simmer, stirring, for about 10 minutes. Remove from the heat and let it cool. Add the meat, cover with plastic wrap, and set in the refrigerator along with the snow peas and rice.

One hour before dinner, preheat the oven to 350°. Take out the rice, snow peas, and Blanquette from the refrigerator. Place the rice in a gratin dish and stir it with a fork. Sprinkle a few dots of butter and a bit of water on top. Bake for about 30 minutes, stirring delicately with a fork once. With a turned-off oven it will keep warm and firm. Meanwhile, reheat the snow peas with a little butter in a covered saucepan on a very low flame.

With a spoon, carefully remove and discard the congealed layer of fat that has accumulated on the top of the Blanquette. Reheat slowly for about 30 minutes, stirring once with a long-handled wooden spoon. Add the mushrooms and onions after 15 minutes, cover, and cook 5 to 10 minutes more.

Meanwhile, beat the egg yolks and heavy cream with a whisk. Gradually stir in a ladle of the hot broth, then pour the mixture into the warm meat and broth pot. The sauce should thicken a little while the meat and vegetables blend with the sauce, but never simmer.

Check to see if everything is thoroughly heated. Add additional lemon juice, if desired, grated lemon zest, nutmeg, and capers. Stir gently. Add salt and freshly ground white pepper, if needed. The sauce should be very flavorful.

Remove the rice from the oven, stir it with a fork, and remove the bay leaves. Place the dish wrapped in a pretty kitchen towel on a rolling table, side table, or dinner table. Pour the warm snow peas into a bowl and place it on the table. Place the chopped chervil on the table along with the warm plates. Bring the Blanquette casserole wrapped with a large kitchen towel.

Serve each guest 2 pieces of meat, a few onions, some mushrooms, and capers in the center of each plate. Spoon the velvety sauce over this and add rice and snow peas around it. Sprinkle the whole plate with chopped chervil. When passing a plate to each guest, suggest that he or she start at once. This delicate dish is at its best when served piping hot.

What to Serve Before and After Blanquette de Veau

APPETIZERS TO BE SERVED WITH THE DRINKS BEFORE SITTING AT THE TABLE:
1. Gougère, page 49
2. Crudités à la Tapenade, au Saussoun, à l'Anchoyade, page 48

WHILE SEATED AT THE TABLE BEFORE SERVING THE BLANQUETTE:
1. Jambon Persillé, page 54
2. Terrine aux Herbes, page 73
3. Pissenlits aux Lardons, page 65, or a plain tossed salad

DESSERTS
1. Poires, Pruneaux, Oranges au Vin Rouge et aux Épices, page 289
2. Grand Baba, page 273, with Compote de Poires, page 266
3. Granité au Vin, page 278
4. Mousse au Chocolat Glacée, page 282
5. Tarte au Citron et aux Amandes, page 291

WINE   Generally, a white wine is advised, but many people prefer a good red wine or even a chilled rosé with Blanquette, so follow your whim and discard the rules.

Decoration of the Table

The meal is a metaphor for all the rich, cozy family treats one longs for in efficient, sleek, insipid times. It is a Sunday best kind of meal, and since it is not messy to serve, you may use a rich printed pique or solid quilted fabric on your table. Make sure you have a lot of warm colors because Blanquette is all white. You may like to scatter tiny bowls of cut flowers across the table or weave a delicate narrow wreath of cut flowers or leaves between the glasses.

Display your most precious salt and pepper shakers, butter pots, tiny plates filled with nuts, decanters, and all the napkin rings you own. Your table will be the setting for a rich and festive performance, filled with delicious food and lively participants. Make sure sparkling glasses, graceful flowers, and a bold use of colors give the cradle your glorious Blanquette Feast deserves.

STRATEGY FOR THE SUGGESTED MENU

• Guests invited for 7:30 P.M.
• Meal served at 8:30 P.M.

• One day before the Feast: Prepare the Blanquette, snow peas, rice, and Poires, Pruneaux, Oranges au Vin Rouge et aux Épices.

• On the day of the Feast:
· 6:45 — Prepare the Gougère and bake it.
· 7:30 — Your first guests arrive.
· 7:45 — Bring the Gougère with drinks to the living room. Place the rice in the oven. Reheat the Blanquette on a low flame. Reheat the lima beans. Prepare the tossed salad and dressing.
· 8:15 — Add onions and mushrooms to the Blanquette. Light the candles. Bring the chilled wine and cold water to the table.
· 8:30 — Ask your guests to sit at the table. Add cream, egg yolks, and lemon to the Blanquette. Bring warm plates, rice, snow peas, and tossed salad to the table. Bring in the Blanquette.
· 8:50 — Bring the Poires, Pruneaux, and Oranges dish and a platter of thin cookies to the table.

· Later — Coffees and teas.
· Later — Cold water, fruit juices, or Perrier.

LEFTOVERS

1. Soup: Chop the pieces of leftover meat and place in a saucepan. Add the Blanquette sauce, lima beans, and the rice. Pour in some good chicken or beef broth or milk and gently bring to a boil, stirring. Correct the seasoning with more salt, pepper, and nutmeg before you serve this luscious soup.

2. Crêpes: Fill salty crêpes with the chopped leftover meat and

vegetables. Roll them, place them in an oven-proof dish, and spoon Blanquette sauce, thinned with a little milk, on top. Dot with butter and reheat.

BOEUF À L'ORANGE NIÇOISE

A marinated beef simmered with vegetables in red wine, herbs, garlic, and orange rinds.

SUGGESTED MENU

Pissaladière

Boeuf à l'Orange Niçoise
Boiled New Potatoes
Green Salad

Oeufs à la Neige et
aux Fruits

Pinot Noir

This is a traditional beef stew revisited by the good fairies of Nice and Provence. They brought fresh orange peel, herbs, and garlic for a sharp and distinctive accent. They simmered the wine marinade for a more mellow and more fragrant taste. They cooked the whole dish very slowly and evenly to let the flavors mingle and enhance one another. They skimmed the fat for a moist, lean, and lively stew, and thanks to them we now have a perfectly accented dish, truly worthy of a Provençal *festin*.

A few points to remember in case the fairies are not looking over your shoulder during the entire operation: The meat must be of good quality, trimmed, and well cut. It must be thoroughly sautéed and then simmered in a tasty marinade to absorb slowly all the spices, herbs, and wine flavors. A gentle, even cooking is essential, and a careful degreasing of the sauce after a night in the refrigerator will make for a light and delicious dish. Start this two days ahead for a perfect blending, but note that it is very easy to prepare; nothing can go wrong with this dish. Remember, cooking is not as holy (or as grave) as a Mass, it is a Feast, so relax and enjoy it.

Boeuf à l'Orange is traditionally served with boiled noodles seasoned with a little olive oil or with new, unpeeled potatoes. Nice's little black olives or good firm green or purple olives can be bought at gourmet counters of some department stores and in local Italian, Spanish, or Greek markets. Never use the soft, watery, canned olives.

FOR *8* PEOPLE

UTENSILS
Skillet
Enameled cast-iron casserole, 9 by 12 inches, or *Doufeu*

MARINADE
4 tablespoons olive or vegetable oil
4 onions, peeled and sliced
1 carrot, peeled and sliced
2 stalks celery, peeled and chopped
Salt
One 3-inch piece dry orange rind (if you do not have dry rind, place a
  fresh piece in a low oven for 15 minutes)
3 cups hearty red wine
2 garlic cloves, peeled and crushed
3 bay leaves
Twig of thyme

BOEUF À
L'ORANGE
5 pounds boneless beef (rump pot roast or sirloin tip or tip of roast beef
  or top round), trimmed of all fat and gristle and cut into 1½-inch cubes
3 teaspoons thyme or marjoram
3 tablespoons vegetable oil
16 fresh baby onions or small white onions
8 ounces lean salt pork or bacon, with no rind and cut into sticks ¼ by 1½
  inches or ½-inch dice
1 tablespoon flour
3 tablespoons cognac brandy or grappa
2 cups beef broth or red wine
3 garlic cloves, peeled and sliced
Salt
Freshly ground pepper
8 carrots, peeled, cut in half lengthwise, and then sliced on the bias
Rind of 1 large orange (orange part only), finely grated
3 tomatoes, plunged into hot water and peeled, seeds removed, and then
  diced
1 cup small Nice black olives, unpitted, or firm, unwatery, large green or
  purple olives (optional)

ACCOMPANIMENTS   *Boiled new, unpeeled, potatoes or noodles*
A bowl of greens, either chicory or endive and watercress or arugula and
escarole (page 301), with a vinaigrette dressing (page 302)

GARNISH   *3 tablespoons chopped parsley*
1 cup grated Parmesan cheese

To make the marinade: Heat 4 tablespoons of oil in a cast-iron skillet. Add the onions, carrot, and celery. Sprinkle with salt and sauté for a few minutes. Add the orange rind, wine, garlic, bay leaves, and thyme, and cook for 15 minutes. Remove from the heat and cool to room temperature.

Place the pieces of beef in a large bowl and pour the cooled marinade over them. Cover and keep in the refrigerator overnight.

Remove the pieces of meat from the marinade and dry with paper towels. Sprinkle the meat with a little thyme. Heat 2 tablespoons of the oil in a cast-iron skillet and sauté the meat, a few pieces at a time. They should brown on all sides for about 10 minutes. Turn them carefully using tongs. Meanwhile, heat the remaining tablespoon of oil in a large enameled cast-iron casserole or *Doufeu*. As the pieces of beef are browned, transfer them to the casserole. You will have to make several batches.

When all the meat is browned, add the onions to the skillet, sauté on all sides until golden, and then pour into the casserole. Sauté the salt pork on moderate flame for a few minutes, then add to the casserole. Sprinkle the flour over the casserole and stir carefully.

Pour the brandy in the skillet, scrape the bottom, and transfer the contents to the casserole. Pour the marinade and the beef broth into the skillet, heat for 1 minute, and transfer to the casserole. Add the garlic, salt, and pepper to the casserole and bring to a simmer on top of the stove, uncovered. Cover and simmer for $2\frac{1}{2}$ hours. Add the carrots and cook 20 minutes more. The dish is cooked if a fork can pierce the meat easily, but the carrots should not be mushy. Remove from the heat. You should have about $3\frac{1}{2}$ cups of sauce, and it should coat a spoon lightly. If you seem to have too much sauce, pour it into a skillet and reduce it over a medium flame for a few minutes. Pour the sauce into the meat and vegetable casserole. Cool, cover, and refrigerate.

Wash and dry the greens for your salad. Wrap and keep them in the lower part of the refrigerator.

One hour before serving the meal, remove the items from the refrigerator. Discard the bay leaves, thyme, and orange rinds from the beef stew in the casserole. The fat that has accumulated on the surface, which should have a waxy texture, is easy to remove with a spoon. Discard as much as you can. Stir a tablespoon of water into the sauce and bring it to a simmer. Cover and cook slowly, basting twice with a wooden spoon.

Bring a large pot of salty water to a boil and cook the accompaniment (potatoes or noodles).

Check and correct the seasoning of your stew, if necessary, and just before you are ready to serve, stir in the grated orange peel, diced tomatoes, and olives. Turn off the heat at once.

Drain the potatoes and transfer them to a basket or dish (or drain the noodles, sprinkle them with a little olive oil or butter, and transfer them to a dish).

Place the dressing, spoon, fork, and then greens in a salad bowl.

Wrap the casserole with a towel and take it, covered, to the table along with the warm plates, potatoes, and bowls of tossed greens, chopped parsley, and Parmesan cheese.

Place a few pieces of beef, a few dice of bacon, 2 onions, a few carrot slices, a few tomato dice, and a few olives on each plate. Spoon some sauce over this and sprinkle a little parsley on top. Add some potatoes (or noodles) and hand the plates to your guests. Pass the bowl of Parmesan and a bowl of greens around the table and leave the covered casserole, as well as the basket of potatoes (or noodles) and the bowl of tossed green salad, for your guests to help themselves to seconds.

WINE   Any red wine, Bordeaux, Bourgogne, Côtes du Rhône, American Pinot Noir, will be welcome as long as it is generous and potent. If you can, use the same wine for cooking as you serve with the meal.

What to Serve Before and After Boeuf à l'Orange Niçoise

APPETIZERS   1. Pissaladière, page 63
2. Poireaux Tièdes Vinaigrette, page 67
3. Jambon Persillé, page 54
4. Crudités en Panier, page 45
5. Pissenlits aux Lardons (Greens), page 65

DESSERTS
1. Oeufs à la Neige et aux Fruits, page 284
2. Grand Baba, page 273
3. Crêpes Normandes, page 269
4. A bowl of raspberries or strawberries surrounded with sliced lemons, sprinkled with lemon juice and sugar, and served with Crémets, page 267
5. Sliced peaches or raspberries sprinkled with orange and lemon juice and a few mint leaves

DECORATION OF THE TABLE

They are displayed appetizingly and bright: carrots, fresh parsley, white onions, shiny black olives. One is overcome by the sight and tantalizing smell of Boeuf à l'Orange Niçoise. Therefore, the setting will be whatever inspires you as long as it is unfussy, inviting, and cheerful: a sharp tablecloth, perhaps a simple Indian fabric, so Provençal in feeling, or a beautifully printed king-size sheet; lively napkins; a bowl filled with lots of fluffy cut flowers, with a few long, sinuous twigs of ivy or honeysuckle stuck among them and wandering toward the guests; deeply colored candles in simple earthenware, wood, white china or crockery holders; two pretty bowls filled with grated cheese; pretty baskets filled with both fresh and oven-dried breads; two or three decanters of wine; and perhaps wooden or earthenware salt and pepper shakers.

STRATEGY FOR THE SUGGESTED MENU

- Guests invited for 7:30 P.M.
- Meal served at 8:30 P.M.

- Prepare Boeuf two days in advance. Prepare Pissaladière, greens for the salad, and Oeufs à la Neige the day before or the very morning of your dinner.

- On the day of the Feast:
· 7:00 — Preheat the oven. Take the Boeuf out of the refrigerator. Place the Pissaladière in the oven to warm up.
· 7:30 — Your first guests arrive. Serve Pissaladière with drinks in the living room.

· 8:00 — Cook potatoes. Arrange the salad bowl. Reheat the Boeuf on a medium flame.

· 8:30 — Light the candles. Ask your guests to sit at the table. Bring warm plates, a basket of warm potatoes, the Boeuf, and bowls of chopped parsley and Parmesan cheese to the table.

· 9:00 — Remove Oeufs à la Neige from the refrigerator. Heat the caramel and dribble it over the bowl of egg whites. Bring to the table.

· Later — Coffees and teas.

· Later — Cold water, fruit juices, or Perrier.

LEFTOVERS

1. Stew: Add sliced carrots, quartered turnips, fresh onions, and quartered potatoes to your leftover stew. Reheat it slowly, adding a little broth if needed. Sprinkle with parsley and serve.

2. Ravioli: Mince the leftover beef and salt pork (a small cup). Add five ounces of cooked spinach, one egg, a little cheese, and stir well. Use this mixture to fill your ravioli according to your favorite recipe with this smooth mixture. Cook in a pot of boiling water, drain, and serve with the beef sauce and grated Parmesan. You should have about forty ravioli.

3. Boiled green croquettes: Cook one cup of spinach and one-half cup of rice. Drain well, then add one cup of finely chopped leftover beef. Stir in one egg, salt, pepper, and three tablespoons of grated Parmesan or Swiss cheese. Make small round balls. Sprinkle a tray with flour and roll them in it. Drop the balls in a large pot of boiling water for ten minutes. They rise to the surface as soon as they are cooked. Drain, sprinkle with olive oil and Parmesan cheese, and serve at once.

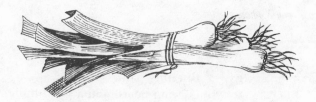

BOEUF FROID EN TRANCHES

Slices of marinated beef cooked to pink and then served cold in their juices with a raw tomato and tarragon sauce.

SUGGESTED MENU

*Poireaux Tièdes
Vinaigrette*

*Boeuf en Tranches
Gratin Dauphinois
Watercress Salad*

Crêpes Normandes

A Full-bodied Red Wine

Whether your guests are "meat and potato" people or normally shun spicy, foreign preparations for other reasons, this will be a winning combination: seasoned cold beef with a fragrant sauce, peppery watercress salad, and luscious Gratin Dauphinois. This menu is a gourmand's delight but is still simple and healthy. For a lighter meal, Gratin d'Aubergines (page 51) or a warm Ratatouille (page 68) can replace the Gratin Dauphinois. Cold beef can be the best or the most mediocre of dishes. When it is rolled in cracked pepper, carefully cooked, thinly sliced, basted in its deglazed roasting juices, and served with a fresh sauce of raw tomatoes and tarragon, it is a delicious dish and the perfect counterpoint to a mellow Gratin Dauphinois.

Boeuf en Tranches is prepared entirely the day before your party and needs no last-minute touch to ensure its success. A wonderful addition to an all-cold summer meal for a buffet, a picnic, or a late dinner.

FOR 8 PEOPLE

UTENSILS

Roasting pan
Carving board and a good knife
Platter

BEEF

One 3-pound beef fillet, 4 inches in diameter, trimmed of all fat, or one
    3-4-pound beef tenderloin, the central section preferably, about 3 inches
    in diameter, trimmed of all fat
Olive oil
Coarsely ground peppercorns
4 tablespoons red vermouth or sherry, approximately
Salt
Freshly ground pepper
Vermouth

SAUCE

3 tomatoes, peeled, seeded, and diced
3 tablespoons tarragon, chervil, or flat parsley leaves cut with scissors
1 tablespoon coarsely ground coriander
Salt to taste
¾ cup virgin olive oil

WATERCRESS
SALAD

2 or 3 bunches of watercress
1 tablespoon minced chervil
10 tablespoons olive oil
3 tablespoons red wine vinegar
Salt
Freshly ground pepper

Remove the meat from the refrigerator at least 3 hours before you
are ready to cook it. Dry the surface with a paper towel. Rub with
the olive oil and coarsely ground peppercorns, pressing them firmly
into the meat with the palms of your hands. Cover with waxed paper
or foil, and leave for a few hours at room temperature.

Preheat the oven to 425°.

Remove the foil or waxed paper, place the meat in a large roasting
pan, and slide it into the hot oven for 10 minutes, turning once so all
sides are seared. Discard the fat from the pan, lower the heat to 325°,
and cook 20 minutes more.

Remove the roast from the oven and cool to room temperature.
Meanwhile, add a little vermouth to the roasting pan and scrape the
coagulated juices in the bottom of the pan with a fork. Pour the juices
into a large bowl with the roast, cover carefully with foil or plastic
wrap, and refrigerate.

A few hours before you are ready to serve the dinner, remove the
meat and juices from the refrigerator. Discard any fat from the

juices. Place the meat on a board. Cut the beef crosswise into slices about ¼ inch thick. Pour any juices into the cooking juices. Carefully spoon some juice onto each slice of meat. Replace the slices tightly against each other, wrap them in foil, and place them on the serving platter. Leave them so they willl be at room temperature when you serve them; the meat will soak up some of the juices.

Meanwhile, prepare the cold tomato and herb sauce. Plunge the tomatoes in a bowl of boiling water for a second before peeling off their skin, then open and seed each tomato. Cut each one into ½-inch dice and place them in a bowl. Pluck the tarragon leaves from the stem and place them in the bowl. Add crushed coriander, salt, and olive oil. Stir and check to correct the seasoning. Cover and leave for later in or out of the refrigerator.

To prepare the salad, remove the tough ends of the watercress, wash, and drain. Add the chervil. Combine the oil, vinegar, salt, and pepper together to make the dressing.

One and a half hours before serving the meal, prepare the Gratin Dauphinois according to the recipe on page 53. Put the Gratin in the oven.

When you are ready to serve, bring the towel-wrapped Gratin to the table along with the watercress salad, the platter of sliced meat, and the bowl of sauce. Sprinkle a little salt and pepper on the meat and spoon a little of its juices on top. Serve each guest 2 slices of beef and a portion of Gratin. Spoon a little cooking juice and then some of the tomato and herbs sauce on top of the meat. Pass the bowl of sauce around the table.

WINE   Any good red wine you like

WHAT TO SERVE BEFORE AND AFTER BOEUF EN TRANCHES

APPETIZERS   1. Crudités en Panier, page 45, with a variety of sauces
                 2. Poireaux Tièdes Vinaigrette, page 67
                 3. Jambon Persillé, page 54

DESSERTS   1. Grand Baba, page 273
                 2. Crêpes Normandes, page 269
                 3. Tarte Tatin aux Poires et aux Pommes, page 292

Decoration of the Table

This is truly the most workable of menus and the easiest to serve. This kind of meal is bound to be a happy one since there is truly no last-minute worry.

You may have as elaborate and busy a table as you choose since this is an unfussy menu. You may like a pretty blue and honey-colored scheme: a fresh, flowered, chintz cloth, and blue and ochre votive candles mixed with tall, thin candles in glass candlesticks. You may like to put a huge hollowed pumpkin in the center of the table filled with an assortment of blue cornflowers, blue bells, peonies, marigolds, and tea roses — all carefully arranged in a glass container and then placed in the pumpkin. You may tie each blue napkin with an ochre or yellow ribbon and slide a name card in it.

You may like to wrap a blue or white napkin on the neck of each bottle and arrange two linen-lined baskets of bread, a few tiny bowls of mustard, and a few small pots of fresh whipped butter on the table.

Strategy for the Suggested Menu

- Guests invited at 7:30 P.M.
- Dinner served at 8:30 P.M.

- On the day before the Feast: When the meat is at room temperature, dry the surface carefully and rub with a little olive oil and cracked peppercorns. Wrap in foil and keep in a cool place a few hours. Preheat the oven to 425°. Cook the beef. Deglaze the coagulated juices in the baking pan with vermouth. Cool and place in a dish, pour juices over it, cover and refrigerate overnight.
- Prepare Gratin Dauphinois or Caviar d'Aubergines and a basket of Crudité vegetables. Prepare the Crêpes Normandes. Cover with foil and refrigerate.
- On the day of the Feast:
- 6:00 — Slice the meat. Dip each slice into the juices. Cover and set aside at room temperature.
- Prepare the Gratin Dauphinois.
- 7:00 — Bake the Gratin. Prepare the watercress and dressing but don't toss.
- 7:30 — Place the Gratin or Caviar bowl(s) and Crudités with the

drinks as your guests arrive.

· 8:30 — Bring the warm Gratin, sliced beef, bowl of sauce, and watercress salad to the dining room. Put the Crêpes in the oven and reheat. Start the meal.

· 9:00 — Add a little currant sauce on top of the Crêpes. Change plates and bring the warm Crêpes to the table with dessert plates.

· Later: Coffees and teas.
· Later: Cold water, fruit juices, or Perrier.

LEFTOVERS

1. Hachis Parmentier, page 186.

2. Brown and cook some sliced onions. Cut the beef into slivers and add to the onions. Cook for a few minutes, season, then serve with chopped parsley, a few drops of red wine vinegar, and with or without boiled potatoes.

3. An omelet: Sauté one sliced onion in a little warm oil. Cut the leftover meat in small pieces and sauté for a minute. Pour a few beaten eggs on top and stir until the omelet is set.

4. Cold salad: Mix diced boiled potatoes, diced leftover beef, and quartered hard-boiled eggs. Season with a hearty vinaigrette (page 302) and sprinkle with fresh herbs.

5. Pasta: Sauté a sliced onion. Add the finely chopped leftover beef and pour in a good tomato sauce. Serve with al dente spaghetti and a bowl of Parmesan cheese.

BOUILLABAISSE ROYALE

A spectacular fish and vegetable soup — or is it a stew? — heady with saffron and herbs, and served with a red pepper and garlic sauce.

This heady and high-spirited fish stew, this glorious mythical dish is truly a Feast by itself. Nothing timid, nothing cautious about it. Bouillabaisse embodies the excess, the joy, the fire of Provence; it speaks of "Pétanque" ball players under silvery plane trees, of cypresses and olive groves, of the purple sea and the rocky jagged coast. With its delicate combination of fish, herbs, vegetables, and olive oil cooked on a high flame, this potent broth is the magical golden soup that Venus invented to please and distract her husband Vulcan while she attended to questionable matters with a young shepherd.

Labelled Marseille's very own specialty, it is such a great combination that every fisherman, every restaurant's chef, every housewife along the French Mediterranean coast is proud to claim his or her very own "authentic" version.

Originally, of course, a fisherman's Bouillabaisse depended solely on what the nets brought that day, though everybody seems to agree there should never be mussels or clams in a serious Bouillabaisse. But should there be potatoes? Garlicky rounds of toasted bread? Pastis? Which Rouille is acceptable? Fierce arguments, endless quarrels persist.

There are fifty ways to make the "right, the only" Bouillabaisse. The "royale" version may include bass and lobster; the "fisherman" version insists on four different kinds of fish; others are made with dry cod, sardines, sorrel, spinach, Swiss chard, and squid. There is even a "one-eyed bouillabaisse," made with poached eggs and no fish at all! Fresh firm fish and a light, pungent broth emulsified for a few minutes with a good olive oil ("bouillabaisse" means brought to a quick boil and cooked quickly) and served with a fiery sauce are the sensible basics of success.

Rascasse (the coarse, horrible-looking rockfish) is traditionally considered the core and soul of this glorious soup, but it cannot be purchased here, nor are weaver (*vive*), girelle, John Dory, favouilles crabs available either. But since they are in no way essential to our dish, there is no point lamenting them. Whiting, red snapper, varieties of rockfish, sole, conger eel, haddock, sea bass, fresh cod, mullet, and soft-shell crabs are readily abundant for a spectacular Bouillabaisse. We also have leeks, fennel, tomatoes, saffron, garlic Pernod, and fruity olive oil. As long as you avoid mackerel and sardine (both when you prepare the broth and as a fish) and depend on striped bass, butterfish, codfish, red snapper, bass and, if you can, sea spiders and soft-shell crabs, you will have a superb dish.

"Rouille," the glossy, peppery, garlicky sauce, comes in many versions. Sometimes it is made with a variety of small fish caught in the rocks; they are coarsely cut up and then crushed, cooked with herbs, and blended with a boiled potato and seasoned with saffron, cayenne, and olive oil. Most of the time it simply is a saffron and garlic mayonnaise or a red pepper and garlic sauce that must be very hot and have a smooth consistency in order to enhance and challenge the strong flavor of the Bouillabaisse. In the eighteenth century this fiery, intense sauce, because of its antiseptic and antibiotic qualities, was even used to fight plague.

The broth and the fish are presented as two separate courses in restaurants. The broth is served and then the Rouille is spread on fried or oven-dried bread rounds and floated on the soup. One must wait for a second before biting. Plates are changed; the platter with its combination of fish is presented, head and all; then each fish is filleted and served with the potatoes on a large platter along with a bowl of Rouille and a bowl of warm broth.

At home things are conducted differently. This is, after all, a fisherman's dish, and the ritual does not have to be so elaborate. Broth, fish, shellfish, served together with potatoes, make for a crammed but splendid plate, and a simpler process allows less opportunity for the fish to be overcooked. Although mussels and lobsters are not traditionally used in Provence, you may like to add them. But for practical reasons lobster must be served in a separate dish, which is some trouble when you serve eight or ten people on your own.

The rich, dark, intense broth, the sweet shellfish, the tasty fish, and the saffrony potatoes make for a glamorous combination. Miracles occur when this "golden broth" appears on the table. The pungent aroma and the bright colors exalt life and radiate joy and energy. It is a spectacular, exciting sight, a truly euphoric process. Nibbling, sipping, smelling, mopping up the last drops of sauce, marveling with unrestrained abandon make the sharing of this dish a total vital experience.

In the galaxy of glorious superdishes Bouillabaisse stands high, extracting with gusto the savor and the essence of the sea and converting all the guests around a table into grateful disciples. Nothing could be more conducive to conviviality and animated conversations than Bouillabaisse.

FOR *8* PEOPLE

UTENSILS

Large soup kettle
Skillet
1 or 2 wide shallow serving dishes
Mortar and pestle and/or food processor for the Rouille
Small finger bowls filled with lukewarm water to pass after the
    meal and/or a stack of paper napkins

FISH

*8 pounds fish, cut into 2 by 4-inch chunks or thick slices; flavorful fish:
    striped bass, fresh cod, sea bass, halibut, eel, haddock, hake, porgy;
    delicate fish: whiting, sole, flounder, red snapper*
2 tablespoons olive oil
2 tablespoon dry thyme
Salt
*2 teaspoons saffron, according to taste and depending on the quality you
    use*
2 tablespoons fennel seeds
*1 pound shellfish: 8 soft-shell or small crabs; 8 large shrimp or gambas,
    unpeeled if possible, peeled if your guests are finicky*
1 tablespoon Pernod or 2 tablespoons anise extract

BROTH

3 tablespoons of raw olive oil
6 onions, peeled and chopped
2 large leeks, white part only (optional)

5 tomatoes, chopped
6 garlic cloves, peeled and crushed
Parsley stems
*2 pounds fish bones, fish heads, and trimmings; the fish man will give
    them to you after he has filleted sole, cod, or any other lean fish*
Bouquet garni (1 sprig parsley and stems, 1 sprig thyme, and 1 bay leaf)
Few twigs of dry wild fennel or fennel seeds or extract anise
One 3-inch orange peel (dried in the oven for 15 minutes)
8 thyme twigs or powder
Salt to taste
4 cups (approximately) dry white wine
2 quarts water
Freshly ground pepper

SAUCES

ROUILLE 1   *8 garlic cloves, peeled, crushed*
6 red chili peppers, peeled, crushed or Tabasco to taste
1 slice of bread, crust removed, moistened and squeezed
5 tablespoons of olive oil
Salt
3 tablespoons broth

ROUILLE 2
(THE EASIEST)   *2 cups Aioli sauce, page 87*
Tabasco to taste
1 teaspoon saffron (optional)
1 tablespoon broth

VEGETABLES   *8 potatoes*

GARNISH   *20 very thin slices of French bread, approximately; oven-dried to crisp*
2 garlic cloves
Grated Swiss cheese

Trim and cut the fish into big chunks. Pat them with a paper towel. Make the marinade with the olive oil, thyme, salt, saffron powder, and fennel seeds. Rub each piece evenly with the marinade and leave in the bowl overnight, covered.

Prepare the broth: Heat a little oil in a thick-bottomed skillet. Add the chopped onions and cook for a few minutes until golden. Add the leeks after a few minutes, then the chopped fennel, tomatoes, the crushed garlic cloves, and the parsley stems. Add the fish bones, fish heads, a bouquet garni, the twigs of fennel (or some seeds), the orange peel, thyme, salt, white wine, and water. Bring to a boil. Lower the flame and simmer, covered, for 1 hour.

Meanwhile prepare the Rouille:

If you choose Rouille 1, put the garlic and peppers (or Tabasco) in a mortar and pound them until crushed and blended. Add the pressed bread, stir until you have a smooth paste. Work in the oil slowly. Add a dash of salt to taste. Stir in the fish broth. Your sauce should not be liquid but have the consistency of a light custard. (You may use a food processor for this.)

If you choose Rouille 2, prepare an Aioli sauce and add Tabasco and saffron to taste. It should be a fiery sauce. Add the broth. Pour the entire mixture into a bowl, cover with plastic wrap, and refrigerate.

You should make $1\frac{1}{2}$ to 2 cups of Rouille for 8 people.

Pass the broth through a Mouli mill or thick sieve, pressing with a spoon against the mesh to extract as much as you can from the mixture. Discard the herbs and bones. Taste the broth and add freshly ground pepper and more salt if needed. Cool, cover with plastic wrap, and refrigerate.

One hour before the meal remove the broth and the marinated chunks of fish from the refrigerator. Remove the fish chunks from the marinade.

Peel the potatoes and cut them into 1-inch-thick slices. Dry well.

Pour enough fish broth to cover the potatoes and bring to a boil; lower the flame and cook.

Meanwhile, heat the soup plates and rub the slices of oven-dried bread with a clove of garlic.

Remove the Rouille from the refrigerator. Put the Rouille and the grated cheese in pretty bowls. Put the garlicky, crisp bread in a basket and bring to the table.

Bring the rest of the broth in the big soup kettle to a boil, uncovered. Add the flavorful fish first, along with the shrimps and crabs. Five minutes later add the delicate fish and a little olive oil (about 3 tablespoons). Add the Pernod or anise extract at the last moment.

Check if the potatoes and fish are ready. Lift out the fish but not the shrimps or crabs with a wide skimming spoon and place in a shallow dish. Do the same with the potatoes and pour a ladle of broth over each. Bring the dishes of fish and potatoes to the table along with the kettle of broth, crabs, and shrimps, and of course the warm soup plates.

Make sure everybody has seen and smelled the whole Technicolor display of your dramatic production, then start serving. Pass the Rouille bowl around.

Place 2 pieces of fish, 1 shrimp, 1 crab, and 1 slice of potato in each dish and pour some hot broth on top. Ask each guest to pass the Rouille bowl, the crisp, garlicky bread, and the grated cheese.

Put the leftover fish, potatoes, and shellfish into the kettle, cover, and keep for second helpings. Meanwhile, pass some warm broth to pour over the guests' plates as they are enjoying their first helping.

WINE   A semi-dry or a mellow white wine is good. A rosé is often served in Provence. Bordeaux Anjou, Monbazillac, and Jurançon white wines are also recommended.

What to Serve Before and After Bouillabaisse Royale

A Bouillabaisse, whether sophisticated or simple, is truly a *plat unique* except perhaps for a tossed salad and a light dessert, but you may choose the following:

APPETIZERS TO BE SERVED WITH THE DRINKS BEFORE SITTING AT THE TABLE:
1. Bowl of Olives Sautées, page 61
2. Bowl of warm almonds
3. Pissaladière, page 63

DESSERTS
1. Mélange de Fruits, page 281
2. Cervelle de Canut, page 265
3. Panier de Frivolités, page 286
4. Granité au Vin, page 278

Decoration of the Table

This extravagant, brilliant dish dazzles and scatters its bright colors and aromas generously all around; in other words, it is a beautiful but quite messy dish. Your table could be covered with a bright blue oilcloth for a safe and pretty meal, and you could place a pile of large shells in the center filled with green leaves. Or you may wish to use a Provençal, heavy, quilted fabric and set a white tureen filled with fruit in the center. Blue, ochre, or bright yellow could make a pretty backdrop. You should place baskets all around the table to discard shells, and use an assortment of pretty bowls to serve the Rouille, grated cheese, and oven-dried bread. If you can, don't forget to have finger bowls or a stack of paper napkins, and, of course, nice wide, all-cotton napkins.

STRATEGY FOR THE SUGGESTED MENU

- Guests invited for 7:30 P.M.
- Meal served at 8:30 P.M.

- One day before the Feast: Marinate the fish for a few hours, then prepare the Bouillabaisse, the Rouille, and the Frivolités.

- On the day of the Feast:
- 7:25 — Remove the Bouillabaisse from the refrigerator and reheat it on a low flame. Peel and cook the potatoes. Prepare Olives Sautées.
- 7:30 — Your first guests arrive.
- 7:40 — Bring Olives Sautées along with drinks.
- 8:00 — Oven-dry the bread, take the Rouille out of the refrigerator, and add the fish to the hot broth. Rub garlic on the crisp, oven-dried rounds of bread.
- 8:25 — Add shellfish and final ingredients to the hot broth. Light the candles. Place the Rouille bowl, grated cheese bowl, and bread basket on the table. Ask your guests to sit at the table.
- 8:30 — Bring to the table the potatoes, the fish moistened with warm broth in two shallow dishes, and the kettle of broth and shellfish.
- 9:00 — Bring to the table the basket of Frivolités.

- Later — Coffees and teas.
- Later: — Cold water, fruit juices, or Perrier.

LEFTOVERS   1. An interesting and unusual way to serve Bouillabaisse is cold-jellied in its own broth on a bed of bitter greens.

2. You can reheat the leftover Bouillabaisse and add a few potato slices and a little white wine

BRANDADE

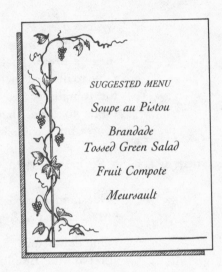

SUGGESTED MENU

Soupe au Pistou

Brandade
Tossed Green Salad

Fruit Compote

Meursault

A fluffy, dried codfish, potato, and milk mousse seasoned with nutmeg and raw olive oil.

Cod is a voracious creature that lives in deep waters, loves cold climates, and feeds on fish and shellfish. Because Norwegian sailors dried it in the wind and sun and brought it to the coasts of Provence as an exchange for olive oil, fruit, and vegetables, it has become a staple in Mediterranean cuisine. Its flesh is rich in protein and mineral salts. It is prepared with tomatoes, spinach, carrots, leeks, onions, potatoes, peppers, or anchovies in an endless variety of dishes.

Brandade, an unctuous purée of shredded dried cod, lukewarm milk, and oil, is a ritual food in Provence. Stirring the warm mixture with a wooden spoon for hours in a slow, steady movement tests your patience and teaches you that one should work hard at one's pleasures. And the metamorphosis of gray cod into this smooth, ivory mousse is one of the mysteries we depend on to be happy.

Whether the original idea came from Venice or Béziers or Nîmes is of little importance. The traditional Provençal recipe is now made with shredded cod, twice as much olive oil as cream, and with an addition of either truffles or parsley. Garlic, potatoes, and even a drop of orange juice are added according to taste and custom.

Brandade is served lukewarm or cold, either in a crisp pastry shell or piled in a white dome. It is eaten throughout Provence on Fridays, on New Year's Eve, and on Christmas night.

There is no need to possess special keys; there is no secret to unlock as you prepare the Brandade. The cardinal fact about this dish is your ability to unsalt dried cod and your patience to check and correct texture and flavor as you go.

Instead of pounding the codfish in a mortar with oil and milk, we use a food processor or a blender for a fluffier texture. We also use more potatoes, less oil, and more spices in our Brandade so that we can serve it as the core of a Feast.

Dried or salt codfish is readily available in Greek, Italian, Chinese, and Spanish markets (where it is known as bacalao or baccalà). It also comes in little wooden boxes packaged in Canada and sold in gourmet shops in the East. Always taste codfish with the tip of your tongue before boiling it to make sure it has soaked enough and is not too salty. Count on one-third pound of dried cod per person. The flesh should be white brown on one side, gray blue on the other. Count about twenty-four hours in water but always check with information on the package.

FOR *8* PEOPLE

UTENSILS — Food processor or blender

BRANDADE

3 pounds dried salt cod
3 large potatoes
Salt
2 bay leaves
1 onion, studded with a clove
1 cup olive oil
1 cup warm milk or half-and-half
3 garlic cloves, peeled and crushed
Pinch of nutmeg
Pinch of freshly ground white pepper
2 tablespoons lukewarm cream or milk
Lemon juice to taste

ACCOMPANIMENTS

3 slices of bread cut into toast points or 9 slices of French-type bread, oven-dried
1 tablespoon olive oil
1 tablespoon chopped parsley
2 tablespoons firm Niçoise or Greek black olives, pitted
Bowl of arugula or chicory or endive tossed greens with a vinaigrette dressing (page 302)

Place the salt cod in a large basin of cold water. Soak to cover for 10 to 24 hours, changing the water at least 4 times. Drain.

Cook the unpeeled potatoes in a large pot of lightly salted boiling water until soft.

Place the cod in an enameled or stainless-steel saucepan and cover with cold water. Add the bay leaves and onion, and bring slowly to a boil. Lower the heat and simmer for 3 minutes, then let it cool in the water. Drain. Remove skin and bones, and shred. You should have about 4 cups of shredded cod.

Heat the cups of olive oil and milk in 2 separate pans. They should be warm, not hot. Peel the potatoes. Place 1 potato and a few pieces of cod in a food processor and whip briefly. Add the crushed garlic, more flaked cod, another potato, and continue processing, alternately pouring in milk and oil. Finally, add the nutmeg, pepper, and even salt, if needed. You should have a white smooth purée. Spoon and scrape into a bowl. Cover with plastic wrap and place in the refrigerator.

Thirty minutes before serving, stir in the 2 tablespoons of warm cream and reheat on medium flame, stirring. Add pepper, salt, and lemon juice to taste.

Meanwhile, prepare the bread: Preheat the oven to 350°. Place the slices (rounds of bread or triangles) on a cookie sheet. Sprinkle a little olive oil on top and bake until brown. Turn them on the other side after 2 minutes and turn off the heat after about 3 minutes.

Pour the Brandade purée into a warm dish, add a few drops of cold olive oil on top, and stir. Dip a tip of the triangular or round crouton in Brandade and then into chopped parsley, and place them all around the edge of the serving dish. You may like to place a handful of pitted black olives in the center of the dome of Brandade.

Serve along with a large bowl of tossed greens seasoned with vinaigrette dressing.

WINE Because of the milk or cream in the Brandade, you should serve a mellow white wine, Bordeaux for instance, or Barsac, Anjou, or Monbazillac, but because of the garlic you should choose a dry white wine such as a Pouilly-Fuissé, Cassis, Bellet, or Meursault so choose according to your taste and to the amount of garlic used.

WHAT TO SERVE BEFORE AND AFTER BRANDADE

DESSERTS   1. Panier de Frivolités (page 286) served with either Granité au Vin
                    (page 278) or Mélange de Fruits (page 280)
                 2. Poires, Pruneaux, Oranges au Vin Rouge et aux Épices (page
                    289)
                 3. Grand Baba (page 273) served with apple compote

DECORATION OF THE TABLE

    A delicious dish but not a very colorful one in spite of the parsley
croutons and the black olives. Therefore, it would be best to choose
a cheerful tablecloth and a bright centerpiece, perhaps a bunch of
short fluffy roses or bright geraniums gathered in a shallow basket.
You may also like to spread tiny glass containers of multicolored cut
flowers around the table. Along with the salt and pepper shakers, put
tiny bottles of olive oil so each guest can add a few drops of cold oil
to his warm Brandade.

STRATEGY

- Guests invited for 7:30 P.M.
- Meal served at 8:30 P.M.

- Prepare the Soupe au Pistou, Brandade, greens for the salad, Frivolités, and cooked fruit ahead of time.

- On the day of the Feast:
· 7:30 — Your guests arrive.
· 8:00 — You reheat the soup on a low flame. Reheat the Brandade on
a low flame. Oven-dry the bread triangles, sprinkling a little oil on
top. Prepare the greens.
· 8:30 — Light the candles. Ask your guests to sit down at the table.
Bring the linen-wrapped soup kettle and bowl of Pistou.
· 8:50 — Bring the Brandade, its toasts, and the tossed green salad to
the table.
· 9:10 — Bring a basket of Frivolités and a bowl of cooked fruits to
the table.

· Later: Coffees and teas.
· Later: Cold water, fruit juices, or Perrier.

LEFTOVERS   1. Crêpes: Fill crêpes with leftover Brandade, cover with a light
cream sauce, and bake.

2. Omelet: Stuff an egg omelet with the leftover Brandade. Add a little milk if it is too dry, and sprinkle with chopped black olives and a drop of olive oil just before serving.

3. Croquettes: Add two eggs to the leftover Brandade and stir. Make into small round patty cakes, dip in bread crumbs, and fry. You may want to fry a few twigs of parsley and serve them with the Croquettes.

4. Oeufs Benedict: Poach eggs and serve on top of a tablespoon of leftover Brandade. Cover with a well-seasoned Hollandaise sauce in individual dishes.

5. Flan de Brandade: Add a little milk and two beaten eggs to the leftover Brandade. Pour into a baking dish, sprinkle with a small amount of bread crumbs, and bake for one hour in a 350° oven. Serve along with cooked spinach, or sautéed mushrooms.

CANARD FARCI

Crisp pieces of duck served with a stuffing of apples, liver, prunes, ham, and herbs and with a light, crisp garnish of chestnut, lemon, and scallions.

SUGGESTED MENU

Pissenlits aux Lardons

Canard Farci
Puréed Cabbage

Grand Baba

Alsatian White Wine

In the eighteenth century women of quality were always given three orations for their funeral. One was delivered by a philosopher (a must in the century of enlightenment when philosophers were what the stock exchange raiders or the haute couture wizards are to us now). The other two orations were given by regular guests at her table. It was not a case of social disease, such as "dining out as an alternative to living," as some Washingtonians or New Yorkers practice, but rather dining out as an intensification of

life, a fulfilling of all senses, an effort at making civilized contact—a
desire to give soul and heart to daily life.

Once you have served this Canard Farci you may rest assured that
when the time comes and you have to leave this valley of tears or
joys, your orations will all be of the very best quality. Canard Farci
may well be your Passeport Gourmand to immortality.

But back to the nitty-gritty of things. Unless you have a farm or
live near a farm, most of the ducks available are frozen Peking ducks
at your local supermarket. However, fresh ducks can be found in
butcher shops, especially in large cities, or ordered with a day's
notice. These ducks weigh about five or six pounds and have big,
heavy frames and high fat content. You need a whole bird for every
two people, so for eight people you will buy three or four frozen
ducks. If you can find duck thighs only, buy nine thighs and cut each
in half at the joint; these will be easier and neater to cook, degrease,
and serve than whole ducks.

Note: Long roasting allows the excess fat to be removed. You will
be happy and grateful to have it later to pour onto sautéed potatoes,
chestnuts, and vegetables of all kinds.

Three or four cooked stuffed ducks on a platter in a dining room
are a lovely sight, but they spell trouble for the hostess. They are a
problem to carve, to slice, to scoop out the stuffing, and then to
serve. It is a complicated process during which most of the meal gets
cold and guests get impatient.

The following preparation solves the difficulties that make Canard
Farci difficult to deal with when one has no help and insists on
serving this dish piping hot, crisp, and moist.

The cut-up duck is cooked slowly and pricked frequently to rid it
of all excess fat and to produce a crisp skin. The stuffing is baked
separately until the very end when the crisp duck is added for a few
minutes. Meanwhile, the chestnuts and scallions brown in duck fat.

This is a precise process tested over and over by generations of
generous mothers eager to provide unforgettable feasts for their
families, with the result being a preparation with no last-minute
surprise or virtuoso tricks, and a harmonious dinner that flows
gracefully around a sumptuous platter.

Everything in a successful Feast is based on planning, planning,
and planning, and that is why we are so elated when the Canard
Farci is set on the table. There is nothing left to plan or worry about.
We can enjoy it and go along with the flow of happiness running

through the room. You may feel pedestrian and disciplined during this rather long preparation in the solitude of your kitchen, but as the platter of Canard Farci appears, it will seem as if it had been created by no less than a whole brigade of gourmand guardian angels.

FOR 8 PEOPLE

UTENSILS	Large roasting pan with a rack
	Skillet
	9-cup terrine, 4 inches deep, or a 9-cup oven-proof dish with a lid or covered with foil

MEAT	*4 ducks, thawed if frozen*
	Freshly ground black pepper to taste
	2 teaspoons dried thyme or 3 sprigs of fresh thyme
	Juice of 1 lemon
	2–3 tablespoons kosher salt

BROTH	*2 onions, studded with cloves*
	2 carrots
	1 celery stalk
	Salt to taste

STUFFING	(about 9 cups are needed)
	Two 10-ounce cans whole chestnuts in water
	12 ounces (1½ cups) prunes, pitted
	6 tablespoons unsalted butter
	1½ pounds tart apples, peeled, cored, and thinly sliced to make 3 cups; you can use Granny Smith, Greening, Jonathan, or Early MacIntosh
	Salt
	Freshly ground pepper
	¾–1 cup duck or chicken livers, cut in half
	3 large onions, peeled and thinly sliced
	Vegetable oil
	6 ounces good country ham (Smithfield, Virginia, Kentucky, or plain country-cured ham), trimmed of fat and cut into ¼-inch cubes
	1½ cups chopped parsley
	2 tablespoons brandy
	1 cup red vermouth or port
	3 eggs, slightly beaten

ACCOMPANIMENTS   *3 tablespoons duck fat (approximately)*
40 whole chestnuts (part of the 2 cans bought for the stuffing)
5–10 scallions, trimmed, with 2 inches of green stem on, and halved lengthwise
1 lemon peel, finely grated
Cabbage or *Fennel Purée (page 299–300)* or *Ratatouille (page 68)*

SAUCE   *1 cup dry white wine (approximately)*
1 cup duck broth
2–3 tablespoons unsalted butter, softened
1–2 tablespoons vegetable oil

GARNISH   *Parsley* or *watercress*

Defrost the duck according to the directions on the package. Pull away the excess fat from the tail end of cavity. Cut away excess neck skin. Remove the wishbone, the wing tips, backbone, breastbone, and neck; you will use them along with the gizzard to prepare a fragrant broth. Separate the legs from the body and cut each leg in 2 parts across the joint. Cut down the length of the breastbone on either side of the ridge and lift each breast out in one piece. Rub the breast and legs (16 pieces altogether), with pepper, thyme, lemon juice, and salt. Keep refrigerated until ready to use.

Trim the 8 breasts and 16 legs and thighs of any fat, keeping the skin intact. Place in a roasting pan large enough to hold all the pieces flat in one layer. Use 2 pans if necessary. Season with salt, pepper, lemon juice, and thyme. Cover and refrigerate for 4 hours or overnight.

To prepare the duck broth: Place the gizzards, wings, and necks in water with the onions, carrots, celery, and salt. Bring to a boil and then simmer for 1 hour, covered. Drain. Cool. Remove top fat cover with plastic wrap.

To prepare the stuffing: Open the cans of chestnuts and set aside about 40 whole ones for the garnish. Add the broken pieces to the stuffing. Soak the prunes in lukewarm water to cover for 30 minutes. Melt 2 tablespoons of the butter in a large skillet. Add the apples. Cook quickly over moderately high heat, stirring often, until soft and lightly colored, about 10 minutes. Season with salt and pepper. Transfer to a large bowl.

Add 2 more tablespoons of butter to the skillet. Add the livers and cook for about 1 minute on each side. Add to the bowl of apples. Melt more butter and cook the onions for 5–10 minutes, or until soft. Transfer to the bowl of apples. Melt a little vegetable oil and quickly sauté the diced ham. Add to the bowl. Combine with the apples, livers, onions, and ham, the broken chestnut pieces, parsley, and pepper to taste. Drain the prunes and add them. Pour over the vermouth. Mix well, cover, and refrigerate for 2 to 4 hours, or until ready to cook.

Prepare the Cabbage or Fennel Purée or the Ratatouille. Cover and refrigerate.

Three hours before the party, preheat the oven to 350°. Prick the duck breasts and leg pieces and place on a rack in a pan. Cook, uncovered, for 30 minutes, then pour off the fat into a skillet and reserve in a bowl. One hour later pour off the accumulated fat again and put into the bowl. Continue cooking about $1\frac{1}{2}$ hours more. Prick the duck with a fork and check to see that the juices run clear, indicating that the duck is done. Remove from the oven. Slice the breasts on the diagonal about $\frac{1}{4}$ inch thick. Arrange the slices to overlap one another in a big oven-proof dish, then place the thighs and legs alongside. Cover carefully with a large piece of foil and leave in a 200° oven. Pour the excess fat into the bowl of duck fat.

To make the sauce: Place the roasting pan over a medium flame on top of the stove. Add wine and brandy to the pan. Scrape the coagulated juices at the bottom of the pan and stir vigorously. Simmer for 5 minutes, add the duck broth, and reduce slightly over high heat. Set aside for later use.

One hour before the party, mix the beaten eggs into the stuffing and pour into the terrine. Cover with foil and a lid or just foil, bake in a 350° oven for 40 minutes, and then keep covered in the warm oven.

Just before you begin the first course of the dinner: Heat the duck fat you have stored in a bowl and sauté the whole chestnuts, lemon peel, and scallions on all sides until lightly colored. (Whole canned chestnuts are fragile and break easily if not carefully stirred.) Sprinkle with salt and pepper. Keep covered in a warm oven.

Place the roasting pan with the cooking juices, wine, and broth on the stove over a high flame. Twirl in the softened butter and correct the seasoning. Take the duck out of the oven and add all the pieces to the warm juices, stirring for 1 minute. Arrange on a serving platter and add the chestnuts and scallions around them. Pour the rest of the juices over the whole platter. Cover with foil and keep warm in oven.

When you are ready to serve Canard Farci, take the dish of stuffing out of the oven. Place it on the rolling table with the warm dishes and the Ratatouille or purée. Take the platter of duck out of the oven. Add a bunch of parsley or a little bunch of watercress at one end and roll your table into the dining room.

Each guest should have 2 or 3 pieces of duck with a little sauce over them, a spoonful or 2 of the stuffing, 3 or 4 sautéed chestnuts, a piece of sautéed scallion, a twig of parsley or watercress, and a spoonful of either the Ratatouille or purée along the duck.

Note: This recipe can be prepared with a young 6-pound turkey.

WINE   A full-bodied red or an Alsatian white wine

WHAT TO SERVE BEFORE AND AFTER CANARD FARCI

APPETIZERS
1. Gougère, page 49
2. Pissenlits aux Lardons, page 65
3. Pissaladière, page 63
4. Caviar d'Aubergines, page 43, with warm toast and raw vegetables

DESSERTS
1. Grand Baba, page 273
2. Crêpes Normandes, page 269
3. Mousse au Chocolat Glacée, page 282, with a purée of fruits

DECORATION OF THE TABLE

A patterned tablecloth with rich caramel, warm rust, and mellow ivory colors would look well with such an opulent meal. You may want to add a brass or green pottery vase in the center, fill it with greens, and add a few blue and yellow irises for a cheerful note.

Scatter brown, beige, and green candles everywhere on the table. Set them in partially hollowed tan butternut squash or small pumpkins or acorn squash or green cabbage, digging a neat hole in the center of each vegetable and wrapping the bottom of the candles with two crushed facial tissues to hold them safely in place.

Wrap pretty colored napkins around the wine bottles. Add two brown or green lacquered baskets for bread. Don't forget butter pots and pretty salt and pepper shakers. Slide green or beige napkins in wood, silver, or china rings if you have some or else wrap a piece of coarse beige string or raffia with a wide bow around one and slide a card or a dry eucalyptus leaf with the guest's name under the string.

STRATEGY

- Guests invited for 7:30 P.M.
- Meal served at 8:30 P.M.

- The day before the Feast or earlier: Prepare Grand Baba and freeze; store the syrup and glaze in jars. Prepare the Cabbage or Fennel Purée and refrigerate it. Prepare stuffing and refrigerate it.

- On the day of the Feast: Three hours before the Feast take everything out of the refrigerator. Sauté the diced bacon for the salad and put in a bowl. Wash and trim the dandelions or chicory.
· Warm the Babas at 320° for five minutes while you reheat the syrup. Pour half of the syrup slowly over the Babas. Allow them to rest and absorb the syrup. After a while pour the remaining syrup and allow to rest again until all is absorbed. Sprinkle a little brandy on top. Reheat the glaze and pour it on top of the two Babas.
· Bake the duck. Discard the fat the first and second time and pour the excess fat in a skillet.
· Bake the stuffing.
· Reheat the purée. Sauté the onions and chestnuts in the duck fat in the skillet.

· 7:30 — Your guests arrive.
· 8:25 — Put pieces of duck into the warm sauce and keep warm in the oven, covered. Place dandelions or chicory greens on each salad plate. Heat the vinegar and oil, and add the crisp lardons for one second. Pour the lardons over the greens and sprinkle with pepper. Bring the plates to the table. Light the candles. Ask your guests to be seated at the table.
· 8:30 — Start the meal.
· 8:40 — While your guests finish the Pissenlits, go to the kitchen and bring the Canard with scallions, chestnuts, purée, and stuffing, and the warm plates, to the table. Each serving should include two pieces of duck, three chestnuts, one or two onions, some of the wine and cooking juices, two spoonfuls of stuffing straight from the terrine pot so it is piping hot, and finally a spoonful of purée. Place leftovers in the oven to keep warm.

· 8:50 — Offer the platter for second helpings.
· 9:00 — Change the plates. Bring the Grand Baba to the table.

· Later: Coffees and teas.
· Later: Cold water, fruit juices, or Perrier.

LEFTOVERS

1. Soup: A duck soup with the leftover diced meat and the delicious broth.

2. Curried duck: Chop or slice the leftover duck and sauté it in a little vegetable oil with one or two sliced onions. Sprinkle with curry, correct the seasoning, and add one or two chopped tomatoes. Serve over plain white rice.

3. Salad: Shred the leftover duck meat and serve it with boiled green beans seasoned with a lukewarm vinaigrette seasoning (page 302)

4. Gratin: Chop the leftover meat and stuffing, add a little duck broth, one or two diced tomatoes, and a few diced boiled turnips. Spread in an oven dish, sprinkle bread crumbs on top, dot with butter, and reheat for thirty minutes

CASSOULET

A lavish version of stew that includes beans, pork, duck, lamb, onions, tomatoes, and herbs baked under a fragrant bread crumb crust.

This earthy superdish, Cassoulet (the word comes from *cassole*, the earthenware pot in which it is baked and served), over the centuries has inspired endless quarrels, much praise, and a fair amount of analytical evaluation.

SUGGESTED MENU

Pissenlits aux Lardons

Cassoulet

Granité au Vin
Thin Cookies

Cahors

Cassoulet involves a rather long process and many ingredients but is basically simple to prepare. By starting the shopping and cooking two days ahead you will have a spectacular *plat de résistance* and no problem whatsoever when entertaining.

Among the innumerable one-and-only cassoulets, three stand out. In Castelnaudary, a small city in the southwest part of France where the dish may have arrived in some rough version around the seventh century by the Arabs, it is proudly and religiously prepared with dried white beans, garlic, ham, sausage, and pork rind. The second-ranking "authentic" version is that of Toulouse. In the city of aeronautics where the Airbus and the Concord are made, pieces of *confit*, preserved goose or duck, are added. Finally, in Carcassonne the "genuine" recipe includes lamb and an occasional partridge. In fact, the dish was prepared in all three places with dried lima beans for centuries until other varieties of beans, including the traditional white beans, were introduced to Europe by Columbus in the fifteenth century.

The secret of this legendary dish is that it is made in three separate steps: The beans are first blanched, which makes them easier to digest. Then they are cooked with lean salt pork, raw ham, and sausages in a white wine broth made with very flavorful herbs and vegetables. Meanwhile, the lamb is cooked apart, along with tomatoes, onions, wine, and herbs, and the duck is pan roasted. It is the final fusion of all these elements, slowly baking together and mingling their flavors, that turns this velvety stew into a triumphant dish crowned by its golden crust.

There is agreement in all three important versions that the crust on the top of the Cassoulet *must* be broken and "buried" in the beans and meats at least three but preferably seven times during the baking. The crust thus thickens as it develops flavor and seals the aromatic mixture underneath. This may well be the single most important and typical characteristic of Cassoulet.

Cassoulet is a very hearty, very substantial, quite heavy dish. As tastes and needs have evolved in the last decade, Cassoulet has likewise been altered for more conservative contemporary taste. This is for the better, I think, since I frankly don't see any one around today able to eat, digest, and survive the kind of Cassoulet served at my grandparents' a few decades ago. Then it took days of herb broth and mineral water to recover from an "authentic" Cassoulet.

The following recipe is, I think, a perfect arrangement. I have clung fiercely to what makes Cassoulet unique, discarding only the amount of fat involved in the preparation. There is lean salt pork, sausage, raw ham, and lamb cooked one day ahead, which makes it easy to discard the fat. The duck thighs, cooked slowly, give out their fat into the fragrant cooking juices, which later add to the dish's seasoning. The cooking juices of the lamb, pork, and beans are very highly seasoned; altogether they make for a very tasty, varied, spectacular Cassoulet but not an overwhelmingly rich one. We can enjoy it to our heart's content without transgressing any sensible nutrition rule.

Organization is again of the essence. Cassoulet must be done calmly one or two days ahead. It improves as it reheats, and leftovers are a treat, so make an abundant spectacular display.

By having the time to remove bones, fat, and gristle, to carefully slice the meats, to correct the cooking broth and all the cooking juices, your Cassoulet will be a true masterpiece and an easy one to enjoy. Fit and fully contented, you will notice once more how good times and good food enjoy each other's company.

A Cassoulet has to be very abundant, but remember that it freezes beautifully.

FOR ABOUT *12* PEOPLE

UTENSILS	Large kettle
	Skillet
	Very wide, 6-quart, 5-inch-deep earthenware or porcelain oven-proof container
	Gratin dish or large casserole (to hold 6 quarts; deep enough so Cassoulet does not dry and wide enough so each guest has a good portion of the delicious crust)
	Large long-handled ladle or deep spoon
	8 to 12 soup spoons
DUCK	*6 fresh duck legs (drumsticks and thighs) or 5 pieces of confit of duck or 5 pieces of confit of goose (available in specialty food shops)*
	Kosher salt
	Dry thyme
BEANS	*3 pounds dry white beans, Great Northern beans, or marrow fat beans*
	Several duck, chicken, veal, or meat bones (to improve the broth)

2 pounds lean salt pork or *unsmoked bacon, rind removed and cut into
1-inch pieces*

2 onions, peeled and studded with cloves

3 carrots, peeled and finely chopped

2 celery stalks, finely chopped

3 teaspoons dry thyme or *4 sprigs of fresh thyme*

10 peppercorns

3 bay leaves

Bunch of parsley, stem and all

8 garlic cloves, peeled

2 quarts boiling broth or *water (approximately)*

*2 cooking sausages (about 1 pound) (Toulouse, if you have a French
butcher nearby; salsicetta, cotechino, Polish kielbasa, or a tasty Hungarian sausage)*

*1 pound cured country ham in one piece, preferably a Kentucky or Vir-
ginia ham*

LAMB

6 pounds lamb (leg or stew meat, if available, or lamb shanks), boned

4 tablespoons (or more as needed) olive or *vegetable oil*

6 onions, peeled and chopped (to make about 4 cups)

2 celery stalks, thinly sliced

10 tomatoes, peeled, seeded, and chopped, or *one 28-ounce can tomatoes
with the liquid*

8 garlic cloves, peeled

6 teaspoons dry thyme or *several sprigs of fresh thyme*

3 bay leaves

4 cups dry white wine

2 cups broth or *water*

Salt

ASSEMBLING THE
CASSOULET

Freshly ground pepper

6 teaspoons dry thyme

2 tablespoons chopped fresh mint leaves (optional but lovely)

3 cups bread crumbs, preferably homemade

1 cup minced parsley

4 garlic cloves, peeled and minced

1–2 tablespoons butter or *walnut oil*

Chicken stock, if necessary (to cover the beans and meat before baking or
to moisten the Cassoulet in the oven)

Since confit of duck or goose is very expensive, the following way to prepare duck makes for a reasonable yet delectable Cassoulet.

One day before the party, rub the duck legs with kosher salt and dry thyme. Leave overnight to marinate.

Meanwhile, prepare the beans. (*Note:* Make sure you don't use stale beans; they will burst while cooking. In fact, the dry beans should be this year's crop.) Unless the instructions on the box are different, soak them in cold water for 2 hours. Drop in a pan of lukewarm water, bring gently to a boil, simmer for 2 minutes, remove from the flame, and let stand in the water for 1 hour. The beans should double their volume. Drain and discard the water.

Put the beans in a saucepan with the bones, if any, along with the pieces of lean salt pork, clove-studded onions, chopped carrots, celery, thyme, peppercorns, bay leaves, parsley, and garlic cloves. Cover with boiling broth or water and bring back slowly to a boil. Lower the heat and simmer, covered, for $1\frac{1}{2}$ hours, until the beans are cooked but not mushy. Add the sausages for the last 30 minutes. Add cured ham for the last few minutes.

Drain the beans, pouring them into a large bowl. Add salt and pepper to taste. Keep the broth for later use.

Meanwhile, prepare the lamb; remove the gristle and fat, and dry with a paper towel. Cut into 2-inch cubes (to make about 8 cups). Brown them on all sides in the oil for a few minutes in a big skillet. Remove the lamb cubes from the skillet and pour off all but 1 tablespoon of the fat. Add the onions and celery. Lower the heat and cook about 3 minutes, until the onions are translucent. Add the tomatoes, garlic, thyme, bay leaves, white wine, broth, and salt. Return the browned lamb to the skillet. Bring to a boil, then lower the heat and simmer for 1 hour, partially covered.

Remove the meat and set aside for a few minutes. Strain the broth, pressing down on the vegetables to extract as much juice as possible. Bring to a rapid boil and reduce, uncovered, until the liquid measures about 4 cups. Return the meat to the broth and cool to room temperature. Cover with plastic wrap and refrigerate.

Refrigerate the beans and other meats.

On the morning of the party, take everything out of the refrigerator. Wipe the pieces of duck with a dry paper or cloth towel. In a heavy skillet pan roast the duck legs in a little vegetable oil for $1\frac{1}{2}$ hours, covered, on a low flame, turning it from time to time while you prepare the rest of the Cassoulet. When the duck is cooked, remove from the skillet and add a little white wine or water. Scrape the bottom to melt the coagulated juices and set the skillet aside. When the duck is cold, cut each leg in 2 parts.

Remove all fat from the lamb pieces and from its broth. Remove the fat from the top of the beans.

Slice the sausages in 1-inch slices. Cut the cured ham in pieces 1 by 1 inch. Check the taste of the bean and pork cooking broth, and season with salt and pepper if necessary.

Put a layer of cooked beans on the bottom of the casserole. Sprinkle with a little pepper and a little thyme. Add the lamb and cured ham, more beans, a little pepper and thyme, then the pieces of duck, sausage slices, and finally the rest of the beans. Season with pepper and thyme. Add mint leaves if you have them. Carefully pour the juices of the duck and the lamb, and enough of the broth that the beans cooked in, to cover the ingredients in the Cassoulet dish. The level of the liquid should reach $\frac{1}{2}$ inch or $\frac{3}{4}$ inch below the rim.

Keep the remaining broth to add to the Cassoulet as it bakes. Sprinkle the bread crumbs and all but 6 tablespoons of minced parsley over the surface of the Cassoulet. Dot with butter. Cover with foil and refrigerate.

Set aside the remaining parsley and minced garlic in a piece of aluminum foil for sprinkling at the last minute before serving.

Two and a half hours before the dinner preheat the oven to 350°. Take the Cassoulet out of the refrigerator. Place the broth near the oven. Unwrap the casserole and set it in the upper third of the oven. As soon as a golden crust forms about 15 minutes—lower the temperature to 300° and break the surface of the crust with the back of a spoon. Push it down into the beans and baste with the casserole liquid. Carefully add some of the reserved broth at the edges of the dish so the beans remain moist and the liquid remains always just under the level of the crust.

Break and baste the crust 3 to 7 times depending on your patience. The beans must be very moist at all times. (I think 3 breakings of the crust is adequate and sufficient, but allow the last crust to form and turn gold and crisp before serving.)

Wrap the Cassoulet dish with a beautiful towel. Add the minced parsley and garlic on top and bring it to the table along with the warm plates. You may like a fresh tossed salad served on half moon plates with this.

Place the large Cassoulet dish on a side table, and either ask your guests to come and help themselves or, for a quicker and more efficient serving, place on each warm plate a piece of duck, a slice of sausage, a piece of lamb, a piece of bacon, a piece of ham, some beans, a bit of juice to moisten, and a piece of crisp crust with the parsley and garlic sprinkling.

After serving bring the Cassoulet dish at once to the oven. Remove the napkin from around it and keep warm until your guests are ready for second helpings. This must be an unhurried kind of meal, so make sure your dishes and your Cassoulet arrive at the table piping hot so you can linger to your heart's content.

WINE   A light red wine, such as a Cahors or Beaujolais, a strong chilled rosé, a dry chilled white wine, or a full-bodied red wine, such as Bordeaux or a Burgundy.

WHAT TO SERVE BEFORE AND AFTER CASSOULET

APPETIZERS   For this hearty, solid dish, experts recommend very little before and a very light dessert. In France raw oysters or clams on the half shell are often served on a platter with sliced lemons and buttered country bread.

1. Crudités en Panier with one sharp sauce, page 45
2. Pissenlits aux Lardons, page 65
3. Beef or chicken broth with thin warm toast

DESSERTS   1. Granité au Vin, page 278, with two platters of thin cookies
2. Mélange de Fruits, page 281
3. Cervelle de Canut, page 280
4. Lemon, coffee, or mint sherbet

DECORATION OF THE TABLE

Such a generous superlative country feast needs a warm and rich table setting. It is an unhurried kind of meal; people take time to enjoy life. Everything on the table is useful and also lovely and interesting enough to contemplate for a long time.

You may use, of course, the predictable rustic red-and-white-checkered cotton, but for a more interesting combination you may prefer a quilted cotton tablecloth in shades of rich brown. Or you may like a dark red, deep blue, and cream paisley fabric. A brass, copper, or silver tureen in the center filled with either dahlias, plump roses, anemones, or peonies and an abundance of blue, ivory, and red candles of different heights all over the table may be lovely.

Make sure there are at least three bottles of wine on the table. Wrap their necks with little napkins. Choose big off-white or colored cotton napkins. Add a soup spoon to each place setting.

STRATEGY FOR THE SUGGESTED MENU

- Guests invited for 7:30 P.M.
- Meal served at 8:30 P.M.

- One day before the Feast: Prepare the first part of Cassoulet. Prepare the Granité au Vin.

- One day ahead or on the morning of the Feast: Prepare the dandelions and the dressing. Cut and sauté the bacon dice.

- On the evening of the Feast:
- 6:30 — Preheat the oven. Bake the Cassoulet in the oven. Break the crust and add broth and juices from time to time.
- 7:30 — First guests arrive.
- 8:15 — Light the candles. Bring water, bread, and butter to the table. Take the dandelions out of the refrigerator and divide onto individual salad plates. Sauté the bacon for a minute. Add vinegar and pour on top of each plate of greens. Bring plates to the table.
- 8:30 — Ask your guests to be seated at the table. Meal starts.
- 8:40 — Wrap the Cassoulet dish in a kitchen towel, bring it to the table, and serve.
- 9:00 — Clear the table and change plates. Bring the Granité au Vin with two platters of thin cookies to the table.

- Later: Coffees and teas. After this sumptuous meal an old brandy, preferably an Armagnac or cognac, are welcome.
- Later: Cold water, fruit juices, or Perrier.

LEFTOVERS

1. Add a little broth and some bread crumbs on top, then reheat in the oven.

2. Make a robust peasant soup by chopping the leftover pieces of meat and adding them to some broth.

3. Cassoulet freezes beautifully. Stir in a few tablespoons of canned tomatoes before reheating

CHOU FARCI

SUGGESTED MENU

Pissenlits aux Lardons

Chou Farci

Compote de Poires

A Full-bodied Rosé

Stuffed cabbage.

It is served in bistros, in guinguettes, and in country inns, but Chou Farci remains essentially a jewel of family cooking and a pillar of festive gatherings. Like all traditional festive dishes it was invented to react against the monotony of daily cooking by transforming inexpensive and easily available ingredients in imaginative and original ways. Consequently, Aunt Marie or Cousin Jeanne's Chou Farci was always a shared event worth remembering in the family patrimony of good things.

There are innumerable interpretations of Chou Farci because each region, each bistro, and each cook is confident that he or she follows the very best version. Many combinations have been tried out, eliminated, selected, adopted, and improved in the course of the years, and as a result the choice is wide: The cabbage may be stuffed with pork, lamb, beef, chicken, or ham and also with peas, chestnuts, mushrooms, olives, apples, prunes, rice, and moistened bread. It may be seasoned with garlic, herbs, shallots, or spices. Generally the meats are braised or boiled (leftover Pot-au-Feu is superb) since roasted meats are often too lean for stuffing that must remain tasty and unctuous after its long cooking. Chou Farci may be braised with vegetables or simmered in broth, or it can be steamed in my favorite utensil, the double steamer pot.

Chou Farci may be served with a sauce of cream and fresh herbs, a fresh tomato sauce, or sauce made with wine and puréed vegeta-

bles. Whatever recipe is finally chosen the variations on this theme
are numerous, from hearty to truly refined. Calmly prepared a day
ahead, the Chou improves in flavor, is easy to reheat, and is easy to
serve. It is not quick to prepare, but this is one of those cases in
cooking when the longest way is truly the best in the long run. The
cabbage leaves are first blanched in boiling water to make them
pliable, then a rich stuffing is spread between them, and finally the
whole cabbage is reshaped and placed in a large piece of cheesecloth
to cook. It is truly fun to create a Chou Farci.

The recipe offered here has been proven and has been used as the
center of many generations of Family Feasts. I have tried my Alsatian cousin's version with apples, my Provençal aunt's rendering
with Swiss chard, peas, and artichokes, and my northern neighbor's
variation where the cabbage is stuffed mostly with a variety of meats.
But mine, which is the version offered here, seems to gather a
consensus among friends and relatives for a hearty, highly spirited,
and wonderfully satisfying festive meal. Once "reconstituted," the
stuffed leaves make for a spectacular and majestic plump cabbage.
By now I can do it with my eyes closed, and you will do the same.

Note that although one stuffed cabbage is plenty, two is more fun
if you want an extravagant, truly memorable meal.

FOR *8* PEOPLE

UTENSILS
Skillet
Large piece of cheesecloth
String
Small wooden board to use when slicing the stuffing
Double steamer pot *or* big soup kettle

INGREDIENTS
2 cabbages (about 3 pounds), trimmed
2 tablespoons butter
1 tablespoon vegetable oil
2 large onions, peeled and coarsely chopped (about ½ cup)
8 ounces lean salt pork or lean bacon rind, cut into ¼-inch cubes
1 pound boiled ham, chopped
4 garlic cloves, peeled and finely chopped
3 eggs, lightly beaten
1 cup cooked rice (⅓ cup raw rice)
1 cup chopped parsley

1½ cups of the center leaves of your parboiled cabbage, coarsely chopped
1 teaspoon freshly ground coriander
Freshly ground pepper
Salt
Fresh herbs such as parsley, chives, and tarragon, finely minced

ACCOMPANIMENTS   *3 long celery stalks, peeled and cut into 2-inch pieces*
2 zucchini, trimmed, sliced lengthwise, and cut into 2-inch pieces
3 fennel heads, trimmed, no strings, and cut in half lengthwise
4 small turnips (about 1 pound), peeled, halved, or quartered
4 carrots, peeled, cut lengthwise, and then cut into 2-inch-long pieces
2 large Polish sausages (garlicky or very spicy), pricked with a fork before cooking

SAUCES   The cold sauce is passed around, the warm sauce is spooned over each portion of Chou Farci to moisten it as you serve it.

COLD   *1 cup olive oil*
Salt to taste
1 teaspoon freshly ground coriander
2 tablespoons minced fresh herbs such as thyme, marjoram, chervil, and parsley
1–2 tomatoes, plunged in boiling water for easy peeling, seeded, and diced

WARM   *1 bowl warm cabbage broth*
Minced parsley

GARNISH   *3 tablespoons finely minced fresh herbs: parsley, basil, scallions, tarragon*

Wash and trim the vegetables, then store them in the refrigerator. (The sausages and vegetables are served with the Chou Farci. Add them to the pan during the last 30 minutes of cooking.)

Cook the cabbage leaves. Remove and discard the core and tough outside leaves. Bring a large pot of water to a boil and parboil the cabbage for about 10 minutes in an uncovered pot. Remove the cabbage to a colander and refresh under cold water. When cool, peel off the leaves and drain them on a towel; keep the small center leaves for stuffing.

Heat the butter and oil in a large skillet. Add the onions and sauté until soft. Add the cubed pork and cook 5 minutes more. Transfer to a mixing bowl and allow to cool. Chop the center leaves of the cabbage (to make 1½ cups). Add to the bowl with the ham, garlic, eggs, rice, and parsley. Stir all the ingredients until well combined. Season with coriander and pepper, and add salt if needed. The stuffing should be rather coarse.

Line a bowl with a large piece of cheesecloth or a thin kitchen towel. Spread a few cabbage leaves on the cheesecloth to line the bowl. Sprinkle the leaves with salt and pepper, then spread on a layer of stuffing. Cover with 2 or 3 cabbage leaves, another layer of stuffing, and so on until you have used all your ingredients. Cover with the final 2 cabbage leaves. Gather up the top of the cheesecloth and close it with a string. You will have a neat, compact ball. Leave it in its bowl in the refrigerator until ready to cook.

Prepare the cold sauce: Mix the olive oil, salt, coriander, and herbs in a bowl. Stir in tomatoes. Cover with plastic wrap and refrigerate.

You will prepare your bowl of warm broth at the last minute.

Two hours before the dinner, take the Chou Farci, raw sausages, trimmed vegetables, and bowl of sauce out of the refrigerator.

Fill the bottom part of a double steamer pot with boiling water. (The double steamer is most useful here. It makes for firm vegetables; it enables you to cook three things at once; and it keeps everything warm if your guests are late.) Place the Chou Farci in the first tray of the double steamer. After 1 hour add the trimmed vegetables on the second tray and place the 2 sausages in the boiling water in the bottom of the pan. Cook for 30 minutes more on medium heat. Check once to make sure there is enough water boiling in the bottom compartment. The stuffed cabbage, vegetables, and sausages will be ready at the same time and can wait for about 1 hour if you turn off the steamer but keep the lid closed.

If you are not using a double steamer pot, fill a large soup pan with water and bring to a boil. Proceed as above: Place the stuffed cabbage in the boiling water, lower the heat, and simmer for 30 minutes. Add the vegetables and sausage. Cook 30 minutes more.

When ready to serve the meal, carefully place the cabbage in a bowl. Cut open the strings with a scissor and push away the cheesecloth. Tip the bowl to drain off the excess liquid. Place a large serving platter on the top and, holding on tight to the platter and bowl, turn the bowl and platter together in a decisive gesture. Turn the cabbage upside down once more onto another platter in order to have it top side up. Peel away and discard the cheesecloth.

Pour some of the warm cooking broth in a bowl and sprinkle a little parsley in it before you take it to the table. You will spoon it over each part of Chou Farci.

When all your guests are seated bring the warm plates, Chou Farci, 2 bowls of sauces, bowl of finely minced fresh herbs, steamed vegetables, and sliced sausages to the table.

When everyone has seen the glorious green Chou, take a modest bow and then a deep breath: This is no time for maybes. Armed with a big knife, a wide spatula, a big spoon, and the good wishes of the whole assembly, you are now ready to officiate. Cut 2 wedges of Chou Farci and lay them on their sides on each warm plate. Arrange some vegetables and a slice or two of sausage alongside the Chou. Spoon a little broth over everything and sprinkle some minced fresh herbs over all. Pass the plates along with the 2 bowls of sauce to your guests.

WINE   A rosé or hearty red wine

What to Serve Before and After Chou Farci

With such a rich dish, nothing too distracting or excessive is needed before or after.

APPETIZERS
1. Pissenlits aux Lardons, page 65
2. A salad of arugula, slivers of fennel, and endives with a sharp vinaigrette dressing (page 300)
3. Crudités en Panier, page 45, with a pungent sauce
4. Pissaladière, page 63
5. Warm almonds and Olives Sautées, page 61

DESSERTS
1. Compote de Poires, page 266
2. Mélange de Fruits, page 281
3. Crémets aux Fruits, page 267
4. Granité au Vin, page 277
5. Panier de Frivolités, page 286
6. Poires, Pruneaux, Oranges au Vin Rouge et aux Épices, page 289
7. Piece of ripe fruit with a good ripe cheese, such as grapes, walnuts, and Roquefort cheese served with a Sauternes or any good sweet wine

Decoration of the Table

Your *plat de résistance,* your glorious superdish will give the tone of the meal, and you may like your table to reflect some of the quiet opulence and informal provincial charm of your Chou Farci. Use natural elements: cotton, straw, wood, terra-cotta, ivory-colored candles. You may place in the center of your table a basket filled with chubby red geraniums or a short-flowered shrub or an exuberant pyramid of fruits and vegetables with Queen Anne's lace tucked in. The setting should suggest nature at its most generous.

Since the plates are kept warm in the kitchen, place a folded napkin between the forks and knives as you set the table.

Strategy for the Suggested Menu

- Guests invited for 7:30 P.M.
- Meal served at 8:30 P.M.

- One day before the Feast: Prepare the dandelion greens, diced bacon, stuffed cabbages, cold sauce, trimmed vegetables, and cooked pears.

- On the day of the Feast:
· 6:30 — Take everything but the pears out of the refrigerator.
· 7:30 — Start cooking Chou Farci. Your first guests arrive.
· 8:10 — Add vegetables and sausages to the double steamer.
· 8:30 — Turn off the pot and the double steamer. Keep covered. Light the candles on the table. Ask your guests to sit down around the table. Heat vinegar in the skillet and pour dressing on Pissenlits aux Lardons. Bring Pissenlits to the table.
· 8:50 — Prepare Chou Farci for the table and serve as described.
· 9:10 — Bring dessert and a platter of thin cookies to the table.

· Later: Coffees and teas.
· Later: Cold water, fruit juices, or Perrier.

LEFTOVERS   1. Chou Farci is easy to reheat with a little broth, but it will not be too presentable.

2. Gratin: Chop all the leftovers, pour into a baking gratin dish, and cover with a light cream. Season the cream with a little broth and a little tomato. Sprinkle bread crumbs on top. Dot with butter

and bake for thirty minutes in a 375° oven.

3. Farcis: Stuff halves of tomatoes and onions with the chopped leftovers moistened with a little broth or tomato sauce. Sprinkle the top of the vegetables with grated Swiss or Parmesan cheese before baking for thirty minutes.

COQ AU VIN

SUGGESTED MENU

Jambon Persillé

Coq au Vin
Celeriac Purée
Watercress and Endive
Salad

Compote de Poires

Côtes du Rhône

A splendid marinated chicken sea-soned with red wine, vegetables, and herbs.

This is one of the most pop-ular of traditional dishes. In se-rious bistros, in country inns, and in families throughout France, Coq au Vin is served for big occasions. All the varia-tions of this potent sauce and moist chicken dish are interest-ing, whether cooked with white wine or red wine, whether thickened with rooster blood, with yolk and cream, with puréed chicken livers, or with a *beurre manié.*

Apparently it all started when the prosperous Gauls under siege by the Roman troops sent to Julius Caesar a thin, old rooster wearing around its neck an ironic message: "Bon appetit!" As we came to learn, Caesar was big enough to take a joke and turn it to his advantage. He responded by a dinner invitation to the Gaul leaders. They accepted and were served a Gaul rooster simmered with Gaul herbs in Roman wine. They loved it, and they saw the Gallic-Roman relationship with a new eye. According to the legend, this Coq au Vin marked the beginning of a long civilization and the beginning of a cautious but lasting friendship.

Today it is easy to find full-bodied wines and good vegetables when we prepare our Coq au Vin, but one-year-old rooster is diffi-cult to come by if you are not raising it yourself. The following recipe takes into account the shortcomings of our times and compensates for them. We heat the marinade first; for concentrated flavor we marinate the chicken overnight. We first cook the legs and thighs of the chicken, which need longer cooking, and add the breasts later because they are fragile but absorb the juices wonderfully. We cool the chicken in its sauce.

Note: By the time it is served, the young fryer has absorbed as much flavor from the herbs, vegetables, and wine as possible; the sauce is potent and velvety, the meat aromatic.

Since we cannot find chicken blood or even pork blood, as is sometimes advised, the sauce is thickened with chicken livers and a small amount of butter and flour mixed and pureed together to form a pasty mixture (*beurre manié*).

Prepared one or two days ahead, this is a foolproof dish that keeps improving when reheated and needs no attention before the meal. You can serve Coq au Vin with a basket of boiled potatoes. The following menu includes Celeriac Purée because it is made entirely ahead of time, is easy to reheat, and adds a little extra charm. A tossed green salad is also suggested, but of course Coq au Vin needs no trimmings and can be served by itself.

FOR *8* PEOPLE

UTENSILS	Large skillet
	Large cast-iron casserole with a lid
BROTH	*Chicken necks, bones, and innards*
	1 onion, stuck with 3 cloves
	Bouquet garni
	Salt to taste
	Thyme
	Peppercorns
	3 cups water or *2 cups very good store-bought stock*
MARINADE	*4 cups hearty, young, tasty red wine*
	2 onions, sliced
	1 carrot, peeled and sliced
	Bouquet garni
	2 garlic cloves, peeled and crushed
	4 teaspoons dry thyme

10 peppercorns

3 tablespoons olive oil

CHICKEN

8 large chicken thighs

8 chicken breasts

6 drumsticks

2–3 chicken livers, trimmed

20 mushroom caps, or more if tiny

24 pearl onions or 12 shallots, peeled

4 large carrots, peeled and cut into thick slices

3 celeriac 7-inch-long celery stalks, trimmed and cut into 1-inch pieces

2 cups chicken broth

1 cup red wine (if meat is not covered by liquid when it starts cooking)

4 ounces lean salt pork or bacon rind removed and cut into $\frac{1}{4}$ by
  1-inch-long pieces (about 2 cups)

3 tablespoons vegetable oil

3 tablespoons butter

Salt

Freshly ground pepper

3 tablespoons dry thyme

1–2 tablespoons flour

Bouquet garni (a bay leaf, 2 parsley sprigs, 1 thyme sprig)

2 large onions, peeled and sliced

4 garlic cloves, peeled and crushed

3 tablespoons flour

3 tablespoons butter, softened

2 tablespoons cream

Pinch of freshly grated nutmeg

Juice of 1 lemon

3 tablespoons good brandy: Marc or Plum brandy or Cognac

GARNISH

3 slices of buttered bread, crustless and cut into 24 triangles

3 tablespoons parsley or chives, finely minced

ACCOMPANIMENTS

Choose from the following suggestions:

Basket of boiled unpeeled potatoes

Celeriac Purée (page 300)

Dish of rice (page 303)

Fennel Puree (page 300)

and a tossed green salad (page 301)

If you are making the chicken broth: Put the chicken parts, onion, bouquet garni, salt, thyme, peppercorns, and water into a large skillet and cook for 30 minutes, uncovered. Correct the seasoning.

For the marinade: Combine the red wine, onions, carrot, bouquet garni, garlic cloves, thyme, peppercorns, and olive oil in a saucepan. Bring to a boil, lower the heat, and simmer for 5 minutes. Let cool to room temperature.

Pour the cooled marinade over the chicken pieces. Set aside the chicken livers. Cover and leave the marinating chicken in the refrigerator overnight, turning 2 or 3 times.

Meanwhile, trim the mushrooms, onions, carrots, celery stalks, and celeriac. Prepare the salt pork. Cover and refrigerate.

On the morning of the Feast, remove everything from the refrigerator. Remove the chicken from the marinade. Reserve the liquid.

Heat the oil and butter in a large skillet. Pat dry each piece of chicken. Sprinkle each piece with salt, pepper, and thyme, and brown on all sides for 5 minutes, starting with the thighs and the drumsticks which require longer cooking. Cook the breasts only 2 minutes on each side. Then sprinkle each piece lightly with flour and cook 1 minute more. You will have to make several batches so all the pieces are crisp and golden. Remove the chicken from the skillet and set aside.

Prepare the salt pork or bacon. Add to the warm skillet over a low flame. When the pieces are crisp and brown, remove and put aside. Pour off the extra fat. Add the pearl onions, carrots, and celery to the skillet for a few minutes, turning them with a wooden spoon. Remove the vegetables and set aside. Sauté the mushrooms in the skillet for a few minutes. Sprinkle them with salt, remove from the skillet, and set aside.

Remove as much fat as you can from the liquid left in the skillet and pour any remaining cooking juices into a large casserole along with about 2 tablespoons of butter or oil. Heat the juices and oil, add the browned chicken thighs and drumsticks, the reserved marinade liquid with the vegetables, and the chicken broth. Bring to a boil, lower the flame, and add the bouquet garni and sliced onions. Simmer for about 30 minutes, until the juices of the chicken run pale yellow when you prick it with a fork. Add the chicken breasts to the warm dish, making sure they are submerged in the liquid. Cool the Coq au Vin to room temperature and then refrigerate.

Cook and purée the celeriac, then cool, cover, and refrigerate.

Preheat the oven to 400°.

Spread the bread triangles with butter, toast in the oven for 2 minutes on each side, then turn off the oven. You will reheat the croutons at the last minute.

Note: These things don't need refrigeration if kept in a cool spot, otherwise refrigerate.

One hour before the meal, take everything out of the refrigerator: Celeriac Purée, chicken in its sauce, mushrooms, onions, bacon, and sautéed but uncooked onions, carrots, and celery. Remove the skin and any gristle you see from the chicken. Remove the fat from the surface of the chicken cooking juices with a spoon and taste the broth; it should be highly aromatic.

Pour the cooking juices from the chicken into a large casserole and bring to a boil. Make the *buerre manié* by working the flour and softened butter into a paste. Whisk it bit by bit into the hot sauce. Cook for a minute or so, uncovered. Add the onions, carrots, and celery. Lower the flame and cook for 10 minutes. Add the chicken, cover, and simmer 10 to 15 minutes more.

Cook the potatoes in a separate pan of salty water.

Reheat the Celeriac Purée on a low flame in a covered pan with 2 tablespoons of cream.

Meanwhile, cut the chicken livers into very small pieces with a pair of scissors and add them to the casserole. Slide in the mushrooms, bacon, onions, crushed garlic cloves, nutmeg, and lemon juice. Cover and cook 2 or 3 minutes more.

Discard the bouquet garni. Check the seasoning. Add the brandy, turn off the flame, and keep the casserole covered in a warm spot.

Reheat the bread croutons for a few minutes in the oven. Make sure the guests are seated.

Pour the potatoes into a basket or dish. Pour the Celeriac Purée into a side dish. Place the salad greens in a bowl over the dressing and on top of the crossed serving spoon and fork. Take the croutons out of the oven. Rub them with a clove of garlic and dip one corner of each bread triangle into the Coq au Vin sauce, then into the minced parsley. Place them on a side dish. Put the remaining parsley in a bowl to take to the table.

At the table, serve a breast and a thigh or a drumstick, a few onions, a few mushrooms, some celery and carrots, and a few pieces of bacon on each plate. Spoon the sauce over, sprinkle with the chopped parsley, and add 2 croutons on the side. Add 1–2 spoonfuls of Celeriac Purée to each plate. Pass the basket of boiled potatoes around the table. Toss the green salad and pass it around.

WINE A red Burgundy, Beaujolais, or Côtes du Rhône, or a hearty, young, full-bodied red wine. Best to use the same wine in cooking and with the meal.

What to Serve Before and After Coq au Vin

APPETIZERS 1. Jambon Persillé, page 54, served with toast fingers
2. Poireaux Tièdes Vinaigrette, page 67
3. Terrine aux Herbes, page 73

DESSERTS 1. Compote de Poires, page 266
2. Grand Baba, page 273
3. Crémets aux Fruits, page 267

Decoration of the Table

This is a hearty, colorful dish but not a messy one. A tablecloth in various shades of ochre, yellow, or peach would be pretty. You might choose a rich paisley or a bold flowery print for your tablecloth, and you might place in the center of the table a wide terracotta or pottery bowl filled with large Granny Smith apples, some thin green pears, and tiny clusters of black and white grapes, in which you can put a few fluffy yellow and pink roses (in little glasses stuck between the fruit). If you can find them, add a few twigs of greens or, better still, a few twigs of those small black and dark blue berries that grow wild along roads and in garden hedges.

You may want to use an assortment of pale green, ochre, or yellow candles, and wrap napkins around the necks of your wine bottles. Set out individual butter pots, or two larger ones for the boiled potatoes, big cotton napkins, and two green or ochre lacquered bread baskets. If you serve tossed salad, it may be wise to use a separate plate; little crystal half moons are nice for this.

Strategy for the Suggested Menu

• Guests invited for 7:30 P.M.
• Meal served at 8:30 P.M.

• On the day before the Feast: Cook the marinade the day before or even earlier. Prepare the Jambon Persillé. Marinate the chicken for at least twelve hours. Trim all the vegetables. Cook and purée the celeriac. Prepare the bacon. Mince the parsley and chives and put in a bowl. Cook the pears and ginger. Cover and refrigerate everything.

• On the morning of the Feast: Sauté the chicken, bacon, mushrooms, pearl onions or shallots, carrots, and celery, and set aside. Add the marinade and its vegetables and cook for about thirty minutes. Cool.

• One hour before the Feast: Remove the fat from the chicken juices. Remove the skin from the chicken. Toast the croutons and leave them in the turned-off oven. Boil the potatoes. Prepare the salad dressing and salad bowl.

· 7:30 — Your first guests arrive.
· 8:00 — Finish the Coq au Vin according to the recipe. Reheat the Celeriac Purée on a low flame. Cook the potatoes.
· 8:30 — Turn off the Coq au vin, Celeriac Purée, and potatoes. Light the candles. Ask your guests to be seated at the table. Bring the Jambon Persillé to the table.
· 8:45 — Reheat the toast for a minute and finish according to the recipe. Wrap the covered Coq au Vin casserole with a pretty towel. Pour the potatoes into a basket. Pour the Celeriac Purée into a dish. If possible, place these on a rolling table along with the bowl of minced parsley, tossed salad, and warm plates. Holding each crouton between your fingers, dip it into the chicken sauce and then into the parsley and place it on a dish on the rolling table.
· 9:00 — Take everything to the dining room and serve.
· 9:30 — Clear the dinner plates. Bring the cooked pears. Pass the crème fraîche bowl around the table along with 2 platters of thin cookies.

· Later: Coffees and teas.
· Later: Cold water, fruit juices, or Perrier.

LEFTOVERS   1. Omelet: Drain the pieces of chicken. Debone it and chop it up. Mix it with a few tablespoons of parsley, a few eggs, and salt and pepper. Cook as an omelet and dot with butter before serving.

2. Croquettes: Chop up one leftover chicken. Mix with the left-

over Celeriac Purée and a few leftover potatoes, mashed. Mix in salt, pepper, and two eggs. Make some flattened little balls, roll them in bread crumbs, and fry until golden crisp.

3. Reheat gently all the Coq au Vin leftovers. Add a cup of boiled sliced carrots and boiled sliced potatoes at the last minute and serve sprinkled with chives or parsley.

4. The leftover chicken meat with the mushrooms, onions, and bacon can be gently reheated in their own sauce and used as sauce over hot pasta

COUSCOUS

A fragrant meat and vegetable stew.

Steamed vegetables, crisp herb-seasoned shish kebabs, warm chick-peas, and a spicy tomato sauce are served with the fluffy, steamed, hard wheat couscous grain.

It is, of course, a celebrated North African dish, but sunny, spicy, exotic Couscous has in the last decades become one of

SUGGESTED MENU

Olives Sautées
Roasted Almonds

Couscous

Compote de Poires

Rosé

France's national dishes, as much as Pot-au-Feu or Onion Soup. Couscous is one of the choices whenever a spectacular extravaganza is needed. Everyone—including grandmothers, infants, and the most severe nutrition-minded guests—can indulge happily in Couscous because it is made with the best wheat grain and offers a variety of fresh vegetables. The chick-peas are full of nutritive qualities; the broiled lamb in the stew is meticulously lean and tasty; the tomato sauce is barely cooked. In short, all the ingredients of a major Couscous Feast are thoroughly healthy. For once, what is good for you is also finger-licking good.

Far from a fickle fashion or a silly experiment this traditional dish is as satisfying as it is exalting. It is the kind of meal you leave quoting the old proverb: "Fate cannot harm me; I have dined today."

The word "couscous" probably comes from the sound made by the steam passing through the perforated tray and the bubbling of the broth. Like Pot-au-Feu, Cassoulet, and Bouillabaisse, it is one of those great dishes that can be done in a more or less elaborate way. A large variety of vegetables may be included: yellow and orange squash, lima beans, chili peppers, artichoke bottoms, eggplants, leeks, turnips, carrots. A few highly seasoned meatballs may be cooked in the broth. A large piece of lamb ribs sprinkled with herbs and broiled, a few fiery "merquez," the thin, spicy sausage, some crisp lamb, onions, bacon, and peppers, shish kebabs, or a cumin-flavored beef, lamb, and vegetable stew may be added to the steamed vegetables and the couscous grain for an opulent display.

The only drawback of this truly sumptuous dish is that it can be very messy to eat. Along with the pile of couscous grain, there are many vegetables on the plate and then, when the various stews are added, the whole plate tends to turn into a mushy battlefield full of lamb, beef, and chicken bones. It can make for a difficult situation to tend to with grace at a dinner table.

And so I have selected my favorite rendering of a Couscous. The flavors, variety, and abundance are there, but the bones, fat, and gristle are not. The steaming pyramid of fluffy grain can be enjoyed peacefully as a gentle counterpoint to the fragrant dishes of meats and vegetables and to the fiery sauce.

We have chosen diversity in color: red, green, orange, white. For variety of texture there is boiled as well as crisp broiled meat, crisp vegetables and soft vegetables. For complements of flavor there is bland grain and bland vegetables, fiery stew and fiery sauce.

The spirit is there, the smell and the taste, but all the meat is cooked ahead of time, and on the day of the party before reheating everything we discard all bones, fat, and gristle.

The preparation of such a dish is long—at least two hours—but most of it can be done a day ahead and simply reheated unattended while the couscous grain steams.

A philosopher once declared that life was an effort that deserved a better cause. The following preparations may also seem like an elaborate effort, but to all Couscous food groupies, such an end amply justifies the means.

FOR 8 PEOPLE

UTENSILS

10 or 12 large skewers

Large skillet to sauté meat and some vegetables briefly

Large soup kettle or casserole for meats and vegetables

"Couscoussière," a pottery or stainless-steel pot with a perforated top, or a double-decker steamer or a colander fitted on top of a pot of boiling water. The main thing is for the steam to escape through the perforated tray and the couscous grain not to touch the boiling water.

Wide shallow bowl

Platter 20 inches wide or bigger, if you have one, to use when sprinkling dry couscous, rolling it, and then serving the cooked couscous in a glorious pyramid

2 wide serving dishes

2 bowls for sauces

CHICK-PEAS

1 pound chick-peas

4 shallots or young onions, minced (about 3 tablespoons)

¼ cup olive oil

Salt

Freshly ground pepper to taste

MEAT AND
VEGETABLE STEW

3 pounds beef, chuck or round, cut into 2-inch pieces and trimmed of fat

3 pounds beef short ribs, trimmed of fat

3 pounds lamb shanks, trimmed of fat

4 tablespoons olive oil

2 tablespoons unsalted butter

2 onions, peeled and sliced

1 large green pepper, seeded and cut into 1-inch squares

1 eggplant (1–1½ pounds) cut into 2-inch chunks

2 zucchini (approximately 8 ounces), cut lengthwise and sliced into 2-inch chunks

3 garlic cloves, peeled and sliced

2 large beef bones (ask the butcher to cut into 4- or 5-inch-long pieces)

3 bay leaves

Sprig of thyme

4–6 cups water or beef broth

1–2 tablespoons cumin powder

Salt

Freshly ground pepper
Tabasco
2 tablespoons minced fresh coriander or parsley

SHISH KEBABS   1 leg of lamb (7–8 pounds), trimmed and boned (approximately 4 pounds
of meat remain)
Five ¼-inch-thick slices (about 8 ounces) lean bacon, with rind removed and
cut into 1-inch pieces.
5 small onions, peeled and quartered
2 green peppers, seeded, trimmed, and cut into 1-inch pieces
2 tablespoons mixed dry herbs (such as thyme, oregano, rosemary)
2 lemons
3 tablespoons olive oil

TOMATO SAUCE   2 tablespoons olive oil
1 medium onion, peeled and finely chopped
One large 28-ounce can tomatoes with their juices
2 garlic cloves, peeled and crushed
3 bay leaves
Salt
Freshly ground pepper
For flavoring the sauce:
2 garlic cloves, peeled and finely chopped
½ teaspoon ground cumin
½ teaspoon ground coriander
½ teaspoon powdered ginger
1 teaspoon Tabasco or Harissa sauce
½ cup virgin olive oil
3 tablespoons finely chopped parsley
Salt
Freshly ground pepper

STEAMED   4 small onions, peeled and halved
VEGETABLES   8 carrots, peeled and cut into 4-inch-long sticks
2 turnips, peeled and quartered
3 celery stalks, cut into 4-inch-long sticks
4 zucchini, cut lengthwise and then into 1-inch slices
4 big leeks (white only), cut in half lengthwise and then into 4-inch-long
pieces; tie together with string in a neat bundle for easy handling
4 fennel bulbs, core removed and quartered

COUSCOUS GRAIN   *2 pounds hard wheat medium or fine couscous grain (Fine is generally more delicate and makes for a fluffier dish, but I find medium safer and more interesting in texture and taste.)*
1½ cups water
2 teaspoons salt
4 tablespoons butter (approximately)
5 tablespoons olive oil (approximately)

GARNISH   *Twigs of watercress*

And now let us start. We are going to prepare:
1. chick-pea dish
2. meat and vegetable stew
3. shish kebabs
4. tomato sauce
5. steamed vegetables
6. couscous grain

To prepare the chick-peas: Soak the chick-peas overnight in cold water. Drain and place the chick-peas in a large pan with enough cold water to cover. Bring the water to a boil, lower the heat, and simmer for 1½ to 2 hours, until tender but not mushy. Drain and discard the water. Cool. Add the minced shallots, olive oil, salt, and pepper. Cover and refrigerate until ready to reheat for serving. The chick-peas can be prepared to this point up to 3 days in advance.

To prepare the stew: Sauté the pieces of meat in small batches in hot oil and butter for about 5 minutes, in a large skillet, making sure they brown on all sides. Drain the browned meat on paper towels and transfer the pieces to a deep casserole. Reserve.

In the same pan, add the onions, green pepper, eggplant, and zucchini. Cook over medium heat about 10 minutes, until all the vegetables are soft. Remove the vegetables with a slotted spoon to paper towels to drain. When cool, transfer to a bowl and refrigerate.

Add the garlic, beef bones, bay leaves, thyme, and water or broth to the pieces of sautéed meat in the casserole. Sprinkle with cumin. Cover, bring to a boil, then simmer for 2 hours, removing the lid for the last hour. Cool.

To prepare the shish kebabs: Alternate pieces of lamb, bacon, onion, and green pepper on 10 or 12 large skewers. Set the kebabs in a shallow dish and season with the herbs. Pour over the olive oil and lemon juice. Cover and set aside in the refrigerator until ready to cook. These can be prepared a day ahead.

To prepare the tomato sauce: Cook the chopped onion in the oil about 10 minutes, until soft. Add the tomatoes, garlic, bay leaves, salt, and pepper. Bring the liquid to a boil, then lower the heat and simmer for 5 minutes, uncovered. Remove the bay leaves, put the sauce in a blender and process until smooth. Set aside to cool.

Meanwhile, prepare the flavoring for the sauce. In a small bowl, combine the garlic cloves, cumin, coriander, and ginger. Stir in the Tabasco, olive oil, and parsley. Season with salt and pepper.

Add to cooled tomato sauce. Cover with plastic and refrigerate.

Prepare the vegetables and set aside until ready to steam and serve.

Two hours before the meal, take out the chick-peas, sautéed meat, cooked vegetables, shish kebabs, tomato sauce, and prepared raw vegetables from the refrigerator. At this point you can begin to assemble the meal. First, spread the couscous grain into a wide shallow bowl or a big round tray. Sprinkle with 1 cup of water to which has been added 2 teaspoons of salt. Toss with your hands and make sure all the grains are wet. Let it rest for 30 minutes.

Meanwhile, remove the fat from the top of the meat stew and all visible gristle and fat on the meat. Discard the bones and bay leaves. Bring to a boil, then add the sautéed vegetables. Lower the heat and simmer, covered, for 30 minutes. Check and correct seasoning with salt, pepper, and cumin. Set aside and keep warm.

To prepare the vegetables: Place all the trimmed raw vegetables in the first perforated tray of a steamer. Cover and steam over boiling water for 30 minutes, or until tender.

Heat the plates. Reheat the meat and vegetable stew in one saucepan, and the chick-peas with some broth in another saucepan.

Fill the bottom part of the double steamer pot (or couscoussière) with water and bring it to a boil.

Line the top tray with a piece of folded cheesecloth. Spoon the couscous grain on it, fold the four corners of the cloth together loosely, and steam for 20 minutes.

Open the cheesecloth and with a fork break any lumps of couscous. Sprinkle with the remaining $\frac{1}{2}$ cup of water a little salt, 1 tablespoon of olive oil, and 1 tablespoon of butter. Toss with 2 forks so each grain is coated. If you see any lumps, roll the grain between your fingers quickly and lightly so you don't burn yourself. Grains should be separated. Cover and let it rest for 20 minutes.

Broil the shish kebabs for about 5 minutes on each side.

Pour some of the cooking broth from the meat and the vegetable stew into a serving bowl to pass along with the tomato sauce, then pour the meat and vegetables into a deep serving dish. Sprinkle with fresh coriander or parsley. Cover and place on the service table.

Take the vegetables out of the steamer tray and place them in a long serving dish. Pour a spoon of hot stew broth over them, cover, and place on the service table.

Remove the couscous grain from the steamer tray. Open the cheesecloth, toss in the remaining butter and oil, and roll with your fingers or with 2 forks, making sure all is fluffy and there are no lumps. If it is too warm, take a kitchen towel and roll the grain between the pieces of cloth.

Pour the couscous grain into a wide bowl, spoon a little hot broth over it. Cover and place on the service table. Place the chick-peas in a dish and then on the service table.

Place the shish kebabs in a narrow dish so it fits on your service table and place a few watercress twigs in a corner. Place the tomato sauce in a bowl on a platter along with a bowl of steaming cooking broth and a bowl of Tabasco mixed with broth.

Light the candles. Ask your guests to be seated at the table.

Remove the covers from all the dishes, add the warm plates to the service table, and roll it into the dining room.

Make sure everybody sees the splendid display, then either ask your guests to help themselves from the service table or serve them yourself, placing on each warm plate 2 or 3 tablespoons of fluffy couscous, three-fourths of a shish kebab, a twig of watercress, a few steamed vegetables, some chick-peas, and 2 tablespoons of the meat and vegetable stew.

Pour a little broth over everything. Sprinkle some coriander or parsley over the meat and pass along to each guest. Pass around the tray with the hot broth and spicy tomato sauce. Meanwhile, gather the leftover meat, vegetables, and broth and bring back to the kitchen so they will be warm when you offer the platter of second helpings later.

This time you will pass the serving dishes around the table from guest to guest along with the 2 bowls of seasonings.

WINES   A very chilly rosé wine or a hearty red wine

What to Serve Before and After Couscous

APPETIZERS TO BE SERVED WITH DRINKS BEFORE YOU SIT AT THE TABLE:
1. A few Crudités, page 45, and warm nuts
2. Pissaladière, page 63
3. Olives Sautées, page 61

DESSERTS
1. Compote de Poires, page 266
2. Granité au Vin, page 278
3. Mélange de Fruits, page 281, with Panier de Frivolités, page 286, if you have time to prepare them
4. Tarte Tatin aux Poires et aux Pommes, page 292

How to Decorate the Table

Couscous, with its golden dome of grain, its stews, and its sauces, will make for a busy table even if you use a service table, so make the centerpiece as visible and as attractive as possible but keep it quite small.

A pyramid of oranges, tangerines, and kumquats piled on a flat basket and then dotted with streams of winding greenery or cut flowers would be lovely. You may also like to use a glass bowl filled with branches of candied dates, litchis on their twigs, and kumquats, all very airy and light in the center of your table. Scatter white votive candles around the centerpiece.

Choose a busy pattern with warm colors for the tablecloth; tomato sauce and the various stews will be passed around with more abandon and insouciance by your guests if you don't have a delicate, pristine cover. Choose big, dark, red or rust or brown cotton napkins. Place the bottles of wine in terra-cotta coolers or with a rust or brown napkin around their necks.

One basket of bread is enough because couscous grain takes its place in such a meal, but butter is needed on the table to use on the grain or on the steamed vegetables as a gentle counterpoint to the fiery sauces. Make sure there are enough butter pots around the table.

- Guests invited for 7:30 P.M.
- Meal served at 8:30 P.M.

- On the day before the Feast: Prepare the meat and vegetables, tomato sauce, marinated shish kebabs, and chick-peas, and trim the raw vegetables and keep refrigerated.

- Early on the day of the Feast: Prepare the olives, almonds, and a few long-stemmed young onions or radishes. Leave to be warmed later.
- 6:00 — Take everything out of the refrigerator.
- 6:15 — Prepare and spread the couscous grain according to the recipe.
- 7:30 — Put the hot water in the bottom of the steamer. Reheat a few almonds in oven.

  Your first guests arrive. Sauté the olives. Warm the almonds for a few minutes.
- 7:40 — Bring olives, almonds, and onions along with a stack of paper napkins to your guests.

  Arrange the couscous grain in the steamer. Broil the shish kebabs, turning once. Reheat the chick-peas.

  Gently reheat the meat stew with its eggplant, zucchini, and peppers.
- 8:00 — Finish the couscous grain, cover, and let it rest.
- 8:20 — Place the couscous grain in steam.
- 8:30 — Light the candles. Ask your guests to be seated at the table.

  Prepare the service table. Add a little butter and a ladle of warm broth to the couscous grain. Fluff with two forks and pour into a wide, deep bowl in a pyramid shape. Pour steamed vegetables into a dish. Pour meat into another dish. Pour warm chick-peas into a third dish. Place broiled shish kebabs on a narrow, flat dish or around the meat stew. Place the bowls of sauce and warm plates on the table and then roll the table into the dining room.

  When everybody has admired the dish, either ask your friends to come and help themselves or serve three tablespoons of couscous, some meat, some chicken, some broiled lamb, and some vegetables on each plate. Spoon a little warm broth over everything. Once everybody is served and seated, pass a bowl of boiling cooking stock and a bowl of fiery tomato sauce around the table.

Bring leftover Couscous to the kitchen and keep warm.

· 8:45 — Bring one or two platters of second helpings of Couscous and leave on the table for easy serving.

· 9:00 — Change plates. Serve the cooked pears, crème fraîche, and a platter of thin cookies. You may add a bowl of store-bought bitter chocolate sherbet.

· Later: Coffees and teas.

· Later: Cold water, fruit juices, or Perrier.

LEFTOVERS

1. Reheat Couscous leftovers by steaming them or simmering them in broth. They improve and are better than on the first day.

2. Hachis Parmentier (page 186) with the chopped leftover meats and a good mashed potato purée.

3. A rich soup: Chop all the leftover vegetables and leftover meats. Add a little water to the broth to reach the desired consistency.

4. Gratin: Dice the leftover meats and vegetables. Add tomato sauce (one-third spicy tomato sauce and two-thirds plain tomato sauce, or three canned tomatoes, drained and chopped), and stir. Check and correct the seasoning, cover with bread crumbs and a little olive oil, and bake until crisp (325°, about 20–25 minutes)

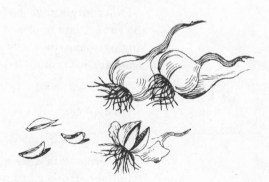

DAUBE DE BOEUF EN GELÉE

SUGGESTED MENU

*Crudités à la Tapenade
and à la Rouille*

*Daube de Boeuf en Gelée
Gratin Dauphinois
Green Salad*

Grand Baba

Bordeaux

A highly seasoned, marinated, and simmered pot roast of beef served cold in its natural jelly.

The word "daube" comes from the oval-shaped covered casserole traditionally used in Provence to prepare stews. This marinated and slowly cooked beef makes a splendid summer dish at an alfresco meal, but for best results you must prepare it at least a day and a night ahead.

An even simmering plus vibrant herbs, and a carefully chosen piece of beef, at once a bit gelatinous and lean, will make for a splendid Daube. And since it is cooked many hours before you taste it, its flavors will have time to mingle and enhance one another, and the unmolded dome of gelée will stand firmly on a platter.

The counterpoints of the fragrant Daube de Boeuf en Gelée are a crisp and bitter Green Salad (chicory, arugula, or dandelions mixed with other greens) and a luscious Gratin Dauphinois. This menu is so effective and so glorious that your guests will leave your table convinced that the world is a perfect place created only to provide man with endless ineffable pleasures.

Don't forget that if you prepare the dish too late and the gelée is too runny, you may of course serve it as a warm dish. And for your singing tomorrows, the leftover Daube can be reheated again and again for everyone's happiness.

FOR 8 PEOPLE

UTENSILS   Skillet
Large enameled cast ironware or heavy earthenware or copper
    casserole with a tight lid
Bowl about 11 inches in diameter and 4 inches deep or 2 large
    charlotte molds approximately $6\frac{1}{2}$ by 4 inches

MARINADE

4 cups dry white wine
1 cup red wine vinegar
2 tablespoons cognac or eau de vie or brandy or gin
2 tablespoons olive oil
2 teaspoons dry thyme or a few twigs
1 carrot, peeled and sliced
2 garlic cloves, peeled and crushed
2 bay leaves
10 juniper berries (optional but lovely)

MEAT

5 pounds lean, trimmed rump roast or combined chuck and shank, cut
    into 1 by $\frac{1}{2}$-inch pieces (make sure meat has no nerve, fat, or gristle)
Salt
Freshly ground pepper
$\frac{1}{2}$ cup olive oil and vegetable oil, approximately (enough to sauté meat)
8 ounces lean salt pork or lean slab bacon, with rind removed and diced
    into $\frac{1}{4}$-inch pieces
3 cups onions (about 2 pounds), peeled and sliced
4 garlic cloves, peeled and crushed
5 bay leaves
2 sage leaves
2 teaspoons dry thyme or 1 large sprig of fresh thyme
2 cloves
1 veal bone, cracked (optional)
One 2-inch piece dry orange peel or one 4-inch piece fresh orange peel
Bundle of parsley stems and leaves tied with a string
1 teaspoon dry powdered ginger or one 2-inch chunk of fresh ginger
10 peppercorns
Salt
3 cups carrots (about 1 pound), peeled and thickly sliced
5 large tomatoes (about 2 pounds), peeled, seeded, and chopped
$\frac{1}{2}$ cup Madeira, port, or a good sweet red or white sherry
$\frac{1}{2}$ cup firm green and $\frac{1}{2}$ cup black olives, pitted
3 tablespoons chopped flat parsley
Tiny stems of parsley

SAUCE

3 anchovy fillets
2 firm tomatoes, peeled, seeded, and diced
2 tablespoons capers
Pinch of freshly ground pepper

1 cup olive oil
1 tablespoon parsley, basil, or chives, cut with scissors (not too fine)

ACCOMPANIMENTS   *Gratin Dauphinois (page 53)*
Green Salad (page 301) with a vinaigrette dressing (page 300)

Start the cooking on the morning of the day before you have your Feast. Combine all the ingredients for the marinade. Place the cut meat in a large bowl, sprinkle it with salt and pepper, add the marinade, cover with plastic wrap, and keep in the refrigerator at least 4 hours or overnight, turning the pieces 3 or 4 times.

When you are ready to start cooking, drain the meat and reserve the marinade. Carefully dry each piece of meat with a paper towel. Heat 3 tablespoons of olive and vegetable oil in a thick-bottomed skillet and sauté the pieces of meat over high heat on all sides to brown. Lower the flame and cook a few minutes more. You will have to do this in 2 or 3 batches. Pour the sautéed meat into a bowl and set aside.

Add a little oil to your skillet and sauté the diced pork and onions for a few minutes; pour into the enameled cast-iron casserole. Add the sautéed pieces of beef, garlic, 2 of the bay leaves, sage, thyme, cloves, veal bone, orange peel, bundle of parsley stems, ginger, peppercorns, and salt to the casserole. Cook for a few minutes, stirring once, and then add the marinade. The liquid should barely cover the meat. Bring slowly to a boil, uncovered, lower the flame, cover, and simmer for 2 to $2\frac{1}{2}$ hours.

Add the carrots and tomatoes, cover, and cook 1 hour more, or until a fork easily pierces the beef. Add the Madeira or sweet wine. Cook for a few minutes, uncovered, and then turn off the heat. Let cool completely.

Degrease as much of the fat floating on the top as you possibly can. Correct the seasoning. Discard the bay leaves, peppercorns, bundle of parsley, and orange peel.

Rinse a large bowl or 2 charlotte molds with cold water. Place the 3 remaining bay leaves in the bottom of the dish. Surround the bay leaves with a circle of cooked carrot slices from the pot, followed by a wider circle of green olives and another of black olives. Finally use 1 tablespoon or more of chopped parsley to cover any open space on the bottom of the mold. Press gently against these garnishes with your hands so they will adhere to the dish. Taking great care not to

disturb the decorative layer, place the pieces of beef, cooked vegetables, and cooking liquid in the bowl. Press gently against the
surface with your hand so any trapped air escapes. Cover the top of
the mold with a piece of plastic wrap and refrigerate overnight or
longer (up to 2 days).

A few minutes before serving the Daube de Boeuf en Gelée, dip a
kitchen towel in hot water, squeeze it, and spread it around the bottom
and sides of the bowl for a second. Pass a knife around the edges to
loosen the jellied meat. Place a wide platter on top of the bowl (or
molds) and, holding tight to the edges of the bowl and the sides of the
platter, turn it upside down in one decisive and steady movement.
Your dome of jellied Daube should detach easily and stand proudly on
the platter. If you are using the charlotte molds, proceed in the same
calm way with one after the other, placing each dome on its own
platter.

Prepare the cold sauce. Crush the anchovy fillets with a fork. Mix
the tomatoes, capers, pepper, and oil in a bowl. Add the fresh herbs
and stir gently.

Take the Gratin Dauphinois out of the oven and wrap it with a
kitchen towel. Surround the base of the Daube with a wreath of
tightly gathered parsley leaves. Stick three 1-inch pieces of parsley
on top like little flags and bring the Daube, Gratin, cold sauce, and
bowl of greens to the table.

Toss the salad with a vinaigrette dressing and leave it on the table
along with the cold sauce for your guests to help themselves when
they choose.

When all the guests have seen the beautiful Daube dome, serve
every plate yourself very carefully, using a wide spatula and a big
spoon, and placing a section of crisp, mellow Gratin on each plate
alongside the Daube. Have your guests help themselves to the sauce
and tossed salad.

WINE   Any generous full-bodied red wine, not a light one, preferably a
Bordeaux, a Bourgogne, or a Côtes du Rhône

WHAT TO SERVE BEFORE AND AFTER DAUBE DE BOEUF EN GELÉE

APPETIZERS SERVED WITH DRINKS BEFORE YOU SIT AT THE TABLE:

1. Crudités à la Tapenade, page 45, and à la Rouille, page 114
2. Pissaladière, page 63

3. Two or three small, flat, cold omelets made with tomato and basil, onions, and herbs or chopped spinach and cheese, cooled, then cut into little pieces and presented on a bed of small lettuce leaves.

4. Paper-thin slices of sausage and prosciutto (or good country ham) with slivers of toast and thin bread sticks.

5. A tray of cucumbers, peeled, cut lengthwise, and filled with Tapenade, page 48, then sliced into 1-inch pieces.

DESSERTS

1. Grand Baba, page 273
2. Cervelle de Canut, page 265
3. Crémets aux Fruits, page 267
4. Granité au Vin, page 278
5. Mélange de Fruits, page 281
6. Flan au Caramel, page 272, and a platter of thin cookies

DECORATION OF THE TABLE

Daube de Boeuf en Gelée can be served as an outdoor informal dish or as the core of a more elegant indoor meal. Outdoors you may like to use a brown or faded green quilted tablecloth. A basket of crisp and enticing vegetables punctuated with long-stemmed scallions or radishes makes a perfect centerpiece. Or place a piece of wicker filled with fruit in the center for a simple, lived-in, drowsy, informal country feeling. Three pretty jugs for the wine, wood or terra-cotta salt and pepper shakers and candleholders, and a plain wooden tray for sliced bread would create a nice, lazy, summery feeling. You may also like to use for the bread some faded green baskets (any dime store spray can turn an ordinary basket into a lovely faded green in a jiffy). *Note:* Let Monet, Renoir, or Colette be your good angel and inspire you as you set your table—and your mood.

If you eat indoors, you may want to create a rhapsody in yellow: a sunflower yellow tablecloth, yellow butter pots, yellow crockery, yellow candleholders, and a yellow basket (dime-store sprayed) filled with yellow fruit—grapes, plums, lemons, pears. And perhaps here and there a touch of blue or brown to counterpoint the dazzling yellow symphony. *Note:* Set an engaging table, serene, cheerful, and warm, and remain vigilant to avoid the very worst of sins in a Feast: overdoing things and looking pretentious and fussy.

STRATEGY FOR THE SUGGESTED MENU

- Guests invited for 7:30 P.M.
- Meal served at 8:30 P.M.

- Two days or one day and a night ahead: Marinate the meat.

- On the day before: Prepare the Crudités, sauces, Daube, chopped shallots for the Gratin, greens for the salad, salad dressing, and Grand Baba. Refrigerate.

- On the day of the Feast:
- 6:45 — Preheat the oven. Remove everything from the refrigerator. Heat the milk, slice the potatoes, and prepare the Gratin Dauphinois and put it in the oven. Pour salad dressing into the bottom of a salad bowl and put the serving spoon and fork on top, ready to be tossed later. Place wine, water, bread, and butter on the table. Place the basket of Crudités and bowls of sauces on the living room table with drinks.
- 7:30 — First guests arrive.
- 8:25 — Unmold Daube on a platter. Light the candles. Ask your guests to be seated at the table.
- 8:30 — Take the napkin-wrapped Gratin, tossed green salad, Daube and its bowl of sauce to the table.
- 8:50 — Bring Babas to the table along with a small decanter of good rum.

- Later: Coffees and teas.
- Later: Cold water, fruit juices, or Perrier.

LEFTOVERS

1. Omelet: Sauté a chopped onion in a large skillet. Add the chopped leftover Daube and cook for one minute, stirring. Pour the beaten eggs (according to how much leftover Daube you have), salt, and pepper, and cook a rich country omelet. Dot the top with some cold leftover sauce.

2. Croquettes: Beat two or three eggs. Add the chopped leftover Daube and a boiled potato if you feel the mixture is too liquid. Form 2-inch balls, roll them in flour, and then fry until golden.

3. Pasta and beef: Dice the leftover Daube meat and reheat it gently in its sauce, correcting the seasoning. Cook the pasta or

spaghetti and toss the warm Daube into the pasta. Sprinkle with a few drops of olive oil and grated Parmesan or Swiss cheese. Serve at once.

4. Farcis: Parboil eggplants, zucchini, and tomatoes. Scoop out the flesh of each and chop the vegetables roughly. Add the chopped leftover Daube and correct the seasoning. Fill each vegetable shell with a teaspoon or so of the mixture. Sprinkle with bread crumbs, dot with butter or olive oil, and bake for thirty minutes in a 375° oven

FONDUE BOURGUIGNONNE

SUGGESTED MENU

Pissaladière

Fondue Bourguignonne

*Madeleines Tièdes
aux Fruits*

A Full-bodied Red Wine

Marinated diced pieces of beef and chicken dipped in a warm oil pan and served with a variety of sauces.

The ultimate convivial dish — a cheerful gathering around a fire and a joyous ritual — Fondue will please all ages and will ensure a lively and friendly Feast. Generally, one burner will do for eight people if you have a round table, but you should have two burners if you have a long table. Prepare a variety of breads, many bowls of capers, pickles, sliced onions, and gherkins, a platter of sauces, and a set of long forks. Remember to warn your guests: Anyone who lets a piece of meat fall into the oil deserves a fine (a bottle of champagne, a bottle of good wine, or the rendering of a song).

The following "peasant" version of Fondue Bourguignonne includes marinated diced chicken breasts along with diced pieces of beef. You may also want to include diced lamb.

The Fondue is served with a large bowl of tossed greens, a dish of warm potato chips, and a basket of tiny new boiled potatoes, and it is followed by a mixture of egg and grated cheese that each guest dips into the boiling oil until golden.

Once more you will notice how things executed at the table bring joy and lively participation by all the guests sharing this good-natured ceremony.

FOR *8* PEOPLE

UTENSILS	8 long-handled fondue forks 8 regular forks 1 or 2 burners and accompanying enameled cast-iron pot or pan
MEATS	*3 pounds tender beef, with no fat or gristle, cut into 1-inch dice* *2 chicken breasts, cut into ³⁄₄ to 1-inch dice*
MARINADE	*Olive oil* *Peppercorns, coarsely cracked* *Thyme*
SAUCES	*Select 3 of the following:* *1. Pistou, page 47* *2. Three differently seasoned types of mayonnaise (see below)* *3. Sour cream, mustard, and lemon* *4. Raw tomatoes, anchovies, and olives* *5. Olive oil, lemon, salt, pepper, and coarsely chopped olives* *6. Egg yolks, mustard, oil, and chopped gherkins*
COOKING OIL	*2 cups vegetable oil* *Twig of thyme* *1 garlic clove* *1 bay leaf*
GARNISH	*1 cup gherkins* *1 cup onions* *1 cup capers* *1 cup black or green firm olives with pits or stuffed with anchovies or peppers* *1 raw onion, peeled and sliced*
CRUDITÉS	*Select from lists on page 45*

Place all the diced pieces of meat in a bowl. Sprinkle with olive oil, cracked peppercorns, and thyme, and stir. Cover with plastic wrap. Keep refrigerated and marinate for a few hours.

Meanwhile, prepare the 3 sauces you have selected.

1. Pistou: Prepare it according to the recipe. Add a little oil or half a crushed tomato to make it more unctuous when you dip the meat in it.

2. Mayonnaise: Make 3 bowls, using:

3 egg yolks
1 teaspoon of Dijon-style mustard
$2\frac{1}{4}$ cups olive and peanut oil at room temperature
1 large lemon (about 4 tablespoons of juice)
Salt
Freshly ground pepper

Pour the egg yolks and mustard in a bowl. Beat with a whip for 1 minute, until sticky, and slowly add the oil. Make sure the yolks are absorbing the oil.

When all the oil is absorbed, stir in the lemon juice to thin it. Season with salt and pepper. Divide among 3 different bowls, and season each one differently.

Stir in 1 teaspoon of curry powder to the first cup of mayonnaise. Add salt to taste and more curry if wanted. Cover with plastic wrap and refrigerate.

Prepare a Rouille, adding garlic and Tabasco to your second bowl of mayonnaise.

Add 4 tablespoons of fresh basil, chives, or flat parsley to the third mayonnaise.

3. Mix 6 tablespoons of sour cream, 1 tablespoon of Dijon-style mustard, and the juice of 1 lemon until smooth. Correct the seasoning.

4. Dip 2 large tomatoes into a bowl of boiling water, remove the skin, seed, and place the tomatoes in a blender or food processor along with 3 garlic cloves, 5 anchovy fillets, 10 pitted olives, 1 teaspoon of capers, 1 tablespoon of fresh herbs, and some pepper. Correct the seasoning, cover with plastic wrap, and refrigerate.

5. Mix $\frac{1}{2}$ cup of pitted black olives, 2 tablespoons of olive oil, and the juice of 1 lemon in a blender. You should have a smooth paste.

6. In a bowl, mash with a fork 2 hard-boiled egg yolks and 2 tablespoons of mustard until you have a smooth paste. Beat in 4 tablespoons of oil slowly, stirring so the yolks absorb the oil and turn into a thick cream. Add the juice of 1 lemon. Squeeze 1 tablespoon of chopped gherkins and 1 tablespoon of capers in a piece of cheesecloth to make sure they are well squeezed. Add to the sauce. Add 1 tablespoon of minced herbs and 2 egg whites passed through a sieve. Correct the seasoning, adding salt and pepper to taste.

Cover the bowls of sauce you have prepared with plastic wrap and refrigerate. Place the garnish—gherkins, onions, capers, and olives—into little bowls. Cover with plastic wrap and refrigerate. Peel and slice raw onion, cover, and refrigerate.

Two hours before the meal, take the marinated meat out of the refrigerator and place it on two platters surrounded with a few small leaves of lettuce or some parsley stems. Keep it covered with plastic wrap.

Cook the tiny new potatoes in a pan of salty water.

Prepare the raw vegetables and place them in a basket or two.

Prepare the dressing for the tossed salad. Pour it in the bottom of a bowl, cross the salad utensils above it, and place the prepared greens on top. Pour a bag or two of potato chips on a cookie tray and heat them in a moderate oven for fifteen minutes.

When you are ready to serve dinner, heat the ingredients for the cooking oil on a high flame in a heavy-bottomed enameled or terra-cotta pan (the oil level must never reach higher than two-thirds of the pan). When bubbling, discard the thyme, bay leaf, and garlic. You are now ready to start the meal.

Place on the table the two platters of diced beef and chicken, baskets of Crudités, bowls of garnish, baskets of bread, bowl of warm potato chips, basket of boiled potatoes, and bowls of sauces along with the large bowl of untossed salad greens.

Each guest will have a long-handled fork to cook his meat. He will then transfer the cooked piece to a regular fork so he can dip it in the various sauces he has spooned around his plate and not burn his lips in the process.

During the meal the platters of meat, crudités, sauces, bread, garnish, and potatoes are constantly being passed around the table along with the salad. Keep the flame at medium and add about $\frac{1}{2}$ cup of warm oil to the cooking pot in the middle of the meal.

WINE   A good red wine. People drink a lot with a fondue, so prepare many pitchers of water and many bottles of wine.

WHAT TO SERVE BEFORE AND AFTER FONDUE BOURGUIGNONNE

Since there is no first course served while at the table with Fondue, you will offer the appetizers before you sit down, with the drinks.

APPETIZERS
1. Gougère, page 49
2. Pissaladière, page 63
3. Sautéed warm almonds and hazelnuts
4. A platter of very small Farcis, page 61, to eat with the fingers
5. For an extravagant all fondue Feast: Fondue Savoyarde, page 172, so the same setting is used twice

DESSERTS
1. Madeleines Tièdes aux Fruits, page 279
2. Tray of cheese (but not if you serve Fondue Savoyarde as a first course)
3. Grand Baba, page 273
4. Crémets aux Fruits, page 267
5. Tarte au Citron et aux Amandes, page 291, or Tarte Tatin aux Poires et aux Pommes, page 292
6. Mélange de Fruits, page 281

DECORATION OF THE TABLE

It will be a very crowded table, so use a simple, bright cotton tablecloth or a brightly colored oilcloth but no synthetic fabric. Choose bright and big cotton napkins along with some paper napkins, large simple glasses, a cookie sheet or metal tray to place under the burners (just in case), lots of water and wine pitchers, a variety of pretty bowls for the sauces and accompaniments, and handsome baskets for the bread. Make sure your table is totally cleared before you bring the dessert, which should be substantial and pretty. Since there is no centerpiece, the color has to come from the crockery and the tablecloth. No flowers and no candles, of course, with a Fondue.

STRATEGY FOR THE SUGGESTED MENU

- Guests invited for 7:30 P.M.
- Meal served at 8:30 P.M.

- On the morning of the Feast: Prepare the Pissaladière, vegetables, greens; bowls of sauces, bowls of gherkins, onions, capers, and olives; cubes of meat; Madeleines and fruit purées.

- On the evening of the Feast:
- 7:30 — Just before your first guests arrive, take everything out of the refrigerator: Pissaladière, meat, vegetables, Crudités, condiments, sauces, and tossed greens for the salad. Add the bread baskets, cold water, wine, and butter to the already set table.
- Cook the potatoes in a pan of salted water.
- Reheat the Pissaladière in a 350° oven.
- 8:00 — Lower the oven temperature to 250°. Bring the Pissaladière along with the drinks to your guests in the living room. Reheat the potato chips in the warm oven.
- 8:20 — Light the candles. Heat the oil, pour it into a pan over the burner, and place it in the middle of the dining room table. Turn off the oven, remove the potato chips, and place the Madeleines in the oven. Transfer the warm potato chips to a side dish. Pour the boiled potatoes into a basket and bring them both to the table along with the platters of meat, baskets of Crudités, bowl of tossed greens, and bowls of gherkins, onions, capers, and olives.
- 8:30 — Ask your guests to be seated. You may start the meal.
- 9:00 — Bring warm Madeleines along with fruit purées to the table.

- Later: Coffees and teas.
- Later: Cold water, fruit juices, or Perrier.

LEFTOVERS

1. Meat and green omelet: Chop the leftover meat in small pieces. Sauté one chopped onion in one tablespoon of oil. Add the meat and when it is golden, pour a few beaten eggs, chopped parsley, salt, and pepper over them. Cook on a high flame. Dot with butter before bringing to the table.

2. Meat sauce for pasta: Make a thick tomato sauce. Sauté chopped leftover meat and one onion. Add to the sauce. Serve with spaghetti and a bowl of grated Parmesan.

3. Gratin: Mix chopped pieces of meat with cooked rice, cheese, and a little tomato sauce or two chopped, seeded, and peeled tomatoes. Cover with bread crumbs and a little olive oil, and bake about 30 minutes in a 375° oven.

4. Hachis Parmentier, page 186

5. White gratin: Make a thick white cream sauce and add leftover finely chopped meat. Pour the mixture between two layers of cooked macaroni. Cover with grated cheese, dot with butter and bread crumbs, and bake.

6. Farcis: Mix cooked rice, one egg, a little chopped parsley, and the finely chopped leftover meat. Sauté with one chopped onion. Fill parboiled zucchini and onions and halves of raw seeded tomatoes. Sprinkle bread crumbs on top and bake.

7. Soup: Add some leftover diced vegetables, two garlic cloves, a twig of sage or thyme, and a bay leaf to the leftover meat. Cook with water, salt, and pepper for thirty minutes. Serve with grated cheese or sautéed diced croutons.

FONDUE SAVOYARDE

A cheese, wine, and brandy fondue served with diced bread and a variety of vegetables.

Fondue Savoyarde is a warm mixture of cheese melted in white wine into which guests plunge cubes of crisp bread. This dish traditionally follows active recreation, but there is no need to ski a slope or climb a mountain to earn it.

SUGGESTED MENU

Terrine aux Herbes

Toast and Gherkins

Fondue Savoyarde

Mélange de Fruits

Fruity White Alsatian

There are some new things under the sun, at least in this realm. Besides the cubes of bread we could, for a lighter, more diverse, and healthier fondue, prepare a basket of carefully cut raw vegetables and dip them along in the cheese sauce. Since the Fondue is shared from a communal dish and kept warm at the table, you will need one large burner for eight people at a round table, and two burners if you use a long table. Custom dictates that whenever a guest drops his piece of bread or his piece of vegetable in the Fondue, he has a fine — generally a song or a bottle of Champagne for the whole gathering to share the following week.

Note: The traditional cheeses for fondue are Emmenthal, Comté, and Fribourg. A good quality Swiss cheese is fine. You may add a little Cantal or even some Roquefort or blue cheese. You may also add a little mustard, a tablespoon of chopped chives, or a pinch of curry. This "varies the pleasures," as the French put it.

FOR *8* PEOPLE

UTENSILS   8 long-handled fondue forks
1 long-handled wooden spoon
Enameled cast-iron or flame-proof earthenware pot
1 or 2 burners

ACCOMPANIMENTS

BREAD: *1 large bowl of diced good white bread (cut into 1 by ½ inch; about 10 dice a person)*

VEGETABLES: *1 large cauliflower, cut into florets and raw and/or parboiled*
4 carrots, peeled, cut into thick slices, and either raw or parboiled for 5 minutes
2 heads broccoli, cut into florets and parboiled for 5 minutes
Bunch of radishes, with 2 inches of stems on, if possible
Bunch of green onions, with green stem on and trimmed
Several celery stems, trimmed and cut into 1-inch pieces
10–15 new unpeeled potatoes, boiled

TOSSED SALAD: *½ cup dressing (vinaigrette, page 302, using about 6 tablespoons olive oil, 2 tablespoons red wine vinegar, salt, and pepper)*
1 bunch of watercress or a few endives, trimmed and washed (about 4 cups)
½ cup coarsely chopped walnuts

FONDUE SAUCE   *2 garlic cloves, peeled and crushed*
2 tablespoons butter
1 tablespoon oil
2½ pounds cheese, all or mostly Swiss, grated (about 8 cups)
2 cups (approximately) dry white wine or fruity White Alsatian such as a
  Gewurztraminer
Salt
Freshly ground pepper
2 tablespoons cornstarch
1 tablespoon cold water
Pinch of freshly grated nutmeg
3 tablespoons kirsch brandy (optional)
2 eggs

Prepare 1 or 2 baskets of vegetables, setting side by side red radishes, creamy white cauliflower, green broccoli, and bright orange carrots in a colorful display.

Divide the bread into 2 baskets

Make the dressing for the salad. Pour the dressing in the bottom of a large bowl. Cross the salad utensils above it, then place the washed and trimmed watercress or endives along with a handful of walnuts on top. You will toss this later.

Thirty minutes before you serve your meal, place the cubes of bread in a 250° oven. Check the bread from time to time; it should become dry but not too crisp. Lower the temperature if necessary. Cook the potatoes in a pot of salty water.

Ten minutes before the dinner is served, prepare the sauce: Rub the thick enameled pan with the garlic cloves, then add them and the butter, oil, grated cheese, and wine to the pan. Cook over a low flame, lifting and folding over the mixture with a wooden spoon and *never* stirring, until it is totally homogeneous. The only rule is that the mixture is smooth, unctuous, and fragrant: It must have the consistency of a warm custard. Simmer the Fondue for a few minutes, then season to taste with salt and pepper. Dissolve the cornstarch in the water and add it. Add the nutmeg and brandy. Check the taste, then pour into the Fondue pot on top of the brazier in the center of the table.

Each guest will spear a cube of bread or piece of cut vegetable with his long-handled fork, dip it in the hot Fondue, coat it with the cheese mixture, and then transfer it to a regular fork to avoid burning his lips. It is best to peel and slice a potato and pour a little Fondue over. The salad can be nibbled along with the Fondue.

Note: After 5 minutes or so, add a little wine at room temperature if the Fondue sauce gets too thick.

Note: In the middle of the meal serve *le coup du milieu,* a tiny glass of kirsch brandy, to all the consenting adults at the table.

At the end of the meal, when there are only 2 tablespoons of Fondue left, add 2 eggs to the mixture, stir, and ladle a bit of this soft mixture onto each guest's plate.

WINE   Have plenty of cold water on hand as well as a fruity Alsatian or dry white wine and perhaps a little kirsch brandy

WHAT TO SERVE BEFORE AND AFTER FONDUE SAVOYARDE

APPETIZERS TO BE SERVED WITH DRINKS BEFORE SITTING AT THE TABLE:

1. Terrine aux Herbes, page 73, with an assortment of toasted bread and a bowl of gherkins
2. Caviar d'Aubergines, page 43
3. Pissaladière, page 63
4. Platter of proscuitto ham and spicy sausage slivers with a bowl of olives sprinkled with thyme

DESSERTS

1. Mélange de Fruits, page 281
2. Granité au Vin, page 278
3. Poires, Pruneaux, Oranges au Vin Rouge et aux Épices, page 289
4. Assortment of sherbets piled in a halved watermelon shell along with Panier de Frivolités, page 286

DECORATION OF THE TABLE

Since you cannot use any centerpiece or candles, and since your table will be very crowded, you should have a very bright and cheerful cotton tablecloth (not synthetic, it is too dangerous), large cotton napkins along with a stack of paper napkins, wide, pretty plates, and an assortment of lovely natural or spray-colored baskets for the bread, the boiled potatoes, and the vegetables.

Note: A tin tray under the burner is a good idea for safety's sake and to catch excess drips.

STRATEGY FOR THE SUGGESTED MENU

- Guests invited for 7:30 P.M.
- Meal served at 8:30 P.M.

- The day before the Feast: Prepare the terrine and the vegetables for the Fondue and greens for salad.

- On the day of the Feast: Prepare the fruit salad in the morning. Refrigerate.
- 7:30 — Toast the bread. Place the terrine and gherkin bowl on a tray.
- 8:00 — Cook the potatoes in a pot of salty water. Dry the bread cubes. Add the warm toasts to your terrine tray and bring it to your guests along with the drinks.
- 8:20 — Prepare the Fondue and bring it with baskets of bread and vegetables, salad, cold water, and chilled wine to the table.
- 8:30 — Ask your guests to be seated.
- 9:00 — When the Fondue is eaten, clean the table completely. Bring the Mélange de Fruits and a tray of thin cookies.

- Later: Coffees and tea.
- Later: Cold water, fruit juices, or Perrier.

LEFTOVERS

1. Appetizers: Gently reheat leftover Fondue and pour over triangular pieces of toast. Sprinkle with lemon juice and a little chopped parsley before serving.

2. Cook some potatoes in a pan of salted water. Slice them, place them in an oven-proof dish, and sprinkle with crushed coriander and a little salt. Reheat the Fondue, thinning it with one tablespoon of milk, if necessary. Pour over the potatoes and bake for thirty minutes.

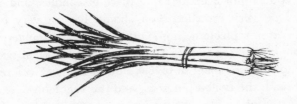

GRATIN DE POULET AU FROMAGE

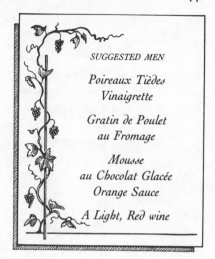

SUGGESTED MEN

*Poireaux Tièdes
Vinaigrette*

*Gratin de Poulet
au Fromage*

*Mousse
au Chocolat Glacée
Orange Sauce*

A Light, Red wine

Chicken fricassee seasoned with mustard, ginger, and cream, cooked with leeks topped with cheese, and baked to golden.

Although this wonderful dish seems to be handed down by the gods to give meaning and pleasure to our Feasts, it is in fact just a present given from man to man.

The ingredients—mustard, cream, ginger, wine—Burgundian in spirit are readily available. Because the chicken, prepared ahead of time, cools in its juice and is reheated later in its sauce, all flavors are enhanced to result in a truly delectable dish. Leeks and celeriac are a superb addition, but if they are not available, use endives and turnips along with the celery. This luscious preparation must include a variety of vegetables.

FOR 8 PEOPLE

UTENSILS

1 or 2 cast-iron casseroles, 9 by 12 inches with a tight lid
2 oven-proof dishes, 8 by 12 inches

FRICASSEE

3 frying chickens, each cut into 8 pieces
6 tablespoons vegetable oil
6 tablespoons butter
Salt
Freshly ground pepper
3 cups dry white wine, or more if needed
2 cups peeled and diced celeriac or turnips (approximately)
6 leeks or endives, white only, cleaned, cut into fourths lengthwise and then into 2-inch sticks (about 5 cups)

2 cups celery stalks, trimmed and cut into 2-inch-long sticks (about $\frac{1}{2}$
    pound bunch)
3 tablespoons Dijon-style mustard
2 cups heavy cream
Pinch of nutmeg
3 tablespoons freshly grated ginger
8 ounces Swiss cheese, grated (about 2 very full cups)
Cayenne pepper
6 tablespoons bread crumbs
1 cup grated Swiss cheese

ACCOMPANIMENTS   Fennel Purée (page 300), or Broccoli Purée (page 299)
Watercress salad (page 301)

Prepare the chicken: Discard the wings, lower part of the back, and extra bits of bones, gristle, or skin (these can be used for broth). Keep only about 19 to 20 attractive, smooth pieces so when the meat is served in a thick sauce it does not hold any bad surprises for your guests. Dry each piece of chicken with a paper towel. If your guests are finicky, use only chicken breasts.

Heat a little oil and butter in a wide skillet and sauté the pieces of chicken, skin side down first, for about 10 minutes. Do not overcrowd the pan; the chicken should fit comfortably in 1 layer. Turn the pieces to the other side with a pair of tongs so they brown evenly. Sprinkle with salt and pepper and set aside. Continue to sauté the chicken in batches.

Place the golden pieces of chicken in the casseroles and cook on a low flame, uncovered, for 40 minutes, turning with a long-handled wooden spoon from time to time so all the pieces cook evenly. Pour out excess cooling fat. Add a little white wine or a little water to the pans and scrape the bottom once or twice.

Meanwhile, prepare the purée you have selected and keep it for later use.

Place the diced celeriac in a saucepan of cold water, bring to a boil, and cook for 10 minutes. Drain and keep for later use. Wash the greens and keep them in a clean towel.

Heat 2 tablespoons of butter and 2 tablespoons of vegetable oil. Add the sliced leeks and celery sticks. Sprinkle with salt and cook on a low flame until soft. Set aside for later.

Pierce the meat with a fork to check its doneness. When it is ready, transfer all the pieces of chicken to a bowl. Discard the fat in both casseroles. Add the white wine, scraping vigorously with a fork the coagulated cooking juices in the bottom of both casseroles. Transfer all the juices into one pan. Beat the mustard, cream, nutmeg, and grated ginger in a bowl. Stir in the wine and cooking juices, then add the 2 cups of grated Swiss cheese, stirring slowly. Simmer for 1 minute; your sauce should be quite thick.

With a pair of kitchen shears cut and discard any piece of loose skin or gristle left on the chicken. Place them back in the casserole, sprinkle with salt and cayenne pepper, and pour the cream and cheese sauce over them, stirring delicately with a long-handled wooden spoon. Add the leeks and celeriac, and stir gently. Check the seasoning. This should be a pungently flavored dish. Pour into 2 buttered gratin dishes. Cover with aluminum foil and put in the refrigerator.

Forty minutes before you sit down to dinner, take the salad greens, purée, and 2 gratin dishes out of the refrigerator. Sprinkle bread crumbs and the cup of grated Swiss cheese on top of the gratins. Cover loosely with lightly oiled foil and bake in a 350° oven. A few minutes before serving, remove the foil so the top becomes crisp.

Heat the plates. Pour the purée into a pan and place it in a bigger pan filled with a little water to prevent the bottom from burning while you reheat it. Or reheat it very carefully over a low flame, stirring the whole time.

Toss the watercress salad with the oil and vinegar dressing.

Bring the purée, watercress bowl, and warm plates to the dining room. Wrap the 2 gratin dishes with kitchen towels and present them to your guests to admire. Each guest should be served 2 pieces of chicken with its sauce and vegetables, then a portion of the purée, and a little bunch of watercress salad.

WINE   A light red wine or a rosé

WHAT TO SERVE BEFORE AND AFTER GRATIN DE POULET

APPETIZERS TO BE SERVED WITH DRINKS BEFORE YOU SIT AT THE TABLE:

     3. Halved tomatoes and halved hard-boiled eggs stuffed with Pistou sauce, page 47

     4. Pissaladière, page 63

DESSERTS

     1. Mousse au Chocolat Glacée, page 282

     2. Flan au Caramel, page 272

     3. Granité au Vin, page 278

     4. Washed and drained strawberries flavored with lemon juice and sugar and served with a platter of Crémets aux Fruits, page 267

     5. Grand Baba, page 273

     6. Panier de Frivolités, page 286

     7. Poires, Pruneaux, Oranges au Vin Rouge et aux Épices, page 289

     8. Tarte au Citron et aux Amandes, page 291

How to Decorate the Table

This is the kind of meal that illustrates best the "too much of a good thing is simply wonderful" principle. The two generous gratins, the bowl of watercress, and the purée will be most inspiring so you don't need to search for effects. You may like to have a fresh *déjeuner de soleil* feeling and give a wink to the painter Claude Monet, his taste for great simple dishes and for the colors he chose in his Giverny house: blue, yellow, and white. Some of the no-iron solid blue, yellow, or flowered sheets are wonderful to cover your table. Avoid a decorated look; the room should have a lazy nonchalant charm. There is no need for everything to match or comply with a scheme. You might want to place a nice polished wooden bowl or plain mushroom basket (the kind the supermarket provides, sprayed in blue or yellow with your dime-store spray or left as is), filled with a pyramid of pears. If you own an old wire wine bottle carrier, you might fill it with glasses of irises, narcissuses, daffodils. You could scatter blue, white, and yellow candles all around, wrap a white napkin on the wine bottles' necks, fold the napkins in a fan shape, and place a leaf or flower on each one. You might write the name of each guest on a dry eucalyptus leaf, too. Cocteau said that elegance is the art of not astonishing, so keep it good-natured and cheerful.

Strategy for the Suggested Menu

• Guests invited for 7:30 P.M.

• Meal served at 8:30 P.M.

• Two days ahead, prepare Poireaux.

• On the day before the Feast, prepare the Gratin de Poulet, Broccoli or Fennel Purée, and Mousse au Chocolat Glacée.

• On the day of the Feast:

· 6:50 — Take the Gratin out of the refrigerator.

· 7:50 — Reheat Gratin in the oven. Reheat purée on a low flame. Prepare the greens and dressing, and place in a bowl ready to toss later.

· 8:30 — Light the candles. Bring cold water to the table and ask your friends to be seated.
Bring in Poireaux Tièdes.

· 8:50 — Bring the napkin-wrapped Gratin, the purée, and the watercress salad to the table.

· 9:10 — Bring Mousse au Chocolat and fruit to the table.

· Later: Coffees and teas.

· Later: Cold water, fruit juices, or Perrier.

LEFTOVERS

1. Croquettes: Add an egg and a little fresh herbs to the chopped leftovers. Make small balls, flatten them a little, roll them in a little flour, fry, and serve piping hot with chopped parsley.

2. Crêpes: Fill the crêpes with boned, chopped leftover Gratin. Add a little of the sauce. Dot the top of the folded or rolled crêpes with butter and bake in a 350° oven for about thirty minutes.

GRATINÉE LYONNAISE

A sumptuous onion soup enriched with cheese, eggs, port, and crisp bread croutons.

Onion soup usually evokes sentimental or vagabond nights, racy late suppers where bons vivants rekindle their forces for new pleasures ahead. Yet in France onion soup traditionally is a family dish, the blessed solution to festive Sunday gatherings, because it is a splendid meal by itself.

There are countless "unique and authentic" renderings of this dish. Some cooks like only the flavor of onion and discard it from the broth after it is cooked; some like to see and taste the slices of onion; some like it puréed, and others, grated. Some like onion soup thin and light; some like it rich and thick. Some serve it in individual tureens; some from a large one. Some grate on a bit of raw onion; some a little grated cheese; some a little onion purée spread on toasted bread before placing it on top of the soup. Some add a poached egg just before serving; some a chopped tomato. Generally Swiss cheese is used but some use Parmesan, and in some regions blue cheese is chosen for a more potent variation. Some add a little milk; some a bit of white wine; some a tablespoon of cognac or port; some a drop of vinegar. Some alternate slices of toasted bread and layers of cheese and then pour the hot broth through a funnel into the pot. Each variation has its virtues.

My favorite version, which is both unctuous and crisp, comes from Lyon, the gastronomical capital of France. This is the one to serve whenever an extravagantly rich onion soup is chosen as the core of a festive meal.

The secret here is the browning of the onion in butter and oil, the slow simmering in broth, the addition of cheese (half slivered inside, half grated on top), and the final addition of egg, port wine, and cognac just before serving.

In France a platter of raw oysters served with a shallot and wine vinegar sauce or a platter of thinly sliced proscuitto, hot sausages, and a tossed green salad are the favorite counterpoints to this heady sweet and mellow soup.

Here again the proportions are for eight people, but since this is the main dish it should be abundant and leftovers are always welcome.

FOR *8* PEOPLE

UTENSILS

Skillet
Soup kettle
Large fire-proof soup tureen or 8 individual oven-proof tureens or little soufflé dishes, either porcelain or earthenware (they must be a good size if you choose individual ones) or two 10-inch diameter soufflé dishes

GRATINÉE

$2\frac{1}{2}$ quarts broth (chicken, beef, or veal; homemade or very good quality store-bought. Use water if you have no broth and correct the seasoning later)
Twig of thyme
2 bay leaves
3 pounds yellow onions, peeled and thinly sliced (about 12 cups)
3 tablespoons butter
2 tablespoons vegetable oil
Salt
1 teaspoon sugar
4 tablespoons flour
2 cups dry white wine
24 slices of French bread (baguette type), 1 inch thick, toasted on both sides, or quartered slices
1 pound Swiss cheese (2 cups grated and 2 cups half grated, half sliced)
4 yolks
3 tablespoons cognac brandy (optional)
4 tablespoons Madeira, port, or sherry
Freshly ground white pepper

Heat the broth. Add the thyme and bay leaves.

Cook the sliced onions in the butter and oil in a large, covered skillet until soft and golden. Sprinkle with 2 teaspoons of salt, sugar, and flour, and cook 5 minutes more on a medium flame, uncovered, stirring, until the onions and flour are brown. Do not let the onions burn. Pour the wine into the onions, stirring carefully. Pour into the broth pan and simmer 30 minutes more. Correct the seasoning. Cool. Cover with plastic wrap and refrigerate.

An hour before the meal, preheat the oven to 400°. Place the slices of bread on a cookie sheet and brown on both sides until crisp. Sprinkle the toast with a little grated cheese and bake for 1 minute.

Spread the bottom of individual-size tureens or the bottom of a large oven-proof tureen or 1 or 2 large soufflé dishes with the slivers of cheese. Pour the soup over them, cover with the toasted bread slices and grated cheese, and dot with a little butter. Bake in a 350° oven for about 20 minutes. To brown the top, broil for a second just before serving if you are using an electric oven.

Beat together the egg yolks, cognac, and port in a little bowl with a pinch of white pepper. Bring it to the table along with the tureen of Gratinée wrapped in a kitchen towel.

Call all your guests to attention: Gratinée Lyonnaise, golden and crisp and preceded by a potent heady aroma, is a breathtaking sight. Then comes the ritual for all your guests to watch as you officiate. Lifting an edge of the cheese and bread crust with a fork, pour the egg yolk mixture into the hot soup and beat it gently as you blend together the rest of the soup. This ritual is called *"touiller,"* and it has been known for years to soften the hardest hearts and wet the hardest eyes.

WINE   A dry white (red is not advisable)

WHAT TO SERVE BEFORE AND AFTER GRATINÉE LYONNAISE

APPETIZERS TO BE SERVED WITH THE DRINKS BEFORE SITTING AT THE TABLE

1. Terrine aux Herbes, page 73, served in its porcelain dish with a spatula and a sharp knife along with toasted bread triangles and paper napkins for your guests to serve themselves
2. Crudités à l'Anchoyade, page 45
3. Caviar d'Aubergines, page 43, along with a basket of trimmed raw vegetables and bread sticks as a dip
4. A platter of thinly sliced prosciutto or Virginia or Kentucky ham and thinly sliced Hungarian or Italian dry sausage wrapped

around bread sticks or served with small slivers of toasted bread and a stack of paper napkins

DESSERTS
1. Tarte au Citron et aux Amandes, page 291
2. Cervelle de Canut, page 265
3. Crémets aux Fruits, page 267
4. One large ripe cheese (such as Brie or Parmesan) or three perfect Coulommiers or fresh chèvres with one or two ripe fruits such as pears, figs, grapes, or apples, or else a large piece of Roquefort with black grapes, walnuts or pecans and a bottle of old port
5. Tarte Tatin aux Poires et aux Pommes, page 292

DECORATION OF THE TABLE

This rich meal deserves a lively and cozy setting. You may choose a thick, colored tablecloth in shades of ivory, faded rose, or green, with wide cotton napkins tied with green ribbons and a low bowl filled with fluffy ivory and tea roses. Scattered around the table should be a collection of small antique baskets or small antique boxes and plenty of faded green and beige-colored candles. You might have pretty individual butter pots, two baskets filled with a variety of bread, pitchers of cold water, and at least two wine decanters.

STRATEGY FOR THE SUGGESTED MENU

- Guests invited for 7:30 P.M.
- Meal served at 8:30 P.M.
- Two days before the Feast: Prepare the Terrine aux Herbes. Refrigerate.

- One day before the Feast or on the morning of the Feast: Prepare the Gratinée and Tarte au Citron.

- On the day of the Feast:
- 7:25 — Heat the Gratinée on a low fire. Warm the toast. Place the Terrine, toast, and gherkins on the coffee table in the living room. Brown the bread for the Gratinée in the oven for a few minutes.
- 7:30 — First guests arrive.
- 8:00 — Bake the tureens.
- 8:30 — Light the candles. Ask your guests to be seated at the table.

Bring the Gratinée tureens or individual tureens and the egg and cognac mixture to the table. Mix in front of your guests and serve.
· 8:50 — Bring Tarte au Citron and a bowl of fresh fruits to the table.

· Later: Coffees and teas.
· Later: Cold water, fruit juices, or Perrier.

LEFTOVERS

1. Soup: Add a little broth and a few sliced potatoes to your leftover Gratinée. Reheat on a low flame.

HACHIS PARMENTIER

SUGGESTED MENU

Pissaladière

Hachis Parmentier
Watercress Salad

Flan au Caramel

A Full-bodied Rosé

A rich beef, parsley, garlic, potato, and cheese gratin.

When André Parmentier brought the potato plant back to France from America, he offered its pretty blue flower to Louis XVI, and the Queen wore it among her jewels in her headdress. The regimes have changed, but the panache of the potato remains high in French cooking.

Of all the culinary creations bearing his name, Hachis Parmentier, which is generally made with leftover beef moistened with broth and mixed with mashed potato, may seem to be one of the most humble. Easy and cheap though it may be to prepare, Hachis is absolutely irresistible, particularly this version. It is made with raw beef, potatoes, cheese, and an inordinate amount of fresh parsley, and it truly represents family cooking at its best. For decades this has been one of the most perfect dishes to offer when children, older people, and hungry adolescents are gathered. Hachis Parmentier may be one of the ultimate crowd pleasers, and it is one of those great simple dishes you can serve and enjoy forever.

When you prepare Hachis, double what seems like a fair quantity, since nobody can remain either sensible or sober in front of this fragrant crisp gratin. Prepared ahead of time and reheated at the last minute, it is served piping hot from its napkin-wrapped baking dish along with a large bowl of watercress seasoned with an oil and vinegar dressing.

Some prefer to spread a beaten egg and a few dots of butter on top of the dish, while others draw lines in the mashed potatoes with the tips of a fork for a wave effect. I like to sprinkle on bread crumbs, grated cheese, and a little olive oil for a crisp, golden crust. Although you will not say what an arrogant cook once declared—"We have done so well that there is no possibility of doing better or of doing otherwise"—you may let your friends whisper it.

This recipe is enough for ten to twelve people, but Hachis looks better when served in two gratin dishes so everyone can have some of the fragrant crust. And there are many exciting ways to use the leftovers, if one is lucky to have some.

FOR *8* PEOPLE

UTENSILS
Skillet
2 oven-proof dishes, 8 by 12 by 2-inch ovals, or 9 inches round by 3 inches deep, or a 9 by 14-inch oval dish

HACHIS
3 onions, peeled and chopped (about $1\frac{1}{2}$ cups)
4 garlic cloves, peeled and crushed
2 large bunches flat parsley, chopped (about 2 cups)
2 tablespoons vegetable oil
3 pounds lean beef, freshly chopped
8 ounces lean salt pork or bacon or country ham, chopped
Salt
3 bay leaves
1 egg, slightly beaten
Freshly ground pepper
5 pounds potatoes, boiled and peeled
3 tablespoons butter
3 cups warm milk (approximately)
Freshly ground nutmeg
8 ounces Swiss cheese, grated (about $1\frac{1}{2}$ cups)
3 tablespoonss bread crumbs

A tossed salad of bitter dandelions or chicory with crisp bacon (page 65), or a tossed salad of endives and watercress seasoned with olive oil and vinegar

Prepare the onions and garlic. Rinse and chop the parsley. (If you don't find the flat variety of parsley, try to add some other fresh herbs such as basil, chives, and fresh thyme along with curly type parsley.)

Heat the oil in a large skillet and sauté the beef, stirring with a wooden spoon so it crumbles and cooks evenly. After a few minutes pour into a dish and keep aside for later.

Add the salt pork to the pan. Cook for a few minutes, until crisp, then pour into the beef dish.

Add the onions to the skillet. Sprinkle with salt, add the bay leaves, and cool for about 10 minutes, until soft. Pour into the beef and bacon dish, and mix in the chopped parsley, crushed garlic, and beaten egg. Check and correct the seasoning, adding salt and pepper to taste. Discard the bay leaves.

Heat a large pot of salty water. Add the washed, unpeeled potatoes and cook for about 25 minutes, until soft. Drain. Wearing kitchen gloves or holding a kitchen towel, peel the potatoes and purée them while they are warm, either in a mill or food processor. Whip in the butter and then some warm milk. The purée should be quite moist. Correct the seasoning, adding nutmeg, salt, and pepper to taste.

Butter the 2 gratin dishes. Pour a layer of potato purée, a layer of the meat mixture, and a top layer of potato purée in each of the dishes. Pat the top of the dishes with your wet hands or the back of a spoon. Sprinkle on the grated cheese and bread crumbs, and dot with butter. Cover with plastic wrap or foil and place in the refrigerator until ready to bake.

Two hours before the beginning of the meal, prepare the greens for the tossed salad. Pour the dressing into the bottom of a bowl, cross the serving spoon and fork on top, and then pile the greens on top of them. You will toss it at the last moment.

Take the gratin dishes out of the refrigerator and remove the plastic wrap or foil. Preheat the oven to 350° forty minutes before you sit down to dinner. Ten minutes later, put the Hachis in the oven and bake for about 30 minutes. Lower the temperature for the last ten minutes if you see the top getting too brown. If your guests are lingering over drinks, cover the gratin tops with foil, lower the temperature to 200°, and don't worry.

Wrap a large kitchen towel around each gratin dish and bring them, piping hot, to the table for everyone to admire and enjoy. Bring the bowl of salad. Toss the salad, place it on the table so everyone can help himself when he chooses, and either serve each guest with some Hachis or pass the 2 dishes, each on its own tray, around the table.

WINE   Any red wine or strong rosé

WHAT TO SERVE BEFORE AND AFTER HACHIS PARMENTIER

APPETIZERS TO BE SERVED WITH THE DRINKS BEFORE SITTING AT THE TABLE:
1. Pissaladière, page 63
2. Crudités à la Tapenade, au Saussoun, and à l'Anchoyade, page 45
3. Caviar d'Aubergines, page 43, with an assortment of Crudités, page 45

DESSERTS   1. Flan au Caramel, page 272
2. Mousse au Chocolat Glacée, page 282
3. Poires, Pruneaux, Oranges au Vin Rouge et aux Épices, page 289
4. Grand Baba, page 273
5. A tray of cheeses along with three ripe fruits

DECORATION OF THE TABLE

A simple honest fabric in either a pretty natural and white striped fabric or a mattress ticking in a red or bright blue and white cloth is what you might want to use on your table with solid-colored cotton napkins.

Hachis Parmentier is not a messy affair, and since you have one dish for each end of the table, serving is easy and neat. Make sure each dish is wrapped with a large and pretty kitchen towel or napkin, and place each on a platter or small tray for easy handling. Fill a large flat basket with three or four potted geraniums as a centerpiece or fill a large bright ceramic bowl with eggplants, peppers, artichoke, and fruits. Insert a few twigs or cut leaves here and there in the bowl.

If you have a pretty collection of old boxes, cans, or mustard jars, you may want to fill them with cut flowers. Natural beeswax candles set in a round country bread or thin, tapered candles set in the center of artichokes, cauliflowers, and squash may be pretty. Set the table with cheerful crockery, three wine decanters, two or three bread baskets, and a pitcher or two of water for an easy, informal, and confident Feast.

STRATEGY FOR THE SUGGESTED MENU

- Guests invited for 7:30 P.M.
- Meal served at 8:30 P.M.

- Prepare the Pissaladière, Hachis, and Flan ahead.
- On the day of the Feast: 6:30 — Take everything out of the refrigerator. Set the table with the bread, butter, wine, and flowers.
- 7:25 — Reheat the Pissaladière in the 350° oven.
- 7:30 — Your first guests arrive.
- 8:00 — Serve Pissaladière in the living room along with paper napkins and place the Hachis in the oven.
- 8:35 — Light the candles and ask your guests to be seated. Bring in ice water, the Hachis, and the green salad. Toss the salad and leave it on the table for everyone to help himself.
- 9:00 — Bring Flan au Caramel with a tray of cookies.

- Later: Coffees and teas.
- Later: Cold water, fruit juices, or Perrier.

LEFTOVERS   1. Croquettes: Stir an egg, a few mushrooms, and a little fresh parsley into your leftover Hachis. Form two-inch balls and flatten them slightly with the palm of your hand. Roll them in a beaten egg and then in bread crumbs. Fry in vegetable oil.

2. Omelet: You can add a handful of chopped basil or parsley and a few beaten eggs to prepare a flat country omelet. When it is cooked, brush the top with a little butter or olive oil and serve with a tossed green salad.

3. Farcis: Parboil zucchini or eggplant, cut them in half, scoop out most of the inside pulp, mix it with the leftover Hachis, and then stuff the vegetable halves. Sprinkle with grated cheese and bake for thirty minutes at 375°

JAMBON EN SAUPIQUET

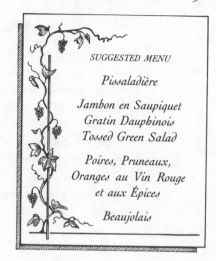

SUGGESTED MENU

Pissaladière

Jambon en Saupiquet
Gratin Dauphinois
Tossed Green Salad

Poires, Pruneaux,
Oranges au Vin Rouge
et aux Épices

Beaujolais

A fresh ham seasoned and mari-
nated with herbs, cooked to crisp-
ness, and seasoned with a light
sauce of vinegar, shallots, and ju-
niper.

Saupiquet is a medieval dish that comes from Burgundy. Traditionally prepared with a light sauce flavored with tarragon and juniper, and enriched with a little light cream, it is both sweet and tart, and totally delicious.

In the following recipe, a fresh, unsalted, unsmoked piece of ham, part of a pork's leg in other words, is used. Generally such a piece is labelled "fresh ham" in supermarkets, but you should read the label carefully to make sure it is indeed raw and not cured or altered in any way.

A five-pound piece of deboned fine-grained meat, for eight or ten guests, firm to the touch with very white fat, is perfect for our Jambon Saupiquet. Part of the hind leg, the upper thigh, the meaty butt end, or the shank end are all fine.

"Tell me what you eat, and I will tell you what you are," goes for pigs, too. Even if the pig sold in your neighborhood market has not fed on chestnuts like those in Corsica and parts of France, or on cheese as in parts if Italy, it will turn into a sumptuous offering after being rubbed with salt, marinated with fragrant herbs, and seasoned with this tangy sauce.

Note: Make sure the fresh ham is cooked enough. When ready to eat there must not be more than the slightest hint of pink in the flesh, but it must be uniformly white or pale gray, and when pricked with a fork the juices should be clear.

Leftover cold pork is delicious as is but can also be used in a great many wonderful dishes. So make a generous display of crisp Gratin Dauphinois, fresh tossed greens, and the glorious *pièce de résistance:* the platter of sliced ham under its lively velvety sauce, with, if you wish, a little paper collar wrapped around its bone and surrounded by tiny apples and herbs. After their first bite your guests will turn into Militant Piggy Groupies and dismiss the everlasting question, "Are the only true paradises the lost ones?" with a contented sigh and another bite of Saupiquet. To live fully the pleasures of the moment is the only thing on their minds from now to dessert.

Note: If time is of the essence and you want to improvise a reasonable facsimile of this, prepare the sauce, pour it over thick overlapping slices of cooked ham, and place the dish, covered with foil, in a slow oven for thirty minutes or so, until the sauce is absorbed and the pork is warm.

FOR *8* PEOPLE

MEAT
6–7 pounds uncooked pork leg or fresh ham, not deboned, salted, or smoked
½ cup kosher salt (approximately)
10 garlic cloves, peeled and cut into slivers
1 tablespoon coarsely cracked peppercorns
5 bay leaves, crumbled or cut finely with scissors
3 teaspoons dry sage
3 teaspoons dry thyme
2 teaspoons coriander seeds

SAUCE
3 cups red wine vinegar
10 shallots, peeled and finely minced
10 juniper berries, crushed
⅔ cup dry white wine
Cracked peppercorns to taste
2 cups light cream
2 tablespoons fresh tarragon leaves or 1 tablespoon dry tarragon

ACCOMPANIMENTS
Gratin Dauphinois (page 53), or Gratin d'Aubergines (page 51)
Watercress, field lettuce, and endive tossed salad seasoned with a vinaigrette (page 300) and garnished with crumbled egg yolks and minced parsley
If possible, small crab apples and cinnamon

Prepare the ham. Remove the rind and trim some of the fat to leave a layer about $\frac{1}{4}$ inch thick. Rub the whole surface of the pork leg with the kosher salt. Leave to marinate for 2 hours. Rinse under cold water until all salt is removed. Dry thoroughly with paper towels. Make deep gashes with a small sharp knife all around the meat and around the bone. Insert the garlic slivers and some of the peppercorns, bay leaves, sage, thyme, and coriander into the slashes. Coat the surface of the ham with the rest, pressing with your palms to make it cling. Cover with a piece of foil. Refrigerate overnight.

Take the meat out of the refrigerator 4 hours before the party. Preheat the oven to 450°. Place the pork, fat side up, on a rack in an oiled, not too large (so juices don't burn) oven-proof dish. Cook for 5 minutes, turn, and lower the oven temperature to 350° (170° inside temperature).

Meanwhile, prepare the Gratin Dauphinois and time it to cook for $1\frac{1}{2}$ hours.

Turn the pork over after 40 minutes and cover loosely with a sheet of foil. If you are using the crab apples, core and peel them, sprinkle them with a little cinnamon, and place them around the pork for the last 30 minutes or so.

Meanwhile, warm the plates.

Prepare the sauce: In a large nonreactive saucepan, combine the vinegar, shallots, and juniper berries. Bring to a boil and, over high heat, reduce until most of the vinegar has evaporated, about 10 minutes. Cool. Pour into a bowl.

Prepare the tossed greens: Pour the dressing into a salad bowl, cross the salad fork and spoon above it, and then arrange the greens on top and leave covered with a wet cloth.

The pork is cooked when its juices run clear and its flesh retains only the slightest hint of pink in its color. Cover with foil and allow to rest for 10–15 minutes before carving. You may want to staple a piece of white paper around the bone.

Pour off the fat from the roasting pan. Place the pan over medium heat on top of the stove and carefully pour in wine. Scrape bits in the bottom of the pan with the back of a fork. Bring the deglazed juice to a boil and let reduce slightly. Pour in the vinegar, shallot, and juniper berry reduction.

Place the ham on a large cutting surface and trim away the fat. Going against the grain, cut slices of $\frac{1}{2}$- to 1-inch thickness. Arrange the slices, overlapping, on a serving platter and keep warm while finishing the sauce.

Gently heat the shallot, vinegar, and juniper berry reduction and deglazed juices mixture. Add the cream and cracked pepper and bring to simmer. Correct the seasoning. Pour over the sliced pork. Sprinkle with tarragon leaves. Cover with foil and keep warm in the oven at a low temperature until ready to serve.

Call your guests to the table. This dish must be served very warm. Bring the warm plates, salad, Gratin, and pork to the dining room.

Arrange 2 slices of pork, a cooked apple, and 2 tablespoons of Gratin on each warm plate. Place the tossed green salad on the table so every guest may help himself.

WINE   A Beaujolais-type red wine, quite light and fruity, a dry white wine, a local rosé, a dry sherry, or a Madeira

WHAT TO SERVE BEFORE AND AFTER JAMBON EN SAUPIQUET

APPETIZERS
1. Poireaux Tièdes Vinaigrette, page 67
2. Caviar d'Aubergines with warm toast, page 43, and Crudités en Panier, page 45
3. Warm Ratatouille, page 68, served with thin crisp toast

DESSERTS
1. Poires, Pruneaux, Oranges au Vin Rouge et aux Épices, page 289
2. Oeufs à la Neige et aux Fruits, page 284
3. Crêpes Normandes, page 269

DECORATION OF THE TABLE

This is an unfussy table since the slicing of the meat and the spooning of the sauce over it have been done in the kitchen. Once everything is served the meal can proceed in an uninterrupted flow, so you may use whatever table setting you want.

Ham is traditionally served for Easter and Christmas, and so any heavy "theme decoration" is to be avoided here. You could perhaps choose a multiflowered cloth that falls to the floor, and over it a piece of lace (square if your table is round, rectangular if it is a long table), fine or coarse or even machine made or macramé and covering only the top of the table. In the center you could fill a round white tureen with Italian poppies, anemones, or ranunculuses in several shades of' pink, yellow, and red. Left in the water for a few hours before the party, their stems will bend into whimsical shapes. Select bright napkins to match one of the shades of the tablecloth and tie each folded napkin with a piece of bright ribbon in a contrasting color, and perhaps a leaf or a cut flower stuck in it. Beware of acute cuteness, but let your table be cheerful and pretty.

You may want to use plain white or pressed glass, terra-cotta or colored crockery accessories for a *festin campagnard* feeling. Use natural baskets for the bread and a little yellow, pink, or red napkin around the necks of your three wine bottles. Make sure there are butter pots, bread in baskets, and two pitchers of cold water on the table.

STRATEGY FOR THE SUGGESTED MENU

- Guest invited for 7:30 P.M.
- Meal served at 8:30 P.M.

- One day before the party: Season the pork as indicated. Prepare the Poires, Pruneaux, Oranges au Vin Rouge dessert, the cooked onions for the Pissaladière, and the greens for the salad. Cover each item and refrigerate.

- On the day of the Feast: Four hours before the dinner, take the bowl of cooked onions, the pork, and the greens out of the refrigerator.
- 5:30 — Preheat the oven and cook the pork. Meanwhile, prepare the vinegar and shallots sauce. Prepare the dough and the Pissaladière.
- 6:30 — Prepare and cook the Gratin.
  Prepare the salad and bowl.
  Bake the Pissaladière.
- 7:00 — Bake the Gratin. Turn the pork, cover with foil, and add apples.
- 7:30 — Your first guests arrive.
- 8:00 — Bring the Pissaladière to your guests.
- 8:30 — Slice the pork. Reheat the sauce. Light the candles. Ask your guests to sit at the table.
  Bring the Gratin, tossed salad, Jambon, and its bowl of sauce to the dining room.
- 8:50 — Offer second helpings. They don't have to be piping hot.
- 9:10 — Change the plates. Bring the dessert.

- Later: Coffees and teas.
- Later: Cold water, fruit juices, or Perrier.

1. Hachis Parmentier, page 186.

2. Wrap the sliced pork in a piece of foil. Place in a 325° oven to reheat. Serve with a spirited Vinaigrette, page 300, and boiled potatoes.

3. A hearty winter soup: Dice the leftover pork. Add some lentils, cooked beans, or chick-peas. Sprinkle with fresh herbs.

4. Cold: Slice and serve with mustard and a cold boiled potato, scallions, and raw celery salad

MARMITE DIEPPOISE

A spectacular stew of mussel, fish, shrimp, leeks, and onions seasoned with curry, white wine, and fresh herbs.

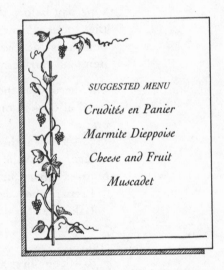

SUGGESTED MENU

Crudités en Panier

Marmite Dieppoise

Cheese and Fruit

Muscadet

Dieppe is France's oldest seaside resort and one of the most interesting towns in Normandy for seafood lovers. History and geography define this dish: Fish, shellfish, and cream abound in the province, and the spices brought by the merchant ships long ago have made curry and cayenne pepper part of the local cooking for centuries.

Marmite Dieppoise, a lusty Norman creation, is a sumptuous chowder prepared with either cider or a dry white wine. It is a simple dish to serve all year round. Although sole, prawns, and turbot are sometimes used in restaurant versions, the traditional ingredients are easily available and make for a delicious, luxurious, dramatic one-dish extravaganza.

Prepared a day ahead, Marmite Dieppoise will gain in flavor and will be easy to reheat at the last moment.

There are many variations of this dish, but the following one is my very favorite. Instead of thickening the broth with flour and butter, I add puréed celery and leeks; this makes the dish lighter, more fragrant, and quite unctuous.

If your broth is very tasty and you truly cannot find fresh fish, then frozen fillets may be used, but the mussels must be absolutely fresh.

FOR *8* PEOPLE

UTENSILS

Large soup kettle or 8-quart enameled casserole
Pretty tureen or large china bowl
8 soup plates

INGREDIENTS

¼ pound (1 stick) butter, plus 2 tablespoons
7–8 leeks, washed, trimmed, split, and chopped
Bunch of celery, washed, trimmed, and chopped
1 onion peeled and sliced, 2 peeled and chopped
12 quarts (about 2 pounds) mussels
4 cups dry white wine
Salt
Freshly ground pepper
1 carrot, peeled and sliced
Parsley stems, washed and chopped
2 bay leaves
10 peppercorns
About 2 pounds fish bones and/or fish heads (approximately)
1 quart hot water
10 pieces fresh codfish or halibut or haddock, cut into 3- to 4-inch chunks
10 flounder or sole fillets
8 scampi or 16 shrimp
2 cups heavy cream
1–2 teaspoons good curry powder
1 teaspoon cayenne pepper
8 large scallops, trimmed and dried carefully

Juice of 1 lemon
8 thin slices of French bread or 5 slices of good whole wheat bread, cut
into 4 triangles, buttered, and ready to be broiled
2 tablespoons finely minced chervil or parsley

Heat the stick of butter in a thick-bottomed pan. Add the leeks, celery, and one sliced onion. Cook over a low flame for a few minutes, until soft. Purée with a food processor or blender; pour into a bowl and set aside.

Pour the mussels into a large sink of cold water and add 1 tablespoon of salt. Leave for 1 hour. Scrub the mussel shells with a hard brush and remove the beards. Place the clean mussels in a large pot. Add half white wine, one chopped onion, salt, and pepper. Cover and cook over a high flame for 5 minutes, tossing occasionally, until the mussels open. Drain and pass the liquid through a sieve lined with cheesecloth. Keep the mussel liquid for later use. Remove the mussels from their shells. Reserve 10 shells and place them in a bowl with the mussels; cover with plastic wrap. Discard the other shells.

Heat one tablespoon of butter. Add one chopped onion, carrot, parsley stems, bay leaves, and peppercorns, and cook for 5 minutes. Add the fish bones and fish heads if you have any and stir. Pour in the rest of the wine and hot water, and simmer for 20 minutes. Pass through a sieve into a large pot, add the strained mussel liquid, and simmer for a few minutes.

Sprinkle the fish with salt and add them to the hot broth to cook for about 4 minutes. Add the fish fillets. Add the shrimp 1 minute later and cook 4 minutes more. Turn off the flame and, using a slotted spoon or skimmer, delicately transfer the fish and shrimp to a dish. Cool, cover with plastic wrap, and place in the refrigerator.

Add the puréed leeks and celery to the warm fish broth, stir, bring to a boil, and reduce for a few minutes; you should have about $4\frac{1}{2}$ quarts of liquid. Stir in the cream, curry, and cayenne powder. Check the seasoning and add salt or spices to taste. The broth should be highly flavored. Let it cool completely, cover with plastic wrap, and place in the refrigerator.

Heat one tablespoon of butter in a skillet. Add the scallops and cook for a few minutes. Sprinkle with salt, turn on the other side, sprinkle with salt, pepper, and the lemon juice, and then turn off the flame. Let the mussels cool, then add them to the bowl of mussels and mussel shells. Cover with plastic wrap and refrigerate.

One hour before your meal, take everything out of the refrigerator. Preheat the oven to 400°. Place the buttered slices of bread on a cookie sheet and bake until crisp. Remove to a basket and set aside.

Reheat the soup gently. Place the chopped fresh herbs in a small bowl. Heat the soup plates and the tureen, which will be used both as a tureen and as the soup kettle for easier serving.

Ten minutes before sitting at the table, add the cooked fish, fillets, and shrimp to the warm soup kettle and reheat for a few minutes. Pour the cooked scallops, mussels, and mussel shells delicately into the warm tureen. Pour about 2 cups of the hot broth from the soup kettle on top and cover to keep warm. Do not reheat them. Bring the tureen to the table.

Wrap a pretty kitchen towel around the large pot of broth and fish, and bring it to the table along with the warm plates, chopped fresh herbs, and bread croutons.

You may prefer to use a rolling table to do all your serving and then pass the plates to your guests. The main thing is to serve in full view so the whole process can be watched and admired by all and the pleasure of this luxurious dish can be fully appreciated. Don't let your guests help themselves with the Marmite: It is messy, and they don't know the variety to be sampled. This is a dish over which you should officiate.

Place a chunk of fish, a fillet of fish, some shrimp, 1 scallop, some mussels, and a mussel shell in each plate. Pour some warm soup on top, sprinkle on a little chopped chervil or parsley, and place a few buttered croutons on top.

When everyone has been served, pour what is left of your tureen into the kettle. Cover and keep warm for second helpings.

WINE   A cool Muscadet, a white Burgundy, a crisp Alsatian wine, or any of your favorite dry white wines served very chilled

What to Serve Before and After Marmite Dieppoise

APPETIZERS TO BE SERVED WITH THE DRINKS:

1. Crudités à la Tapenade, à l'Anchoyade, au Saussoun, page 45, or Pistou sauce, page 47
2. Gougère, page 49
3. Terrine aux Herbes, page 73, served in its porcelain pan with a sharp knife, along triangles of crisp country bread

DESSERTS   1. A tray of selected cheeses with a few perfectly ripe fruits
2. Crêpes Normandes, page 269
3. Tarte Tatin aux Poires et aux Pommes, page 292
4. Oeufs à la Neige et aux Fruits, page 284, with a platter of thin cookies

DECORATION OF THE TABLE

There should be no extra frills, no fussy display here. The charm will operate and the conversation will start going the minute the steaming tureen of Marmite Dieppoise appears.

You may like to set the table with a deep blue or an ivory-colored tablecloth. Place a few large shells filled with tiny shells or pebbles about. Or make a lovely fluffy fresh bundle for your centerpiece. Wrap the bottom parts of three little potted ferns or short geraniums with a large piece of white muslin or cheesecloth and tie the gathered fabric loosely with two thin blue ribbons.

If you have a blue tablecloth and if you own an antique or a reproduction Chinese red-type lacquered box, you may want to fill it with big grayish blue pebbles as a centerpiece, then place ivory-colored candles all around.

Set the flat plates (the soup plates are kept warm in the kitchen), napkins, soup spoons, forks, and knives — all three are needed for a Marmite — on the table along with a pretty water pitcher, three bottles or decanters of wine, or two or three baskets (enameled in a cream color with a spray can) lined with a napkin and filled with a variety of breads. If you are serving at the dining table, make sure it is not too crowded once the kettle and the tureen are on it and that there is plenty of room for you to serve each plate and pass it along easily.

STRATEGY FOR THE SUGGESTED MENU

• Guests invited for 7:30 P.M.
• Meal served at 8:30 P.M.
• On the day of the feast:
· 7:25 — Take everything out of the refrigerator. Bring the Crudités and the bowls of sauce with the drinks to the table in the living room.
· 7:30 — Your first guests arrive.

· 8:00 — Reheat the soup on a low flame.

· 8:15 — Add the fish to the kettle.

· 8:30 — Ask your guests to be seated. Light the candles. Bring the Marmite and the warm plates to the dining room.

· 8:50 — Bring the cheese tray and the fruit to the table.

· Later: Coffees and teas, and a platter of thin cookies.

· Later: Cold water, fruit juices, or Perrier.

LEFTOVERS

1. This stew reheats wonderfully. You can either add a little wine and serve it with fresh croutons or, if you don't have enough leftovers, add diced potatoes, a handful of mushrooms, and a little milk for a light soup.

2. Ramekins: Add sliced mushrooms to the chopped leftovers, fish, and shellfish. Stir in a little cream sauce. Pour into individual ramekins, sprinkle with grated cheese, dot with butter, and bake for thirty minutes at 350°

MOUSSAKA PROVENÇALE

A chopped lamb, herb, and vegetable mixture served with fried eggplants and a light tomato sauce.

SUGGESTED MENU

Crudités en Panier

Moussaka Provençale

Tarte Tatin aux Poires et aux Pommes

White Burgundy

Eggplants are native to India, but ever since Arabs brought them to Spain they have become a staple of Mediterranean cuisine. In Greece, Moussaka is served with a white cream sauce, but the version we use here is part of the traditional Provence repertory, which is lighter and more pungent.

Prepared ahead, reheated thirty minutes before the meal, and served in two different guises—as a glistening dome and as a crisp gratin with a bowl of fresh tomato sauce—it is a sumptuous dish.

Note: If you have a large group, skip the unmolded Moussaka and prepare only two large gratin dishes. They will go directly from the oven to the table and will be easier to serve.

FOR 8 TO 12 PEOPLE

UTENSILS
Skillet
2-quart charlotte mold about 7 inches in diameter
2-quart rectangular oven-proof gratin dish, made of porcelain, earthenware, or Pyrex

MOUSSAKA
4 tablespoons vegetable oil
4 tablespoons butter
2 pounds mushrooms, cleaned, trimmed, and finely sliced
6 pounds eggplants (approximately) (12 elongated violet eggplants; avoid the seedy black ones, if possible), sliced in half lengthwise
Salt
Olive oil
2–3 onions, peeled and finely chopped (2 cups)
3 pounds ground lamb
Freshly ground pepper
3 bay leaves
4 garlic cloves, peeled and minced
8 tablespoons chopped parsley
2 tablespoons dry thyme or savory or oregano
1 28-ounce can tomatoes, drained, seeded, and coarsely chopped
3 eggs, beaten
1 cup chopped fresh mint leaves (optional but wonderful)
½ cup bread crumbs
½ cup grated Swiss or Parmesan cheese

SAUCE
1 28-ounce can whole, peeled, seeded tomatoes or about 6 large fresh to-matoes, peeled, seeded, and quartered
2 bay leaves
1 garlic clove, peeled and sliced
2 tablespoons coarsely cut parsley leaves

ACCOMPANIMENTS   *2 cups cooked rice (page 301)*
3 tablespoons butter or 2 tablespoons olive oil
Bowl of cleaned, trimmed watercress
Vinaigrette dressing (page 302)
Juice of 1 lemon

Preheat the oven to 400°. Heat 2 tablespoons each of the oil and butter in a skillet. Add the sliced mushrooms, stir, and toss on a high flame. When they become a little stiff, lower the heat, add salt, and after a minute turn it off. Cool and set aside.

With a sharp knife cut gashes in the flesh of the halved egg-plants, making sure not to cut them down to the skin. Sprinkle salt over the surface of each half. After 15 minutes, rinse under cool water, dry with a towel, and rub a little olive oil all over each eggplant. Pour water into a large baking dish to measure about 2 inches deep. Bring to a simmer on top of the stove. Place the eggplant halves in the baking dish, skin side down. Bake for 30 minutes, or until tender but not mushy. You may have to do this in 2 batches.

Meanwhile, heat the remaining 2 tablespoons of oil and butter. Cook the onions until transparent and golden but not brown. Add the lamb and cook over high heat, stirring often with a wooden spoon. Sprinkle with salt and pepper. Add the bay leaves, minced garlic, 5 tablespoons of parsley, and thyme. The meat should be evenly cooked and crumbly, without any big lumps. Add the canned tomatoes. Stir with the wooden spoon. After 5 minutes turn off the heat.

Remove the eggplant from the oven. With a large spoon remove the flesh and place all the skins on a plate. Coarsely chop and sauté the flesh for 2 minutes in a skillet with a little olive oil. Add the cooked mushrooms, the onion-lamb-herb mixture, and the beaten eggs, and stir carefully. Check and correct the seasoning with salt, freshly ground pepper, or a little thyme. Discard the bay leaves. Add the fresh mint if you have some.

Oil the charlotte mold and the rectangular gratin dish carefully. Line them with the eggplant skins, dark side against the sides, pointing toward the top of the mold, and slightly overlapping one another. Save any trimmings for the top of the mold. Press with the palm of your hands against the sides to make sure it is well lined, then carefully add the meat and vegetable mixture with a spoon.

Place a few eggplant slices or some of the trimmings over the top of the filled mold and cover with a piece of foil, making sure it is tightly closed. Place in the refrigerator.

Sprinkle the top of the rectangular gratin dish with bread crumbs and cheese. Sprinkle a few drops of oil on top, cover with foil, and place in the refrigerator.

Prepare the sauce: Place the tomatoes in a medium-sized, nonreactive saucepan. Add the bay leaves and garlic, cook for about 5 minutes, then cool. Check and correct the seasoning. Pass through a blender or food processor; it should be a smooth purée. Add the parsley. Cover with plastic wrap and place in the refrigerator.

Cook the rice. Add a little olive oil, cover with plastic wrap, and set in the refrigerator.

An hour and a half before the dinner, remove the Moussaka mold and gratin dish, tomato sauce, and cooked rice from the refrigerator and remove the plastic wrap. Chop remaining fresh parsley and keep in a little bowl for later use.

Preheat the oven to 350°. Place both dishes in a large pan containing about 2 inches of simmering water. Cover loosely with a piece of foil and cook for 45 minutes to 1 hour, until warm. Remove the foil for the last 5 minutes. It may be necessary to use 2 pans of water to hold the molds.

Thirty minutes before the meal, reheat the rice in a saucepan or sauté pan with a little butter and a little cold water. Stir with a fork. Or, if you have space in the oven, spread the rice on a baking dish, dot with butter or sprinkle with olive oil, and leave in a 300° oven for about 10 minutes, until ready to use.

Make the vinaigrette in a large bowl. Add the watercress and place the crossed serving tools on top to use for tossing later.

Place a large plate upside down over the charlotte mold and, holding the edge of the serving plate and the handle of the mold with both hands, turn them over together in a decisive movement. Let the mold sit for a few minutes while you pour the rice into a serving dish and sprinkle it with the lemon juice. Pour the tomato sauce in a serving bowl and wrap a kitchen towel around the gratin dish.

Remove the charlotte mold very carefully. Pour a small line of tomato sauce all around the purple dome of Moussaka and place 3 parsley leaves on top.

Bring the molded Moussaka to the table along with the Moussaka gratin dish wrapped in a towel, dish of rice, bowl of tomato sauce, bowl of chopped parsley, bowl of tossed green salad, and warm plates.

Make sure everyone has time to admire the beautiful purple dome of Moussaka as well as the crisp golden gratin of Moussaka, then start serving. It is a dramatic and beautiful dish that must be seen whole before you begin to give each guest a little white rice, a ladleful of the Moussaka gratin, and a part of the Moussaka dome, sprinkled with a little chopped parsley over all. Pass the bowl of tomato sauce around for everybody to help himself.

Place the bowl of salad greens on the table, toss the salad carefully, and let each guest help himself as he wishes.

WINE   A robust red wine or dry chilled white wine from Burgundy

WHAT TO SERVE BEFORE AND AFTER MOUSSAKA PROVENÇALE

APPETIZERS   1. Crudités à l'Anchoyade, au Pistou, à la sauce Mayonnaise Curry, page 45
                  2. Poireaux Tièdes Vinaigrette, page 67
                  3. Mouclade, page 58
                  4. Lentilles ou Pois Chiches en Salade, page 57
                  5. Olives Sautées, page 61

DESSERTS   1. Tarte Tatin aux Poires et aux Pommes, page 292
                  2. Flan au Caramel, page 272
                  3. Tarte au Citron et aux Amandes, page 291
                  4. Crémets aux Fruits, page 267

HOW TO DECORATE THE TABLE

Follow your feelings and use what you have at hand. This is a very spectacular dish especially when it comes in two different attires, and you should not worry too much about the rest. But a flowered or paisley tablecloth with dark red or dark blue napkins would be pretty with the eggplant and tomato colors of the dish.

You may like to place a large copper, silver, or brass dish filled with blue and red and ivory anemones, or a beautiful arrangement in the center of your table of dark grapes, red apples, and yellow peaches with some greens stuck among them and winding down the sides. Scatter dark red or ivory-colored candles around it. Make sure the two baskets of bread are lined with a fresh napkin and that you have at least two decanters or bottles of wine along with a water pitcher on the table. Once more, a rolling or a side table is useful when you serve the two Moussakas so that the table remains neat and peaceful. But make sure everyone sees the Moussakas before you start serving.

STRATEGY FOR THE SUGGESTED MENU

- Guests invited for 7:30 P.M.
- Dinner served at 8:30 P.M.

- One day ahead or on the morning of the Feast: Prepare the Crudités, sauces, Moussaka, salad greens, cooked rice, crème fraîche, and Tarte Tatin ahead of time.

- On the evening of the Feast:
· 6:30 — Take the Moussaka, rice, tomato sauce, salad greens, and Tarte Tatin out of the refrigerator. Leave the crème fraîche in the refrigerator until you are ready to serve it.
· 7:25 — Place the Crudités and bowls of sauces on the coffee table in the living room. Preheat the oven to 300°.
· 7:30 — First guests arrive. Heat the Moussaka gratin and the Moussaka mold in the oven.
· 8:25 — Reheat the rice. Lower the temperature to 150° and, after you take the Moussaka out of the oven, slide in the Tarte Tatin to warm it in the oven. Reheat the tomato sauce. Prepare the bowl of greens.
· 8:30 — Ask your guests to sit at the table. Light the candles. Bring the warm plates, rice, tomato sauce, and two Moussakas to the table along with the bowl of green tossed salad.
· 9:00 — Bring the warm Tarte Tatin and the crème fraîche to the table.

· Later: Coffees and teas.
· Later: Cold water, fruit juices, or Perrier.

LEFTOVERS   1. Gratin: Gather all the leftover Moussaka into a baking dish. Add a little tomato sauce to thin it, sprinkle with bread crumbs and cheese, and then reheat in the oven at 350° for thirty minutes.

2. Croquettes: Add an egg or two and a little chopped parsley to the leftover Moussaka. Make into two-inch balls, roll them in flour, and fry until crisp

PAELLA

SUGGESTED MENU

Tomatoes and Eggs
filled with Pistou

Paella

Mélange de Fruits

Sangria

A lusty dish of meat, chicken, fish, shellfish, a variety of vegetables and rice seasoned with saffron and lemon.

With its lavish profusion of colors, textures, and flavors, Paella is a perfect party dish, a perfect summer dish, a perfect buffet dish. Always popular in the regions of France bordering Spain, its appeal has spread throughout the country, and Paella, pushing back boundaries, has for the last forty years been totally assimilated into the French patrimony.

No room for discretion or measure here, but a vital exuberant experience. Originally cooked outdoors and eaten with wooden spoons directly out of the pan, Paella is likely to include a wide variety of ingredients: snails, eels, duck, chicken, rabbit, codfish, crayfish, frogs, pork, artichoke hearts, green beans. A less fierce and exotic recipe is now a fixture on most Parisian and country restaurant menus as well as in festive family gatherings. No exotic ingredients, but the *tour de main*, the know-how makes for its quality which is the story of a successful integrated marriage. Fish, meat, vegetables, and spices mingle happily, and the rice absorbs and combines all the tastes.

Paella gets its name from the pan it is cooked in, and if you can find one, do buy it at once—it has dozens of uses. A very large porcelain or enamel cast-iron oven-proof dish will do, but make sure it fits in your oven.

This extravagant dish brings great immediate excitement to the table. Intrigued and baffled by such variety and such abundance, your guests will sail through the meal under its charm and become part of the Feast. And so the proliferation of ingredients is truly essential, and you can vary the combinations according to your taste and what your market offers.

Paella seems more appealing in spring and summer, and is one of my favorite outdoor meals. Small fresh artichokes, green beans, and tiny peas are delicious with Paella. For a hungry group I would include chicken breasts, diced lean salt pork, sausage, shrimp, prawns, hunks of monkfish, and peas, green and yellow peppers, onions, and tomatoes.

It takes a bit of time and organization to get all the ingredients ready, but it is easy to prepare and serve, and truly impossible to ruin. One of the most joyous dishes to offer for a festive gathering.

FOR *8* PEOPLE

UTENSILS

Large skillet
Baking dish about 3 inches deep and at least 14 inches in diameter; use the largest dish that will go in your oven or a paella pan, if you can get one

INGREDIENTS

8 tiny baby artichokes, trimmed, parboiled, and cut in half
2 garlic cloves, peeled and crushed
2 large onions, sliced, plus 1, peeled and chopped
1 green pepper, seeded, trimmed, washed, and cut into strips 1½ inches long by ¼ inch wide
1 large red pepper, seeded, trimmed, washed, and cut into strips 1½ inches long by ¼ inch wide
2 tomatoes, peeled and chopped
8 ounces green beans, cut in half
1 quart mussels
Vegetable oil
Butter
10 half breasts of chicken
Salt
Freshly ground pepper
½ cup dry white wine

1 pound chorizo (hot) or garlicky smoked sausage (an 8-inch piece), sliced
½ cup peas
10 large raw shrimp in their shells
10 gambas or prawns
3 cups rice
½ teaspoon saffron
6 cups boiling water
2 lemons, cut into wedges

Prepare the vegetables. Scrub and wash the mussels.

Parboil the artichokes for 5 minutes, until tender, and slide into a bowl. Heat a little oil and butter in a skillet and sauté the chicken breasts on all sides. Sprinkle with salt and cook 5 minutes more. Sprinkle the crushed garlic cloves on top and cook 1 minute more. Add salt and pepper. Remove to a side dish.

Add a little wine to the pan. Scrape the coagulated juices at the bottom of the pan and pour the liquid onto the cooked chicken.

Add 2 tablespoons of oil to the pan and sauté the hunks of fish on all sides, until cooked. Sprinkle with salt and pepper and set aside. Add a little oil to the skillet and cook the sliced onions until golden. Add the peppers and cook until barely tender. Slide into the large bowl with the chicken.

Add the sausage to the skillet and cook on a medium flame for a few minutes. Discard the fat and pour the sausage into the bowl with the chicken and vegetables.

Add a little oil to the skillet and sauté the chopped onion until soft. Add the white wine and mussels. Cook for 1 minute on a high flame, until the shells open (see Mouclade, page 58). Shake and remove from the heat. Cool, discard the shells (keep 6 pretty ones for decoration), and pour the mussels into the bowl with the chicken.

Cook the peas and pour into the bowl with the chicken and mussels.

Heat 2 tablespoons of oil. Cook the shrimp and prawns with their shells on over high heat for 1 minute on each side, until the shell turns pink. Set aside for later.

Forty minutes before you are ready to serve the Paella, preheat the oven to 350° and take all the prepared ingredients out of the refrigerator.

Heat a little oil in the skillet. Add the chopped onion and diced sausage, and sauté for a few minutes, stirring once. Add the rice and stir with a wooden spoon so it is coated on all sides, then pour it into the large oven-proof paella dish or a very large baking dish. Add the chicken mixture, saffron, and boiling water. Bake, uncovered, for 30 minutes. Turn off the heat and stir in the mussels and peas delicately with a fork. Place the artichoke hearts, gambas and shrimp all around, and leave in the oven 5 minutes more. The grains of rice should be separated and dry.

Sprinkle a little oil and place lemon wedges and a few mussel shells all around. Sprinkle lemon juice on top of everything. Wrap a towel around the paella or baking dish and bring straight onto the table. All your guests must have time to admire this splendid display of colors. Serve each guest because the dish is too big to pass around.

WINE   If you want to go Spanish, a large decanter of chilled Sangria made from a strong red wine, sparkling water, orange juice, a bit of Cointreau or brandy, and sliced peaches—a refreshing and treacherous drink. Or a hearty, full-bodied red wine.

WHAT TO SERVE BEFORE AND AFTER PAELLA

APPETIZERS   1. 8 tomato halves and 8 hard-boiled egg halves, cut lengthwise and filled with Pistou sauce, page 47. Top each with a small black olive and serve on a platter lined with watercress or arugula and tiny leaf or Bibb lettuce leaves.
2. Terrine aux Herbes, page 73
3. Watercress, arugula, and endive tossed salad
4. Pissaladière, page 63

DESSERTS   1. Mélange de Fruits, page 281
2. Flan au Caramel, page 272
3. Cervelle de Canut, page 265
4. Granité au Vin (doux), page 278
5. Plain coffee ice cream with a bowl of ginger-flavored whipped cream

DECORATION OF THE TABLE

This is a summery, joyous kind of meal, so you may like to use a warm rust, a rich brown, or a deep yellow tablecloth and place a large basket of mangoes, oranges, grapes, and yellow peaches in the

center of your table. Then form a loose wreath around the glasses
with pieces of vine, wisteria, honeysuckle, or ivy.

Pass finger bowls, wet towels, or a stack of paper towels along
with the pretty wide cotton napkins you have placed on the
table—shrimp and prawns can be messy. Set the table with forks,
knives, and soup spoons—a *must* for Paella habitués.

STRATEGY FOR THE SUGGESTED MENU

- Guests invited for 7:30 P.M.
- Meal served at 8:30 P.M.

- Prepare the Pistou-filled tomatoes and eggs, Paella ingredients, and
fruit salad the evening before the Feast.

- On the day of the Feast:
· 7:30 — Your first guests arrive.
· 8:00 — Reheat the Paella.
· 8:25 — Light the candles. Ask your guests to be seated.
· 8:30 — Bring the platter of tomatoes and eggs to the table.
· 8:50 — Take the Paella out of the oven. Wrap it with a large towel
and bring it to the table.
· 9:15 — Remove the Mélange de Fruits from the refrigerator and
bring it to the table with a platter of thin cookies.

· Later: Coffees and teas.
· Later: Cold water, fruit juices, or Perrier.

LEFTOVERS   1. You can reheat the leftovers easily. Scatter a diced tomato on
top, sprinkle a little olive oil, cover with a loose sheet of foil, and
bake for twenty minutes.

2. Stuffed peppers: Trim and parboil the large fleshy green or red
peppers. Stuff them with the chopped Paella leftovers. Sprinkle
break crumbs on top, dot with a little olive oil, and bake for about
thirty minutes at 375°.

3. A flat omelet: Stir two beaten eggs into the chopped Paella
leftovers. Add a handful of chopped fresh herbs (parsley, basil,
chives) and make a large flat omelet. When both sides are golden and
firm, slide onto a platter and sprinkle with a little olive oil. Serve with
a tossed green salad

PIETSCH

SUGGESTED MENU

Mouclade

Pietsch

Gratin d'Aubergines
Tossed Green Salad

Flan au Caramel
Thin Cookies

Full-bodied Red Wine

A veal or lamb breast stuffed with vegetables, ham, cheese, and herbs, sautéed, and then cooked with vegetables in white wine.

I think Thurber was wrong when he said that the undisciplined mind was far better adapted to the confused world in which we live than the organized one. Had he known about Pietsch, he might have had another opinion. Here, organization makes for an easy, smooth process leading to a superb dish.

This can be served cold or warm. Have the butcher remove all the bones and cut the pocket into the veal breast. Of course the veal breast may be boned, flattened, filled, and rolled for a more elegant presentation, but it will lose so much of its charm. Serve this with a side dish of Gratin d'Aubergines (page 51) and perhaps a tossed salad of arugula, lamb's lettuce, watercress, and endives.

It will be the focus of your meal, so make sure all may savor the sight and the aroma of this plump and golden bundle before you slice it. Pietsch is the best antidote to stress, exhaustion, annoyance, and anxiety.

As soon as the masterpiece appears, there is exultation, a sense of coherence and happiness around the table. The radiant faces are confident for a moment that their main activity is enjoying life to the fullest.

FOR 8 PEOPLE

UTENSILS
2 wide flexible spatulas
Needle and thread
Long knife
Small wooden board to press against the Pietsch as you are slicing and also to hold each slice as you slide it onto the plate with a spatula

Large skillet
Enameled cast-iron casserole, 9 by 12 inches; Doufeu, for instance

PIETSCH

3 pounds Swiss chard or spinach, cooked and chopped (3 cups)
2 onions, peeled and sliced
Olive oil
4 ounces lean salt pork and country ham, coarsely chopped (1½ cups)
1 cup chopped flat parsley
Salt
Freshly ground pepper
5 garlic cloves, peeled and thinly sliced
Pinch of freshly grated nutmeg
¾ cup grated Romano or Parmesan cheese mixed with Swiss cheese
2 tablespoons moistened bread, well squeezed
2 eggs
5–6 pounds breast of veal
1 teaspoon cracked peppercorns
½ cup white wine
4 celery stems, trimmed and cut into 1-inch pieces
3 carrots, peeled and thickly sliced
2 bay leaves
1 garlic clove, peeled
½ cup water or broth

SAUCE

3 tablespoons olive oil
3 tablespoons chopped fresh herbs
3 tablespoons pitted and chopped black olives
2 tomatoes, peeled, seeded, and diced
Salt
1 tablespoon coarsely ground coriander

ACCOMPANIMENTS

Gratin d'Aubergines (page 51)
Tossed green salad

Bring a large pan of water to a boil. Add the green part of the Swiss chard or spinach leaves. Cook for 15 minutes, until tender. Drain and chop.

Sauté the onions in a little oil until golden. Add the chopped lean pork and sauté for a few minutes. Pour into a bowl. Add the parsley, cooked Swiss chard, salt, pepper, garlic, nutmeg, cheese, and moistened bread. Stir well and then add the eggs and mix in.

Dry the veal breast with a paper towel. Sprinkle the inside and outside with salt and cracked peppercorns. Fill with the mixture and carefully close the opening with a needle and thread. With the tip of a very sharp knife cut some shallow crisscross lines on top of the Pietsch. They will open and make for an attractive design when cooked.

Heat 2 tablespoons of olive oil in a large skillet or cast-iron pan. Sauté the stuffed veal breast on both sides for about 20 minutes. Turn carefully with 2 wide spatulas. Add the white wine and scrape the bottom of the pan with a fork. Transfer the meat into an enameled cast-iron casserole.

To the skillet add the celery, carrots, bay leaves, and garlic. Bring to a boil, add the water, bring back to the boiling point, then lower the flame and simmer, covered, for 2 hours. Uncover for the last 30 minutes. You may serve Pietsch at once or let it cool in its broth, cover with plastic wrap, and refrigerate.

To prepare the tomato sauce: Add herbs and chopped olives to the olive oil. Stir in diced tomatoes. Season to taste with salt and coriander. Cover with plastic and refrigerate.

Prepare the Gratin d'Aubergines but do not bake it yet. Keep it in the refrigerator.

An hour before the dinner, preheat the oven for the eggplant gratin. Remove the fat from the surface of the broth in which the Pietsch has cooked. Slowly bring the veal breast and its broth to a boil, and simmer until warm. Meanwhile, bake the eggplant gratin.

When all is ready, bring the gratin to the table along with the bowl of cold tomato sauce, a bowl of warm broth from cooking the veal, and the vegetables that were cooked with the veal. Place the veal breast on a wide flat platter. Remove the sewing thread with a scissors, surround the veal with parsley, and bring to the table along with a large serving spatula and a large knife.

Note: A small board is useful to place against the meat or the stuffing as you slice the Pietsch. You can make it yourself or wrap a piece of cardboard with a double sheet of foil.

Make sure all your guests have a chance to admire the splendid golden plump "tummy," the gorgeous Pietsch, then place it on a rolling or side table. Cut slices from the Pietsch and serve onto a plate with a wide spatula. Pour a little of the cooking broth over each portion and add some celery, carrots, and a twig of parsley. Pass this to your first guest. Each person will then help himself to some of the tomato sauce and the eggplant gratin.

WINE   A full red wine

WHAT TO SERVE BEFORE AND AFTER PIETSCH

APPETIZERS
1. Mouclade, page 58
2. A finely sliced fennel bulb salad seasoned with coarsely cut walnuts and a dressing of olive oil, mustard, and vinegar
3. Pissaladière, page 63
4. Panier de Crudités with a few sauces, page 45

DESSERTS
1. Flan au Caramel, page 272, and a platter of thin cookies
2. Cervelle de Canut, page 265
3. Tarte au Citron et aux Amandes, page 291
4. Grand Baba, page 273
5. Poires, Pruneaux, Oranges au Vin Rouge et aux Épices, page 289

DECORATION OF THE TABLE

The main thing, to avoid trouble, is not to slice your Pietsch on the table. You will present it, let everyone admire it, and then place it on a rolling or side table for cutting. In this way your tablecloth and table setting can remain quite pretty.

Choose a warm-colored tablecloth, perhaps a simple Indian patterned spread, a rich dark red and blue quilted cotton. You may wish to place an old wicker basket filled with grapes and red apples in the center, or else a good piece of crockery surrounded with colored candles, and then scatter some short-cut flowers on the tablecloth. Remember that the gratin dish and the bowl of tomato sauce will have to be passed around and that you must make room for them as well as for the bread basket, wine decanters and water pitcher, salt, pepper, and butter accessories. Keep the centerpiece bright and distinctive but rather small.

STRATEGY FOR THE SUGGESTED MENU

• Guests invited for 7:30 P.M.
• Meal served at 8:30 P.M.

· On the night before or on the morning of the Feast: Prepare Mouclade, Pietsch, Gratin d'Aubergines, tossed salad, and Flan au Caramel.

· On the evening of the Feast: 7:25 — Preheat oven to 400° and take everything out of the refrigerator. Reheat the broth and Pietsch, as described. Place the eggplant gratin in the oven.

· 7:30 — Your first guests arrive.

· 8:00 — Reheat the Mouclade broth over a gentle flame.
Bring wine, water, bread, and butter to the table.

· 8:30 — Light the candles. Ask the guests to sit at the table.
Add mussels to the Mouclade. Pour into the tureen and bring to the table in its soup kettle along with warmed plates.

· 8:50 — Bring the Pietsch to the table along with the eggplant gratin and bowls of cold and warm sauces.

· 9:20 approximately — Bring Flan au Caramel and cookie tray with dessert plates to the table.

· Later: Coffees and teas.

· Later: Cold water, fruit juices, or Perrier.

LEFTOVERS

1. Cold sliced Pietsch is delicious served with a tossed salad. It is easy to slice and, served with cold tomato sauce, makes for a delicious buffet or picnic meal.

2. Farcis: Chop everything and fill halved tomatoes and halved parboiled zucchini. Sprinkle bread crumbs on top, dot with olive oil, and bake for twenty to twenty-five minutes at 375°.

PLAT DE FARCIS

*A platter of peppers, tomatoes, on-
ions, eggplants, and zucchini
stuffed with vegetables, ham or
chicken, lean pork, parsley, garlic,
and cheese, and sprinkled with bread
crumbs and olive oil.*

SUGGESTED MENU

Soupe au Pistou

*Plat de Farcis
Tossed Green Salad*

*Oeufs à la Neige
et aux Fruits*

A Fruity Rosé

A bountiful display of light,
lean, and tasty Farcis is part of
all Provence's summer *festins*.
Because Farcis can be served
hot, lukewarm, or cold, the
meal is ready whenever you
wish and is perfect for a large family gathering, a buffet, or a picnic.

Far from the ready-made pleasures, the processed or frozen, con-
venient but boring preparations, Farcis feel and taste like real food;
their flavors derive from healthy and intense products; they are
pretty, colorful, and at once moist and crisp. There is variety as well
as quantity on the platter, and it delights the eye as much as the
palate. In the highly evocative theatrical language of Provence, it is
said that when Farcis are well prepared, they make guests think they
have died and are already in heaven.

You can trim and fill the Farcis the night before your party and
bake them while your guests are having drinks, then serve them
piping hot, or you can cook, cover, and refrigerate them to serve
them cold later. Make sure you have at least four different kinds of
vegetables and that they are always the smallest and freshest you can
find. The best choices are small, firm vegetables.

FOR 8 PEOPLE

UTENSILS   Skillet
3 baking pans (or more, if needed), 15 by 17 inches
2 large serving platters

INGREDIENTS

3 pounds raw, chopped Swiss chard (green part only) or spinach
8 small red, yellow, or green bell peppers, stems removed, seeded, and cut
  in half lengthwise
8 firm, shiny eggplants, stems removed and cut in half lengthwise
Olive oil
8 onions, peeled
8 firm zucchini, unpeeled, stems removed
8 firm, fleshy tomatoes
2 onions, peeled and chopped
2 cups chopped meat—Choose any of the following: Virginia, Kentucky,
  or a good local country ham or a good boiled ham or boiled chicken
  (12 ounces)
1 cup chopped lean salt pork or lean bacon
3 teaspoons dry thyme
4 garlic cloves, peeled and crushed
5 eggs, lightly beaten
3 cups freshly grated Parmesan and Swiss cheese
1 cup chopped parsley
Salt
Freshly ground pepper
1½ cups (approximately) homemade bread crumbs

ACCOMPANIMENTS

Tossed green salad (arugula, chicory, or watercress) (page 301)
Vinaigrette dressing (page 300)

Bring a large pot of salted water to a boil and cook the Swiss chard or spinach until tender. Drain and squeeze to extract as much water as possible. Chop and set aside.

Preheat the oven to 350°. Place the pepper and eggplant halves on the baking pans. Put a little oil on the surface of the vegetables and bake for about 15 minutes, until soft. Remove from the oven, scoop out the flesh of the eggplants with a spoon, and put in a bowl. Leave only ½ inch of flesh around the skin for a shell. Set aside.

Meanwhile, bring a large pot of salted water to a boil. Cook the whole onions and zucchini for 10 minutes. Cool and then cut the vegetables in half. Scoop out the pulp of the zucchinis, leaving about ½ inch of flesh so the shell is firm enough to hold the filling. Take out the inner layers of the onions, leaving the outer three as shells. Put the eggplant and zucchini flesh and center layers of the onions in a bowl along with the eggplant flesh.

Cut the tomatoes in half. Scoop out and discard the seeds, and squeeze the excess juice. Don't peel the tomatoes.

Heat 2 tablespoons of oil in a large skillet and sauté the chopped onions for a few minutes. Add the salt pork and meats for 1 minute, then the pulp of the eggplants, zucchinis, and onions that you kept in a bowl. Add a little thyme and cook for a few minutes over a low flame. Turn off the heat, add the Swiss chard greens or spinach, the thyme, garlic, eggs, grated cheese, parsley, salt, and pepper. Check and correct the seasoning.

The stuffing should be firm and smooth. If it is too dry, add a few chopped tomatoes. Place all the vegetable shells — half peppers, eggplants, zucchini, onions, and tomatoes — on 3 or 4 oiled baking pans (or whatever it takes to hold them). Fill each shell with 1 or 2 spoonfuls of the stuffing. Sprinkle the top of each vegetable Farci with some bread crumbs, using up half of them. Do not overstuff. Cover with plastic wrap and refrigerate until ready to bake.

Note: This seems like much too much Farcis as you prepare it: 5 different vegetables for each guest. Because of the diversity of colors, textures, and tastes, and because it is basically a very light vegetable-based filling, you should be prepared for this surprising fact: At the end of your Feast there will be very few Farcis left for your next picnic.

Fifty minutes before you serve your meal, while you set the table and prepare the appetizers, preheat the oven to 375° and take the Farcis out of the refrigerator. Sprinkle them with the remaining bread crumbs and dribble a little olive oil on top.

Place the tomatoes, onions, and peppers on the same tray: They need about 30 minutes. Bake the zucchini and eggplants on another tray: They need about 45 minutes. They should be brown and crisp.

Prepare the tossed salad and dressing.

Transfer the cooked Farcis on a big platter with a spatula and take piping hot or lukewarm to the table along with the tossed green salad. Toss the salad and leave it on the table for your guests to help themselves when they want.

Serve 5 stuffed vegetable halves on each plate, using a wide flexible spatula and a big spoon. Farcis are mostly made with vegetables; they are lean and light, and the proof is in the eating. The leftover Farcis will not be there for long. Gather them on a platter, wait for about 10 minutes after the first serving and the passing of the tossed salad, and then offer the platter of Farcis once more.

WINE   A light red wine or a fresh rosé

WHAT TO SERVE BEFORE AND AFTER PLAT DE FARCIS

APPETIZERS TO BE SERVED WITH THE DRINKS BEFORE SITTING AT THE TABLE:
1. Gougère, page 49
2. Pissaladière, page 63

AND AS A FIRST SEATED COURSE
1. Soupe au Pistou, page 70, for vegetable fans
2. Jambon Persillé, page 54
3. Terrine aux Herbes, page 73
4. Lentille ou Pois Chiches en Salade, page 57, also for vegetable fans

DESSERTS
1. Oeufs à la Neige et aux Fruits, page 284
2. Mélange de Fruits, page 281
3. Panier de Frivolités, page 286, served with cooked fruits or a fresh fruit salad
4. Grand Baba, page 273
5. Mousse au Chocolat Glacée, page 282
6. Compote de Poires, page 266

DECORATION OF THE TABLE

The table must spell summer abandon, so you may want to choose a pretty Provençal-inspired or fresh country print cotton for your tablecloth with terra-cotta or bright crockery accessories. You may use as a centerpiece a shallow crystal bowl filled with water and float a few colored candles, along with stemless pansies, roses, daisies, or geraniums on top. Cut flowers will last for several hours so you can prepare this before you set your table.

Or you may fill a bowl with fruits and put long pieces of ivy or vines between the fruit and winding down on the tablecloth. You may want to fill glass candleholders with colored candles and surround each of them with a twine of green, then make a serpentine wreath of flowers and leaves around the glasses.

Offer two baskets of bread, two or three wine decanters, and a pitcher of cool water. But mostly remember that you can depend on the freshness and variety of your platters of Farcis. They will make your Feast a cheerful one, so don't worry too much about the setting; what matters most is what is on the plate.

STRATEGY FOR THE SUGGESTED MENU

• Guests invited for 7:30 P.M.
• Meal served at 8:30 P.M.

• Soupe au Pistou, Farcis, and Oeufs à la Neige can be prepared ahead of time.

• On the night of the Feast:
· 7:25 — Set the table. Take the soup and Farcis out of the refrigerator. Preheat the oven to 350°. Reheat the soup on a medium flame, covered. Bake the Farcis in the oven.
· 7:30 — Your first guests arrive.
· 8:30 — Ask your guests to sit at the table. Bring the soup plates, Soupe au Pistou, wine, and cold water.
· 8:40 — Bring the Farcis from the oven to the table, along with the bowl of tossed greens.
· 9:00 approximately — Reheat the caramel for a second and dribble it over the Oeufs à la Neige. Bring it, along with the platter of thin cookies, to the table.

· Later: Coffees and teas.
· Later: Cold water, fruit juices, or Perrier.

LEFTOVERS   1. The leftovers can be eaten cold as is and as appetizers, or with cold pork or beef.

2. Gratin: Chop all the leftovers, vegetable shells, and stuffing. Add a little broth or tomato sauce for a moist mixture. Correct the seasoning, pour into a gratin dish, sprinkle with cheese, dribble with olive oil, and bake for thirty minutes at 375°. If you don't have enough leftovers to prepare a gratin, add a cup or two of boiled rice to the mixture

PORC AUX HERBES

SUGGESTED MENU
Crudités with Sauces

Porc aux Herbes
Sautéed Mushrooms
Celeriac Purée
Salad

Madeleines Tièdes
aux Fruits

A White Wine

A loin of marinated pork baked with spices and flavored with a tangy red currant sauce.

The festival of Saint John's Day in June celebrates the coming of summer and its many treasures: tender vegetables, berries of all kinds, peaches, apricots, and plums. And when November comes, it is with Saint Cochon, Saint Piggy's, that the cozy, substantial, reassuring pleasures of winter are announced. On that day the pig is killed and relatives and friends gather to share the traditional preparations done with fresh pork.

Like man, pigs eat meat as well as vegetables. Given a chance it will feed on acorns, hazelnuts, chestnuts, mushrooms, black currants, snails, frogs, roots of all kinds, and on the farm, on oatmeal, lean milk, beets, and potatoes. This is what gives its meat a rich flavor, a firm texture, and fragrant juices.

Pork is considered throughout France the king of animals; farmers still refer to it as "le Monsieur," the gent. It is chosen for impressive festive occasions. Nothing in it is ever wasted; it all turns out into something delicious: pâtés, sausages, and a variety of ham. When properly cooked even a pig that has not been taken to the woods to feed on delicious fruits and vegetables will give a mellow meat and fragrant amber-colored cooking juices.

The following recipe of marinated pork flavored with spices and vegetables is wonderful served with celeriac and mushrooms. We have chosen these and an endive and watercress salad, but you can select any of the accompaniments. The preparation is truly simple and the cooking mostly unattended. As always, remember to have a rich platter of goods on your table and that leftovers are welcome.

FOR *8* PEOPLE

UTENSILS	Oven-proof dish barely bigger than the roast Serving platter

MARINADE

3 onions, peeled and thinly sliced
2 cups red wine
1 cup port or red sweet vermouth
10 peppercorns
10 juniper berries
2 cloves
2 bay leaves
1 tablespoon grated orange zest
1 tablespoon grated lemon zest

MEAT

One 5-pound boneless loin pork roast, about an 8–10 rib portion, trimmed
  of fat and bones, rolled, and tied neatly to keep its shape during cooking
Salt
Freshly ground pepper

GARNISH

16 large prunes, pitted
1 cup port or sweet vermouth

ACCOMPANIMENTS

Choose 1 or 2 of the following:
Buttered celeriac: 2 celeriacs, peeled, diced, boiled, and seasoned with but-
  ter, salt, and pepper
Sautéed mushrooms: 2½ pounds mushrooms, butter, oil, parsley
Purée of celeriac (buttered celeriac puréed and a few tablespoons of heavy
  cream added before serving)
Tossed green salad: 4 cups of trimmed watercress and endives tossed with a
  lemon and oil dressing (page 301)
Ratatouille (page 68)
Gratin d'Aubergines (page 51)
Gratin Dauphinois (page 53)

SAUCE

4 tablespoons Dijon-style mustard
1 tablespoon grated fresh ginger
1 tablespoon grated orange zest
4 tablespoons red currant or cranberry jelly
1 teaspoon cinnamon

Combine the marinade ingredients in a large kettle. Bring to a boil, turn off, and let cool slightly. Meanwhile, dry the pork and rub it with salt. Place it in a bowl, pour the lukewarm marinade over it, cool, cover, and refrigerate. Marinate overnight or longer (up to 2 days), turning a few times.

Place the pitted prunes in a bowl, add the cup of port, cover, and let them soak at least 4 hours or overnight, turning once, until ready to use.

Prepare the vegetables: Peel and cut the celeriac. Cook it for 20 minutes in a large kettle of boiling salted water. When tender, drain, cool, cover with plastic wrap, and refrigerate. Wash, trim, and cut the mushrooms. Sauté in a large skillet with butter and oil. When they are still firm turn off the heat. Cool, add salt, cover, and refrigerate. Wash and trim the endives and watercress, roll loosely in a kitchen towel, and refrigerate.

Two hours before the dinner, take the meat, celeriac, and mushrooms out of the refrigerator. Preheat the oven to 375°.

Lift the roast out of the marinade. Strain the marinade, keeping the liquid of the marinade for later and reserving the onions. Dry the surface of the meat with a paper towel. The roasting pan should be quite narrow so the juices are not wasted or likely to burn during the cooking. Moisten the bottom of the pan with a little vegetable oil, place the pork on top, rub it with a little vegetable oil, and brown in the oven for about 20 minutes, turning it a few times.

Lower the temperature to 350° and cook for 15 minutes. Pour off any excess fat and add the reserved onions and half of the marinade around the roast, not on the meat itself.

Sprinkle the meat with salt and roast for about 1 hour and 15 minutes, turning it a few times. Cover loosely with a piece of foil in the last 30 minutes. Check often and add a little marinade to the bottom of the pan if necessary.

Reheat the diced celeriac for about 15 minutes, adding a little butter, salt, and pepper. Reheat the mushrooms for about 10 minutes, adding salt and pepper, if needed, and freshly chopped parsley.

Place the olive oil, lemon, salt, and pepper dressing in the bottom of a large bowl, cross the fork and spoon on top, and then place the watercress and endive salad on top. Set aside for later.

After the pork has been roasting for 1½ hours, pierce with a fork. If the juices are red, it is not cooked enough, if they are white, the roast is overcooked; if pale pink, place the meat on a warm plate, cover with the foil, and put in the warm turned-off oven. Tilt the roasting pan and remove as much fat as you can from the top of the cooking juices with a large spoon. Roll some paper towels and use to brush the top of the cooking juices to remove whatever fat is left. Deglaze the coagulated cooking juices in the bottom of the cooking pan with the rest of the marinade, scraping vigorously with a fork. Stir in the port in which the prunes were soaking (keeping the prunes for later). Pour the deglazed cooking juices into a saucepan. Bring to a rapid boil and reduce the liquid to $1\frac{1}{2}$ cups. Add the mustard, ginger, grated orange zest, red currant jelly, cinnamon and, finally, the prunes. Cook on a low flame for 1 minute and then turn off. The prunes will absorb the flavor while you remove the strings from the roast and discard them.

Carve the meat in $\frac{1}{2}$-inch-thick slices. Pour the warm sauce you just prepared on top: It will mix with the juices that escaped from the meat as you sliced it. Sprinkle salt and pepper, and place the slices overlapping on a warm platter. If there is too much sauce, pass it in a bowl separately. Cover the meat with foil to keep it warm and so that the sauce will permeate the meat. Pour mushrooms and celeriac purée in separate dishes. Toss the watercress salad.

As soon as all your guests are seated, bring into the dining room the rolling table with the pork platter, sauce, warm plates, celeriac, mushrooms, and bowl of watercress and endives.

Give each guest 2 slices of pork and 2 prunes. Pour 2 spoonfuls of sauce on top and place 2 tablespoons of celeriac and a tablespoon of mushrooms on each side of the meat. Pass around the warm sauce and the bowl of tossed watercress.

You may leave all the dishes on the table so that the guests can have second helpings. Pork is very good lukewarm.

WINE　　　　A white wine, but not too dry

What to Serve Before and After Porc aux Herbes

APPETIZERS

TO SERVE WITH THE DRINKS:

1. Poireaux Tièdes Vinaigrette, page 67
2. Crudités with two sauces, page 45
3. Caviar d'Aubergines, page 43

DESSERTS　　　　1. Madeleines Tièdes aux Fruits, page 279

2. Poires, Pruneaux, Oranges au Vin Rouge et aux Épices, page 289
3. Crêpes Normandes, page 269

DECORATION OF THE TABLE

This is a substantial winter meal, so your table should have a cozy and inviting feeling. You may like a large silver or copper bowl in the center of the table, filled with a mixture of greens, or if you collect them as I do, two birds' nests (there are pretty made-up ones in many shops now) filled with red berries, holly, and greens. Place them at each end of the table. Perhaps you'd like a thick red quilted table-cloth and an abundance of green, red, and cream candles in all sizes (but never too high), some stuck in round green squash, a few pretty lacquered baskets for bread, and bright napkins around the wine bottles. This is a cold-weather dish, so make the setting as warm and cheerful as you possibly can.

STRATEGY FOR THE SUGGESTED MENU

- Guests invited for 7:30 P.M.
- Meal served at 8:30 P.M.

- The day before the Feast: Marinate the pork. Prepare the celeriac, mushrooms, and watercress and endive salad dressing. Trim and wash all the Crudités. Prepare the two sauces, Madeleines, and cooked fruits.

- On the the day of the Feast:
- 6:30 — Take everything out of the refrigerator. Preheat the oven to 375°.
- 6:45 — Brown the pork on all sides.
- 7:05 — Lower the oven and cook the pork.
- 7:30 — Your guests arrive.
- 7:45 — Serve the Crudités and the sauces with the drinks.
- 8:00 — Reheat the celeriac on a low flame. Reheat the mushrooms on a low flame, uncovered.
    Slice the pork, deglaze the coagulated juices, reduce, and finish the sauce. Cover with a piece of foil to keep warm. Pour the celeriac into a serving dish and season with butter. Pour the mushrooms into a dish and cover with a piece of foil. Place the Madeleines in the turned-off warm oven, covered with a piece of foil.

· 8:30 — Light the candles. Ask your guests to be seated. Bring the rolling table to the dining room table with the warm plates, platter of sliced pork, mushrooms, celeriac, warm sauce, and bowl of tossed greens.

· 9:00 — Change the plates. Bring the lukewarm Madeleines and the cooked fruit.

· Later: Coffees and teas.

· Later: Cold water, fruit juices, or Perrier.

LEFTOVERS   1. Mixed salad: Diced leftover pork and cooked lentils served lukewarm with an oil, vinegar, and mustard dressing and sprinkled with minced onion and minced basil or chives.

2. Pasta: Chopped leftover pork mixed with chopped leftover mushrooms and seasoned with plain tomato sauce. Pour this over a dish of warm pasta and sprinkle with grated Parmesan and dribble some raw olive oil.

3. Cold salad: Diced leftover pork mixed with diced fennel and celery and seasoned with a dressing of oil, crumbled hard-boiled egg yolk, mustard, and vinegar.

4. Sliced pork with a fresh tossed lettuce salad is delicious.

POT-AU-FEU

SUGGESTED MENU

Broth from the
Pot-au-Feu
Cheese Toasts

Pot-au-Feu
Chick-pea Salad

Oeufs à la Neige
et aux Fruits

Red Bordeaux

*The glorious boiled dinner of meats
and vegetables scented with herbs
and served with an assortment of
condiments and sauces.*

Pot-au-Feu is France's national dish. It has been called the foundation glory of French Cuisine, and according to Goethe it is also the glory of home cooking. Escoffier redundantly went on to declare it the symbol of family life, and, in fact, whether it deals with a real or an invented family, Pot-au-Feu truly stands against loneliness and division; it creates cohesion and warmth for a suspended moment while a group of friends gathered around a steaming pot share its procession of good things.

Pot-au-Feu is a reassuring and comforting dish. Faced with a pile of vegetables, bones, meats, and a variety of sauces and condiments, man, woman, child, old and young, feel at once secure and confident. Once they have experienced this feeling for a few hours, they are, of course, likely to believe it can happen again and again, and spread this contagious thought around them. Hence, the tonifying importance of Pot-au-Feu in society, to the extent that Mirabeau declared that the foundation of empires lay in the common Pot-au-Feu. But Pot-au-Feu is not only a solid, heartwarming dish, it is a spectacular extravaganza, too.

In the beginning of the century the gourmet writer Marcel Rouff wrote an extraordinary novel about the most refined and gifted of gastronomes, Dodin Bouffant (*The Life and Passions of Dodin Bouffant,* 1925). After being lavishly entertained by the prince of Eurasia who had overwhelmed him with a pretentious meal, Dodin Bouffant decided to serve a "boiled beef garnished with its own vegetables." The prince was insulted at first, thinking it a vulgar dish. But as soon as the splendid display of Pot-au-Feu appeared on the table, he "wavered between the noble desire to create Dodin Bouffant a duke immediately, a wild urge to offer the gastronome half his fortune and half his kingdom and take over the rights of his gustatory administration, the irritation of being taught a lesson, and the haste to cut into the marvel which laid before him his intoxicating promises." When asked to explain this apotheosis of simplicity and sophistication, Dodin simply answered what is indeed the definition and the key of all good food: "A work of choice, demanding much love."

All of France loves Pot-au-Feu, and each region has its variations, but not two villages, not two cooks agree on the ingredients. Of course there must be meat, vegetables, bones, and marrow bones. But some may add lamb, as in Provence, and some include veal or ham. Other possibilities may be a stuffed breast of veal, a stuffed goose neck, duck thighs, turkey legs, a piece of cured country ham, or a preserved goose. Saffron, juniper berries, or garlic may be added to the broth. A variety of vegetables can be selected. Although Pot-au-Feu is generally served with coarse sea salt and mustard, capers, olives, and bitter cherries in vinegar, and a variety of sauces may also be offered, along with a salad of warm chick-peas as an accompaniment.

It is better not to see what the nouvelle cuisine has done with Pot-au-Feu. As usual, its bright chefs never lack ideas and are amused by esoteric variations on this classic theme. But we want pleasures, tangible ones, not rhetoric when it comes to such a festive meal.

Alexander Dumas formally stated that French cooking owed its superiority to the excellence of French bouillon and advised that an old pigeon, a partridge, a rabbit could be added to the broth. He also firmly demanded seven hours of "sustained simmering" for a Pot-au-Feu worthy of its name. He was excessive, but his claims went in the right direction.

Sensibly prepared, the true sophistication of this dish appears at once: It first announces its coming on the table through the nose; it opens everyone's appetite and then offers in abundance the means to satisfy it. It needs no introduction, and its very presence at once overwhelms the senses.

And this glorious meal — a heady broth, moist meats, a selection of well-cooked vegetables, crisp bread rounds spread with marrow — embodies everyone's idea of a good healthy dish. In fact, it has been given for centuries to new mothers, melancholy adolescents, and elderly people.

But preparing Pot-au-Feu also represents the precise orchestration of a great simple dish at its best. The slow simmering of the meat, herbs, and bones requires no attention. The greatest challenges to the cook are the timing and the first-rate quality of the ingredients.

Pot-au-Feu must be done one day ahead, kept overnight in the refrigerator, and carefully degreased the next day. In this way it is also easy to serve and most economical since nothing is lost of the broth, meat, bones, and vegetables, and all can be used in a variety of preparations in the days to come.

And as you finish serving your guests, you will see them, as Dodin Bouffant observed, "extract, in one stroke, between spoon and fork, the quadruple enchantment which is in their share" and later see the whole table "abandon themselves, in all contentment, to the pleasures of taste, and to that sweet, confident friendship which beckons to well-born men after meals worthy of the name."

You may select the sauces, vegetables, and meats you wish from the lists given. Generally each guest should have one marrow bone, some sliced beef, some chicken, one carrot, one potato, one turnip, leek and either a piece of celeriac or some green beans, along with one or two sauces, a few pickles, some good mustard, and coarse salt. But you may add to this more vegetables, a stuffed breast of veal, a stuffed chicken, according to the party you have in mind.

Remember, leftovers will give you a week of delicious menus, so there is no reason not to offer an opulent Pot-au-Feu to your guests.

FOR ABOUT 8 PEOPLE

UTENSILS   Double-decker steamer pot or 2 large kettles
Rolling table or side table
2 extra soup kettles
Variety of baskets
Variety of small bowls
8 tiny spoons
8 small soup bowls or cups
Plenty of cheesecloth

MEATS   *1 pound bones (approximately): a veal knuckle (have the butcher crack it)
and some beef ribs*
2 pounds ox tail, cut into 2-inch pieces (optional)

5 quarts water

1 3-pound brisket, neatly tied with a long piece of string so it can be lifted easily from the broth

3 pounds rump pot roast, tied to hold its shape

1 large piece beef short ribs, trimmed (about 4 pounds or so)

2 onions, studded with cloves

3 sprigs of thyme

3 garlic cloves

Salt

10 peppercorns

Bouquet garni, composed of:

    bunch of parsley

    twig of thyme

    3 bay leaves

    leeks, green part only

    1 carrot

    10 peppercorns

    1 head of garlic, unpeeled

1 4-pound chicken

8 marrow bones, sliced about 1 inch thick

A peppery lean cooking sausage or a garlic sausage (Saucisson à cuire if you have a French butcher nearby) or a Hungarian sausage or "cotechino" sausage

SAUCES

Choose 1 or 2 of the following:

1. *1 cup of mayonnaise seasoned with 1 tablespoon of mustard, 1 tablespoon of minced shallots, 2 tablespoons of capers, 1 tablespoon of crushed coriander, and 1 tablespoon of minced parsley*

2. *1 cup of tomato sauce made with 2 sliced onions sautéed in oil into which 1 cup of drained canned tomatoes and a little pepper are stirred; cook for 30 minutes on a low flame and season to taste with salt and minced basil, chives, or parsley at the last moment*

3. *1 cup of olive oil, 3 tablespoons of minced fresh herbs (such as flat parsley, thyme, basil), 3 tablespoons of chopped capers, 5 tiny diced gherkins, 1 crushed garlic clove, 1 teaspoon of Dijon-style mustard, and 1 teaspoon of red wine vinegar vigorously stirred together before serving*

4. *1 cup of mayonnaise seasoned with 2 tablespoons of tarragon and 1 tablespoon of Dijon-style mustard*

5. *Horseradish sauce: 5 tablespoons of freshly grated horseradish mixed with 1 cup of heavy cream, lightly whipped, 2 teaspoons of mustard, and 2 tablespoons of red wine vinegar*

6. *1½ cups of heavy cream boiled slowly for 15 minutes to reduce, then enriched with 2 tablespoons of Dijon-style mustard and 2 tablespoons of tomato sauce (see #2 above) and sprinkled with 2 tablespoons of chopped chervil or parsley*

7. *1 cup of Aioli, page 87*

ACCOMPANIMENTS   Choose from the following:

Several types of mustards, but mostly Dijon-style

Sour gherkins or small dill pickles

Pickled onions

Sour black cherries in vinegar. Cover ripe cherries and part of their stems with wine vinegar, a few tarragon leaves, peppercorns, and whole coriander; seal and keep for 2 to 12 months. The longer they are kept, the better they are. Can also be purchased in gourmet stores.

Bowl of kosher salt or coarse French "gray sea salt"

10 bread rounds, buttered, sprinkled with grated Swiss cheese, and broiled for a few seconds before serving with the warm broth. These can be prepared ahead and reheated. Have an additional 8 rounds to be oven-dried later.

8 bread rounds or triangles of oven-dried bread to be spread with the warm marrow and coarse salt

Bowl of grated Swiss and Parmesan cheese (for the guests who like it sprinkled on the broth)

Dish of grated celery root (or celeriac) seasoned with a mustardy mayonnaise or a lukewarm salad of chick-peas (page 57).

VEGETABLES   Choose a variety from among the following:

8 carrots, peeled, cut in half lengthwise, then in half crosswise, and tied in a bunch

1 large celeriac, peeled and quartered

6 white turnips, peeled and halved

2 fennel roots, cut in half, or whole if small

3 celery hearts, trimmed and quartered

Savoy cabbage, quartered (optional; cook separately or in the steamer)
8 leeks, white part only, leaving only 2 inches of green, cut in half length-
wise, tied in a bunch, and then wrapped in cheesecloth
10 small potatoes, peeled
1 pound string beans, trimmed

GARNISH   *3 tablespoons minced flat parsley and chives*

Place the veal and beef bones in a hot oven for a few minutes to brown them, then put them on the bottom of a very large soup kettle. Add the ox tail. Cover with water and bring slowly to the simmering point, uncovered. The top of the water should just shiver, or "smile" as tradition calls it. Add the pieces of brisket and rump pot roast. After a few minutes a brown scum will start rising; remove it from the surface continuously until it changes to white and frothy. Add a little cold water from time to time to make sure all the scum has risen to the surface. Continue to skim the broth as necessary.

Add the rest of the meat, 2 clove-studded onions, thyme, unpeeled garlic, salt, peppercorns and bouquet garni to the hot broth. Bring almost to just under a boil and simmer gently for 2 more hours.

Meanwhile place the chicken (stuffed or plainly trussed with just an onion and a bay leaf inside) in a 375° oven for 15 minutes to release some of the fat. Wipe the chicken carefully with a paper towel, add it to the broth, and cook 1 hour more. The meat must cook for at least 3 hours and be very tender. Turn off the flame and cool to room temperature.

Place the meat and chicken on a large platter. Line a strainer with 1 or 2 layers of dampened cheesecloth, then pour the broth through it into a large bowl. Add salt or pepper to correct the seasoning of the broth. If the broth is weak-flavored, place it on a high flame to reduce for a few minutes. Discard the bones, bouquet garni, and onions. Add the cooked beef and chicken to the bowl, cover, and refrigerate overnight.

Pat some coarse salt into both ends of the marrow bones. Wrap them in a large piece of cheesecloth tied with a long string. Refrigerate. Prepare the sauces and accompaniments you have selected. Cover with plastic wrap and leave overnight in the refrigerator.

An hour before the party, remove everything from the refrigerator. The fat will be soldified, congealed on top of the dish, and will be as easy to remove as a piece of wax. Discard any fat and gristle you can see on the cooked beef, mostly on the ribs. Slice the beef across the grain to make ½- to ¼-inch slices. Wrap it in a large piece of cheesecloth with a long string for easy removal and set aside. Cut the chicken, discarding any fat, gristle, or skin. Place the pieces in a large piece of cheesecloth with a long string and set aside.

Bring the broth, sliced meat, and cut-up chicken neatly tied in their pieces of cheesecloth to a boil, lower the flame, and let it simmer gently.

Cook the cheesecloth-wrapped marrow bones in cold water for 20 to 30 minutes. Remove from the heat and set aside in hot water until ready to serve.

If you are using them, reheat the cheese bread rounds and plain bread rounds for a few minutes in a 350° oven. Turn off the oven and keep warm until the meal.

Fill the bottom of the steamer with boiling water. Prick the surface of the sausage with a fork and add it to the water. Place your selections of carrots, celeriac, turnips, fennel cut in half, celery hearts, and cabbage on the steamer's tray. Cover and cook for 10 minutes. Add a second tray with your selections of leeks, potatoes, and string beans on top of the first one and cook 20 minutes more. It will be ready to serve, but if you need to wait, you can keep everything warm and firm for an hour off the stove in the tightly closed steamer pot.

If you don't use a steamer, cook the carrots, celeriac, cabbage, fennel, and turnips in a large pot of salty water for about 10 minutes, then add the potatoes, green beans, sausage, and leeks.

The broth, meat, and chicken will reheat in a separate pot. Ask one of your guests to come and help you. Warm the plates. Warm the large serving platters over a steaming pot or in the oven for a few minutes while you pull the vegetables, meat, chicken, and bones out of the pot. Remove the strings and cheesecloth. Place the sauces and accompaniments on a tray and bring to the rolling table.

Bring cups or small bowls filled with hot broth to the table along with a bottle of port and a basket of warm cheese bread rounds. Your guests may add a drop of port to the broth and sip this delicious amber bouillon with the cheese rounds.

Meanwhile, bring in the sauces and whatever other condiments you have chosen to serve. Arrange the vegetables on 1 or 2 of the warm platters and moisten them with the warm cooking broth. Also arrange the slices of beef and moisten with a little warm broth. Sprinkle with chopped chives. Decorate the platters with some flat parsley.

Slide the sliced sausage and marrow bones onto a warm plate and add a little parsley for garnish. Bring it along with oven-dried bread and a bowl of warm broth. It is good to have little spoons or forks for getting every bit of marrow from the bones; seafood forks or coffee spoons are good for this. This is one of those times when a rolling table or serving cart is very useful, so if you have one by all means load it up with the elements of Pot-au-Feu.

Present the platters in the dining room so everyone can see the abundant colorful display. If you are set up for it, let each guest arrange his own combination of steaming vegetables, meats, and sausage from a sideboard or serving table. Or arrange portions of Pot-au-Feu on each plate yourself, making a full selection of vegetables and meats moistened with a little broth.

The marrow should be extracted from its bones with the little spoons, spread on the warm bread rounds, and sprinkled with coarse salt by each guest. This is a delight to bite into. Pass the various condiments and sauces and a basket for discarded bones. The warm broth is available throughout the meal.

Reassemble the remaining vegetables and meats onto 1 or 2 platters. Add a bit of broth and pass around for second helpings. Lukewarm meat and vegetables from Pot-au-Feu are acceptable. But if you don't mind getting up and you want the second helpings to be piping hot, place the Pot-au-Feu leftovers back on the stove and then bring them back for seconds.

WINE   A good red Bordeaux

WHAT TO SERVE BEFORE AND AFTER POT-AU-FEU

APPETIZERS TO BE SERVED WITH THE DRINKS BEFORE SITTING AT THE TABLE:

1. A bowl of warm broth with old port and cheese toasts. Use thin strips of oven-dried whole wheat or white bread, or slices of French bread, spread lightly with butter and grated cheese. Broil to melt and slightly brown the cheese.
2. Pissenlits aux Lardons, page 65
3. Terrine aux Herbes, page 73
4. Poireaux Tièdes Vinaigrette, page 67

Note: You may wish to serve along with your Pot-au-Feu a dish of lukewarm chick-peas (page 57) or a dish of raw celeriac coarsely grated and seasoned with a mustardy mayonnaise.

DESSERT

1. Oeufs à la Neige et aux Fruits, page 283
2. Crémets aux Fruits, page 267
3. Flan au Caramel, page 282
4. Mousse au Chocolat Glacée, page 282
5. Grand Baba, page 273

DECORATION OF THE TABLE

This glorious dish deserves a warm, festive table. You might like to choose a floor-length quilted tablecloth in a pretty shade of blue, and perhaps choose some salmon-colored cotton napkins, a round lacquered basket filled with salmon petunias, or salmon-colored geraniums or graceful tulips in the center.

Choose pretty bowls for the various sauces and condiments, two baskets sprayed in blue (with your dime-store spray can) and lined with white napkins for the oven-dried bread, and perhaps two plain ones for the discarded bones. Put a white or a salmon-colored napkin around the necks of the red wine bottles and scatter salmon or white votive candles in front of each glass.

Remember, the table will be crowded so keep the centerpiece small and in a distinctive color and shape.

Note: Don't forget to add tiny spoons for the marrow when you set the table.

STRATEGY FOR THE SUGGESTED MENU

- Guests invited for 7:30 P.M.
- Meal served at 8:30 P.M.

- The day before the Feast: Prepare the vegetables, cover with plastic wrap, and keep in the refrigerator. Prepare the sauces and condiments, cover, and refrigerate. Prepare the meat, bones, and herbs. Cover and refrigerate. Prepare Oeufs à la Neige, cover, and refrigerate.
- On the morning of the Feast: Remove the fat from the top of the broth. Remove any fat or gristle left on the beef and chicken. Slice the beef, cut the chicken, and wrap in neat cheesecloth bundles

with long strings for easy fishing out of the broth. Discard the herbs and bones.

· 7:00 — Preheat the oven to 300°. Prepare the breads for the soup course and serve with the marrow bones. Remove everything except Oeufs à la Neige from the refrigerator.

· 7:20 — Warm the plates. Reheat the meat and broth on a low flame in an open kettle. Prepare the steamer or pots for cooking vegetables, marrow bones, and sausages. Turn off the oven, leaving the bread in it.

· 7:30 — Your first guests arrive.

· 7:50 — Cook the vegetables, sausage, and marrow bones according to the recipe. Arrange the platters, sauces, and condiments according to the recipe.

· 8:00 — Serve the broth, cheese rounds, and bottle of port with the drinks.

· 8:30 — Light the candles. Ask your guests to be seated. Present the Pot-au-Feu.

· 9:00 — Take Oeufs à la Neige from the refrigerator at the same time second helpings are served. Heat the caramel and pour it on top.

· 9:30 — Remove plates and platters. Bring the dessert plates, Oeufs à la Neige, and thin cookies to the table.

· Later: Coffees and teas.
· Later: Cold water, fruit juices, or Perrier.

LEFTOVERS

· 1. Pot-au-Feu en Gelée: Remove all bones, gristle, and fat. Cut the meat in small pieces. Take a big wide bowl and spread it as prettily as you can with one-third of the vegetables. Scatter some tarragon leaves on top. Spread half of the meat over the vegetables and scatter a few more tarragon leaves; add half of the remaining vegetables and the rest of the meat, and finally the rest of the vegetables. Press firmly with the palm of your hands. Degrease the broth and reheat it. Add some minced chervil if you have it and pour it over the meat and vegetables. Poke with a fork to make sure the broth has penetrated to the bottom of the bowl. Cool, cover with plastic wrap or foil, refrigerate overnight, and then unmold. Surround the bottom of the dish with parsley.

2. Petite marmite: Cut up the meat and vegetables in small pieces. Reduce the broth for thirty minutes. Check the seasoning, add the meat and vegetables, and reheat gently. Serve with crisp bread

rounds or grated cheese. If you have leftover cabbage, chop it, sprinkle it with salt, and place one-half teaspoon of it on a crisp piece of bread. Sprinkle cheese on top, pass it under the broiler, and float it in each soup plate.

3. Gratin: Sauté a few sliced dry mushrooms, six finely chopped shallots, and two garlic cloves in a little oil and butter until soft. Add one cup of bread crumbs, salt and pepper, and stir. Butter an oven-proof dish and spread half of the mixture in it. Add a layer of sliced leftover beef or chicken and then the rest of the mushrooms, shallots, and bread crumbs mixture. Carefully pour one-half cup of dry white wine into the dish, dot with butter, and bake for at least thirty minutes at 375°.

4. Boeuf en salade: Thinly slice or dice the leftover beef and the boiled potatoes, and layer with a dressing of oil, vinegar, mustard, chopped capers, minced shallots, and minced flat parsley. Place a few hard-boiled egg slices on top. Serve cold or at room temperature.

5. Hachis Parmentier, page 186.

6. Croquettes: Add to the leftover beef and potatoes some chopped parsley and a few beaten eggs. Shape into balls and pan fry in butter and oil.

7. Mironton: Peel and chop or slice a few onions. Sauté in butter and oil, and blend in some red wine vinegar and white wine, about one-fourth cup for each person, and a little broth. Heat, stirring, and add chopped parsley, salt, and pepper. Pour a little of the mixture into the bottom of a buttered oven-proof dish. Add the sliced leftover beef or chicken and spoon the rest of the sauce over. Sprinkle some bread crumbs on top, dot with butter, and bake at 375°. Tomato sauce and chopped watercress are sometimes added to the dish for a more pungent taste.

8. Serve the leftover broth with one poached egg per person and crisp bread rounds.

9. You can serve just the leftover broth, very warm, with the addition of eight tablespoons of port and eight tablespoons of heavy cream just before serving.

10. Leftover broth is the very best choice to precede Gratinée Lyonnaise, page 182.

11. Stuffed tomatoes, page 217, replacing ham with beef or chicken leftovers.

POTÉE

A stew of white beans, cabbage, carrots, leeks, and pork seasoned with herbs and spices.

SUGGESTED MENU

Pissenlits au Lardons

Potée

Granité au Vin

Graves

Once upon a time, because they needed courage, reassurance, and unity, and probably because they also were exceptionally fond of pork and cabbage, the Gauls invented the Potée. They indulged in it for years, and throughout the centuries this satisfying superdish has warmed the hearts and souls of every generation of Frenchmen.

Potée—so-called simply because it is cooked in an earthenware pot—still embodies the very idea of conviviality and cozy pleasures. There is nothing more reassuring than a Potée simmering in a house, nothing more evocative of home sweet home than family and friends around a lavish, generous, and inviting Potée.

By tradition this is a true country dish. The pork comes from the farm, the vegetables from the garden, and they are prepared and cooked in harmony; no ingredient upstages another. Everything simmers together and mingles for hours to give a moist and fragrant Potée.

Each regional version selects and clings to its very own ingredients, so each Potée is unique. Lean salt pork, smoked bacon, rolled pork shoulder, ham, head of pig, quartered, spareribs, breast of lamb, stuffed chicken, plain chicken, red beans, white beans, cabbage (of course), garlic, clove-studded onions, carrots, turnips, leeks, brussels sprouts and sometimes fresh peas, green beans, and young onions, all have their place in a Potée. And when it appears on the table, toasted rye bread may float on the broth while the meats and vegetables follow separately. Or the whole Potée may be presented on a single platter and the broth kept for another day. In some regions one or two whole garlic heads (about eighteen cloves) cook in the broth and are spread, when they are cooked and soft, on slices of country-style bread for a nutty delicious garnish.

The quality of this dish depends on the variety and, of course, the freshness of its ingredients. It also depends on very careful cooking, because just like Pot-au-Feu, Potée should simmer and never be stirred in its slow cooking process. The steps are simple to understand and simple to follow.

But in the following recipe, handed down by generations of attentive cooks, there are a few tiny new tips: Brown the vegetables before simmering them in the broth; blanch the beans and cabbage separately and add them later to the Potée; trim all the meats so there is little gristle and just enough fat; and sauté the sausage before adding it at the last moment. This Potée will then become very tasty and also highly digestible.

At the table you will have sliced meats on one platter, white beans and shredded cabbage on another, which will almost have melted to give a fresh, intriguing, wonderful taste and texture.

You will place all around—gathered in little bunches—the leeks, carrots, and turnips, along with the slices of crisp sausage.

This invigorating dish will conquer all hearts at first sight and first bite and be a candidate for frequent reelection throughout the winter. Potée is neither expensive nor complicated to prepare and cooks mostly unattended, but you must take time to share and enjoy it, for this is for the serene and rich hours. Be generous in your offerings of vegetables and meats; "the most is the bestest here," as the Gauls might have said, and leftovers will turn into succulent preparations for days to come.

FOR *8* PEOPLE

UTENSILS   2 large kettles or Boston bean pots
Skillet

VEGETABLES   *1 pound (2 cups) white beans, such as Great Northern or navy*
Salt
1 large green cabbage (about 2 pounds), shredded

2 tablespoons unsalted butter

2 tablespoons vegetable oil

6 carrots, peeled and cut into 2-inch pieces

2 onions, peeled and quartered

1–2 celery roots (about 2 pounds), peeled and cut into 2-inch pieces, or 5
  small white turnips, peeled and quartered

10 garlic cloves, peeled

4 leeks (white part only), cleaned and tied into a bundle (reserve greens for
  the cooking liquid)

3 bay leaves, crumpled

3 teaspoons dry thyme or a few sprigs of fresh thyme

Freshly ground black pepper

SEASONINGS
1 quart water (approximately) for each pound of meat

Stalk of celery, trimmed

2 medium onions (about 8 ounces), peeled and stuck with 2 whole cloves

10 peppercorns

10 juniper berries

3 bay leaves

4 garlic cloves, peeled

Greens of 2 leeks

MEATS
One 1-pound (or more) cured ham, such as Virginia or Kentucky country

One 2-pound piece lean slab bacon or lean salt pork, with rind removed

3 pounds meaty pork spareribs, trimmed and left in 1 piece

One 2–3 pound boneless shoulder of pork or Boston butt

1 meaty ham bone or blanched smoked ham hock (optional)

1 pound boiling sausage, such as Polish kielbasa or saucisson from Lyon

1 pound thin frying sausage, such as Italian sweet, or hot, garlicky or
  peppery or smoky

ACCOMPANIMENTS
4 slices of whole wheat bread

Mustards: Dijon-style, à l'ancienne (with mustard seeds and a coarse texture), or tarragon

Kosher salt

Small bowl of tiny sour gherkins (cornichons)

Bowl of vinaigrette (page 300) with 3 tablespoons finely minced chives or
  tarragon or fresh coriander or flat parsley

GARNISHES
¼ cup chopped chives and parsley sprigs

Soak the beans in cold water for 1 hour. Drain, rinse, and add cold water to cover. Bring to a boil, lower the heat, and simmer about 1 hour until cooked but not mushy. Drain, cool, and reserve until ready to assemble the Potée.

Bring water to a boil in a large pot. Add salt (about 1 teaspoon for each quart of water). Add the shredded cabbage and bring back to a boil. Lower the heat slightly and cook for 15 minutes. Drain and refresh under cold running water. When cool enough to handle, squeeze out as much water as possible with your hands. Reserve until ready to finish the Potée.

Melt the butter with the vegetable oil in a large skillet over medium heat. Add the carrots, onions, and celery root. Cook, stirring frequently, about 7 minutes, until lightly colored. Add garlic and the bundle of leeks. Continue cooking about 3 minutes more. Season with bay leaves, thyme, salt, and pepper. Remove to drain on paper towels and reserve until ready to assemble the dish.

Bring 8 or 9 quarts of water to a boil and add all the seasonings. Boil for 5 minutes.

Trim the cured ham, bacon, spareribs, and shoulder of pork of as much fat as possible. Place in the pot with the seasonings (and ham bone if you have it) and bring back to a boil. Lower the heat and simmer for 1 hour. Add the lightly browned vegetables, the cabbage, and the bundle of leeks. Simmer for 15 minutes. Add the cooked beans and continue cooking 15 minutes more. Stir with a long-handled spoon so you have meats and vegetables on top of the cabbage to prevent it from floating.

Prick the boiling sausage with a fork to prevent splitting and add it to the pot. Cook 20 minutes more. Remove from the flame, let cool to room temperature, and then refrigerate.

Two hours before the party take the Potée out of the refrigerator. Forty minutes before you sit down to dinner, preheat the oven to 350°. Bring the Potée to a boil and reheat on a low flame, stirring a few times with a long-handled spoon.

When you feel the meat is warm, remove all the pieces from the kettles and slice them, removing all the loose bones, rind, and gristle. Place in 1 or 2 serving dishes. Spoon 1 or 2 ladlefuls of hot broth on top, cover with foil, and place in the oven while you finish preparations.

Toast the whole wheat bread either in a toaster or in an oven until crisp and then slice in half. Brown the frying sausages until crisp and place in the oven to keep warm. With a wide long-handled sieve, remove the beans and cabbage from the broth and put into a shallow serving dish. Place the various boiled vegetables all around. Remove and discard the string from the leeks and cut each into 2-inch pieces.

Spoon warm broth over everything. Sprinkle with salt and pepper and a little chopped chives. Take the sliced meats out of the oven and place a few parsley sprigs in the center. Sprinkle with salt and freshly ground pepper. Spoon a little more broth over the platter. When your guests are all seated, bring the serving dishes, warm plates, slices of toast, and bowl of hot broth into the dining room.

You may let your guests get up and help themselves from a side table, or you can serve each plate yourself. Ask a friend to pass the plates for a quicker service since Potée is better warm. Each serving should have a 2-inch piece of sparerib, a slice of boiled sausage, a slice of crisp sausage, a slice of raw cured ham, a piece of lean salt pork, a piece of shoulder butt, a generous helping of white beans and cabbage, and a few boiled vegetables. Moisten the vegetables with a bit of warm broth.

Pass the different mustards, the kosher salt, gherkins, and Vinaigrette around the table.

Bring what is left of the Potée back to the kitchen at once. Put it on the stove or in the turned-off oven and return to your guests. Ten minutes or so later, bring a steaming lavish platter of meats and vegetables to the dining room for second helpings.

WINE	A dry white wine or a red wine with bouquet from Burgundy, Beaujolais, Médoc, or Graves, or a local one

What to Serve Before and After Potée

This is a hearty country dish, so you should have a light appetizer.

APPETIZERS
1. Pissenlits aux Lardons, page 65
2. Poireaux Tièdes Vinaigrette, page 67
3. Crudités with a sauce, page 45
4. Caviar d'Aubergines with warm toast and crisp vegetables, page 43

DESSERTS
1. Granité au Vin, page 278
2. Cervelle de Canut, page 265, with warm toast

3. Flan au Caramel, page 272, and a platter of thin cookies
4. Mousse au Chocolat Glacée, page 282
5. Panier de Frivolités, page 286

DECORATION OF THE TABLE

With such a glorious offering don't worry too much about the decoration of the table. But you could, for instance, choose a solid brown tablecloth or an Indian brown and caramel tablecloth, and add red accessories for a cheerful and substantial table dressing to fit this impressive Potée meal.

You could choose red napkins and tie each rolled napkin with a piece of brown ribbon and a soft bow. You might like baskets sprayed in rich brown or deep red for the bread. You might also cover a round platter or small tray with one of the red napkins and then place all the mustards, salt, gherkins, and vinaigrette on it.

In the center you may want an antique wooden salad bowl or a tiny wooden crate (the kind mushrooms come in) filled with a mixture of walnuts in their shells, kumquats, and crab apples, and with a few litchis or twigs of greens stuck here and there.

You may like brown and red candles on your table put into stale rolls of country bread or, if you use thin candles, place them in big brown muffins or red apples.

Your wine bottles could have a little brown napkin wrapped around their necks, and don't forget to have one or two pitchers of water on the table.

STRATEGY FOR THE SUGGESTED MENU

- Guests invited for 7:30 P.M.
- Dinner served at 8:30 P.M.

- On the day before the Feast: Cook the Potée and prepare the Granité au Vin if you have time. Trim all the greens and prepare the dressing.

- On the day of the Feast:
- 7:30 — Reheat the Potée over a low flame, stirring once or twice very, very gently with a long-handled spoon. Take the salad greens out of the refrigerator. Prepare the salad plates and cut bacon. Preheat the oven to 350°.

· 7:30 — Your guests arrive.

· 8:15 — Sauté the bacon, toss it on the greens, and arrange on individual plates. Prepare the pork, sausages, and spareribs, cover with broth and foil, and keep warm in a 350° oven. Sauté the sausage; place it with the sliced pork in the oven.

· 8:30 — Light the candles. Ask your guests to sit down to the Pissenlits.

· 8:45 — Arrange serving dishes according to the recipe and bring everything to the dining room. Remove small salad plates, bring in warm plates, and serve Potée as described.

· 9:20 — Change plates and serve Granité au Vin (with a platter of thin cookies).

· Later: Coffees and teas. Armagnac, marc, or cognac.

· Later: Cold water, fruit juices, or Perrier.

LEFTOVERS

1. A country soup: Float some crisp croutons on top of the leftover broth for a delicious soup.

2. Add diced leftover meat and vegetables to the broth and serve piping hot with a sprinkling of chives.

3. Serve the cold sliced leftover pieces of pork with a very tart, lemony mayonnaise, page 168, or a very lively vinaigrette, page 302.

4. Leftover pork can be used for Plat de Farcis, page 217.

5. Leftover pork can be used for Chou Farci, page 137.

6. Leftover pork can be used for the Poule Verte stuffing, page 256.

7. Gratin: A delicious gratin can be made with diced leftover vegetables, seasoned with a little tomato sauce, and covered with grated Swiss cheese.

POULET FRICASSÉE PROVENÇALE

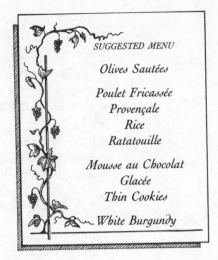

SUGGESTED MENU

Olives Sautées

Poulet Fricassée
Provençale
Rice
Ratatouille

Mousse au Chocolat
Glacée
Thin Cookies

White Burgundy

Marinated chicken sautéed with on-ions and seasoned with a heady purée of chicken livers, garlic, fresh herbs, and capers.

The cornerstone of a good meal is each guest's feeling that he or she is in good hands. This is the case when you serve Poulet Fricassée Provençale. This light and vibrant dish is easy to prepare, easy to reheat, easy to serve. The chicken is marinated with herbs, sautéed in butter, deglazed with wine, and at the last moment a heady mixture is stirred into the dish. Tiny zucchini, spring carrots, and baby turnips or a Ratatouille will complement this Chicken Fricassée, and with everything prepared ahead of time, to be reheated at the last moment, this makes for a confident process.

Le Corbusier said, "God is in the details," and so is the good cook. As always, take care of little things—the crispness of each piece of chicken before you add the wine, the firmness of the carrots, and of the zucchini—and you will soon notice that the big things will take care of themselves.

FOR *8* PEOPLE

UTENSILS

Skillet
Casserole, 9 by 12 inches, with a tight lid

FRICASSÉE

20 pieces of chicken: either three 4-pound chickens cut into serving pieces, discarding the wings and backs, or 20 chicken breasts
Juice of 1 lemon
4 tablespoons thyme

6 tablespoons butter
6 tablespoons olive oil
2 teaspoons marjoram
2 teaspoons sage
Salt
Freshly crushed pepper
2 large onions, peeled and chopped
1 cup dry white wine
1 cup dry white vermouth
1–2 teaspoons peppercorns (a mixture of green, red, and black, if available)
12 scallions (1 inch wide), with stems on
12 ounces chicken livers
1 tablespoon flour
5 garlic cloves, peeled and crushed
$\frac{3}{4}$ cup chopped parsley
3 tablespoons chopped basil or any fresh herb
4 tablespoons capers

ACCOMPANIMENTS
2 cups rice (page 303)
Ratatouille (page 68) or a mixture of turnips, zucchini, and carrots sautéed in butter

GARNISH
4 thin slices of bread, toasted
Olive oil

Dry the pieces of chicken. Sprinkle them with lemon juice and then rub all the pieces with a great deal of thyme, and olive oil. Cover and marinate for a few hours, turning once or twice.

Meanwhile, prepare the accompaniments: Cook the rice. Cool, cover, and keep in the refrigerator. Prepare the Ratatouille and keep it in the refrigerator or prepare the sautéed vegetables: heat the skillet and sauté the crisp vegetables, briefly, truly al dente (they will have to be reheated). Cool, cover with plastic wrap, and leave in the refrigerator.

Heat 3 tablespoons of butter and oil in a large skillet. Sprinkle each piece of chicken with a little marjoram, sage, salt, and fresh crushed pepper. Cook on a medium-high flame for 5 to 10 minutes so each piece is golden on all sides. Do this in as many batches as needed so that each piece has enough room to brown on both sides. Transfer the chicken to a large casserole in which 2 tablespoons of butter and oil are heating and continue cooking, uncovered, for 10 minutes. Cook the chopped onion in the skillet and add to the casserole. When all the chicken pieces are in the casserole discard any excess cooking fat left in the skillet and pour the white wine and vermouth into the skillet. Scrape the coagulated juices in the bottom with a fork and pour this into the casserole on the chicken pieces.

Add the peppercorns and cook on a medium flame, uncovered, for 20 minutes. Turn the chicken pieces with a wooden spoon to make sure every piece is brown and impregnated with the onion-wine sauce. Add the scallions and cook 10 minutes more, uncovered. Check with a fork to make sure the chicken is cooked.

Heat 1 tablespoon of butter and 1 tablespoon of oil in the skillet. Sprinkle the chicken livers with a little flour and sauté for 1 minute or so, until they stiffen. Pour them and the crushed garlic into a food processor or a blender and process for 1 minute. Pour into the chicken casserole, turn off the heat at once, and stir carefully. When cool, cover with plastic wrap and leave in the refrigerator.

One hour before the meal, place the parsley and basil (or other fresh herb) in a bowl with the capers. Remove the Fricassée from the refrigerator and reheat it on a low flame with the lid half covering the dish. This is a *sauce courte*, a short sauce, since most of the sauce has been absorbed by the chicken. Reheat the Ratatouille or sautéed vegetables briefly. Reheat the rice with a little butter, fluffing it lightly. Warm up the plates. Toast the bread slices lightly on both sides and dot with a few drops of olive oil. Cut them in triangles and stack them on a small plate.

When you are ready to serve dinner, stir the chopped parsley, basil (or fresh herbs), and capers into the casserole, turn off the heat, cover, wrap with a pretty towel, and bring to the table along with the warm plates, rice, Ratatouille or vegetables, and crisp toasted bread.

When you serve your guests, each plate should have 2 pieces of chicken with a little sauce poured over them, 1 or 2 baby scallions, 2 pieces of toast, 2 spoonfuls of rice, and 2 spoonfuls of Ratatouille or sautéed vegetables.

WINE   Serve a chilled white Burgundy, a white Bordeaux, or a Côtes du Rhône

WHAT TO SERVE BEFORE AND AFTER THE POULET FRICASSÉE PROVENÇALE

APPETIZERS

1. Olives Sautées, page 61
2. Terrine aux Herbes, page 73
3. Crudités à la Tapenade, page 45

DESSERTS

1. Mousse au Chocolat Glacée, page 282, and a platter of thin cookies
2. Grand Baba, page 273
3. Crémets aux Fruits, page 267
4. Poires, Pruneaux, Oranges au Vin Rouge et aux Épices, page 289
5. Oeufs à la Neige et aux Fruits, page 284

DECORATION OF THE TABLE

You may wish to cover your table with a richly colored table-cloth—either a piece of thick quilted cotton or else an Indian cotton bedspread big enough to reach the floor. You can spread a piece of ivory or white crochet work, macrame, or heavy lace over the long cloth. Then you may place a china or earthenware tureen in the center and set two round, chubby bunches of cut flowers in plain glass vases on either side. Scatter candles and tiny pots of butter all around, along with two wine decanters, two pretty water pitchers, and two baskets filled with an assortment of country bread.

This setting should suggest a feeling of cozy pleasure, of easy, sensual well-being. It should be sensible and cheerful and avoid at all cost the magazine rendering of a utopian "food celebration."

STRATEGY FOR THE SUGGESTED MENU

• Guests invited for 7:30 P.M.
• Dinner served at 8:30 P.M.

• One day before the Feast: Prepare the Poulet Fricassée, Rice, Ratatouille, Mousse au Chocolat, and sliced oranges. Refrigerate.

• On the day of the Feast:
· 7:15—Take everything except the Mousse au Chocolat out of the refrigerator. Sauté the olives.
· 7:30—Your first guests arrive. Serve Olives Sautées with the drinks.

· 8:00 — Reheat the Fricassée, Ratatouille, and rice. Warm the plates. Place the bread in the oven to dry.

· 8:30 — Stir the parsley and capers into the casserole. Turn off the heat. Wrap the casserole with a wide and pretty napkin. Light the candles. Ask your guests to sit at the table.

Bring the warm plates, Poulet Fricassée, toast, Ratatouille, and rice to the table.

· 8:50 — Take the Mousse au Chocolat out of the freezer. Unmold it on a platter lined with a white napkin. Sprinkle it with chocolate shavings and bring it to the table along with the sliced oranges and a platter of thin cookies.

· Later: Coffees and teas.
· Later: Cold water, fruit juices, or Perrier.

LEFTOVERS

1. Paella, page 207.

2. Croquettes: Add two eggs and pass everything through a mill or food processor. Form little balls about one inch in diameter. Roll them in flour lightly, dip them in a slightly beaten egg, and fry for one or two minutes. Drain the croquettes and serve them with lemon wedges.

3. Crêpes: Chop the chicken leftovers and spoon in the center of each crêpe. Roll them, pour a little butter on top, and reheat in the oven at 350°. Serve with a plain tomato sauce.

4. ''eGratin: Pour into a buttered gratin dish, cover with tomato halves, and sprinkle with salt and pepper, bread crumbs, and chopped parsley. Dot with olive oil and bake until warm at 375° for thirty minutes.

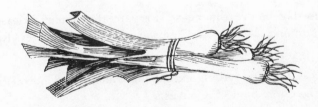

POULET EN GELÉE

Chicken cooked with vegetables and herbs, served cold in its natural aspic and decorated with parsley and lemon.

This is a wonderful dish for summer. It must be patiently prepared a day ahead to allow the chicken to rest in its juice and for all the flavors to mingle. This is not an improvised preparation, nor is it complicated or labored. The cook remains calm knowing nothing can go wrong.

No gelatin is added, so the taste and the texture are wonderful, and it is not rubbery like the plastic fantastic aspic offered in ready-to-eat concoctions in magazine ads. It is a bit harder to serve than the chemically superfirm gelatin, but the flavor makes up for it. All the time and effort devoted to this preparation are rewarded the minute you bite into this luscious and fragrant dish.

Try to use a rather shallow bowl since a deep dome may be more difficult to serve when you have many guests. The chicken should be presented on a very wide round platter so there is room for a wreath of green all around. Both the tossed greens and the lentils or chickpeas should be in bright, pretty ceramic bowls. Have a stack of paper napkins along with wide cotton napkins.

FOR *8* PEOPLE

UTENSILS
Medium saucepan
Soup kettle (6– 8 quarts)
Skillet
Large roasting pan
Wide shallow bowl mold
Piece of cheesecloth

BROTH
3 pounds chicken wings, necks, or backs (gizzards as well), trimmed of skin, fat, and gristle

1 large veal bone, cracked (optional)
1 onion, peeled and studded with 2 cloves
Twig of thyme
3 bay leaves
Salt
1–1½ quarts water
½ cup sherry

VEGETABLES AND   2 cups carrots sliced on the bias (about 1 pound).
CHICKEN   Salt
1 tablespoon oil
2 medium onions, chopped (1 cup)
½ cup diced lean salt pork or bacon
2 cups dry white wine
2 chickens, trimmed and cut in half
Freshly ground pepper
2 teaspoons thyme
½ cup coarsely chopped celery or 2 tablespoons coarsely chopped green pepper
Juice of 3 large lemons
1 lemon peel, grated
5 garlic cloves, peeled and sliced
2 veal bones (optional)
3 bay leaves
1 cup chopped parsley

GARNISH   Bunch of parsley or watercress, with stems removed
2 lemons, thinly sliced
1 lime, thinly sliced (optional)
4 tablespoons minced parsley or chives or basil

ACCOMPANIMENTS   Lentille ou Pois Chiches en Salade (page 57)
Green salad (page 301)

Place the sliced carrots in a medium saucepan with a pinch of salt. Cover with water. Bring to a boil, lower the heat, and simmer about 10 minutes, until soft. Refresh under cold water. Drain.

To prepare the broth: In a large kettle place the chicken parts, veal bone, onion, thyme, bay leaves, and salt. Add the cold water to cover. Slowly bring to a boil. Skim off scum as it rises. Simmer for

1 hour. Pour the contents through a sieve and retain broth. Bring the sieved broth to a boil. Pass through a fine sieve lined with a clean linen kitchen towel or piece of cheesecloth. Add the sherry. Check and correct the seasoning.

Meanwhile, heat 1 tablespoon of oil in a skillet and cook the chopped onions and lean salt pork for a few minutes, until the onions are soft and translucent. With a slotted spoon, add the onions and pork to the chicken broth along with the white wine. Cook a few minutes more, then turn off the flame.

Place the chicken halves flat in a large roasting pan. Sprinkle with salt, pepper, and thyme. Add the chopped celery and then the prepared chicken broth, lemon juice, lemon peel, garlic, and veal bones, if used. The meat should be barely covered. You may need 2 pans. Cover with foil, bring to a boil, lower heat, simmer for $1\frac{1}{2}$ hours.

Remove the pieces of chicken and set aside. Reduce the liquid over high heat for 15 minutes in an uncovered saucepan. You should have about 6 cups of liquid. Correct the seasoning.

Meanwhile, discard the veal bones. Bone and remove the skin from the chicken with a pointed knife and cut into large pieces, $1\frac{1}{2}$ to 2 inches. Place 3 bay leaves in a star pattern on the bottom of a wide bowl. Place a few of the cooked carrot slices around them, alternating with the chopped parsley. Place the chicken pieces and the rest of the cooked vegetables in the bowl, and then pour all the broth on top. The meat will be barely covered. Cool to room temperature, cover with plastic wrap, and refrigerate overnight. It will become firm but tender.

A few minutes before serving, dip the bowl into warm water for a second (or dip a towel into warm water, squeeze, and then place on top of the bowl for a minute). Run a long knife around the rim of the bowl. Place a platter on top of the bowl and, holding the platter and bowl firmly, turn them upside down in a decisive movement.

Tuck twigs of parsley or watercress all around the jellied chicken and arrange very thin slices of lemon and lime on the lower part of the jellied dome. Stick 3 short twigs of parsley on the top of the preparation and sprinkle finely minced parsley or chives or basil all over the dome surface.

Prepare a salad bowl. Pour dressing into the bottom of the bowl, cross the salad spoon and fork over it, and place the greens on top. Pour the dressing over lukewarm lentils (or chick-peas), and pour them into a pretty side dish.

Bring the platter of Poulet en Gelée to the table along with the lentils and the tossed green salad. Make sure all your guests see the pretty chicken dome as you bring it, and then pass it around with a wide flat spatula and a large serving spoon. You may prefer to serve each guest yourself, placing 2 tablespoons of Poulet en Gelée and 1 tablespoon of lentils on each plate. Leave the tossed salad on the main table to be passed around later.

WINE   A light red Burgundy wine, Côte de Beaune or Mercurey, served cool

WHAT TO SERVE BEFORE AND AFTER POULET EN GELÉE

APPETIZERS TO BE SERVED WITH THE DRINKS:

1. Crudités with Anchoyade and Tapenade sauces, page 45
2. Warm salted almonds, hazelnuts, or walnuts
3. Pissaladière, page 63
4. Olives Sautées and/or Olives Farcies, page 61
5. Tiny sliced tomatoes served on a platter along with hard-boiled eggs, sliced lengthwise, with a thick paste of basil, garlic, olive oil, salt, and pepper. Dot each of them with a black olive.

DESSERTS
1. Crémets aux Fruits, page 267, and a platter of thin cookies
2. Granité au Vin, page 278
3. Panier de Frivolités, page 286, and a large bowl of Oeufs à la Neige, page 284

DECORATION OF THE TABLE

This is a summer Feast, and your table should be light and crisp. You may choose an ivory or peach tablecloth, a wide basket (enameled with a dime-store can of spray paint in peach or off-white) filled with a soft bundle of rambling roses and branches of ferns, wisteria, and honeysuckle. You may want to use terra-cotta accessories— butter pots, salt and pepper shakers—and offer two kinds of bread in napkin-lined baskets. Wrap a fresh napkin around the wine bottle necks, and don't forget the pitcher of cold water.

Strategy for the Suggested Menu

• Guests invited for 7:30 P.M.
• Meal served at 8:30 P.M.

• One day or a day and a night before the feast: Prepare the Crudités, sauces, Poulet en Gelée, salad lentil, and Crémets.

• On the day of the Feast:
· 7:30 — Your guests arrive.

Bring Crudités basket and two bowls of sauces along with the drinks in the living room. Reheat the lentils on a very low heat.
· 8:25 — Light the candles. Ask your guests to sit at the table. Season and toss the salad. Unmold the Poulet en Gelée.
· 8:30 — Bring the Poulet en Gelée and the salad to the table.
· 8:50 — Bring the Crémets and fruits to the table, along with the platter of thin cookies.

· Later: Coffees and teas.
· Later: Cold water, fruit juices, or Perrier.

LEFTOVERS

1. Omelet: Add a few eggs, salt, and pepper to the chopped chicken leftovers and make a flat omelet. Dot the surface with a little olive oil or a little butter and serve it with a light tomato sauce.

2. Chicken fritters: Prepare a light batter. Dip one tablespoon of chopped leftover chicken in it and deep-fry until golden. Serve the fritters with lemon wedges.

3. Croquettes: Add two eggs and a little chopped parsley to the chopped chicken leftovers. Check the seasoning. Make balls about one or one and a half inches in size. Roll them in a beaten egg and then in bread crumbs. Fry the croquettes in a large skillet and serve surrounded with twigs of parsley.

POULE VERTE

SUGGESTED MENU

Gougère

Poule Verte and
Stuffed Cabbage
Bundles
with Vegetables and
Their Sauces

Mousse
au Chocolat Glacée

A Light Red Wine

A chicken stuffed with spinach, ham, eggs, herbs, spices, and garlic, and served with eight "baby chick" bundles, a variety of vegetables, and a pungent sauce.

When Carême stated that "gastronomy marches like a queen at the head of civilization," he probably had Poule Verte leading the way.

Spread across a platter like a glorious monarch, the "green" chicken surrounded by her plump "baby chicks" is indeed a dazzling sight with its moist ivory meat, assortment of firm vegetables, thick slices of stuffing, and bowls of pungent sauce and fragrant cooking broth. Toulouse-Lautrec, a fine artist and a superb gourmet, prepared the stuffed hen and her little green bundles in his native Perigord, and celebrated and enjoyed them as often as he could. To him Poule Verte evoked family gatherings and those large Feasts around important occasions when only such an opulent traditional dish will do. It is one of those great reassuring dishes we long to have a few times a year to keep our faith in good things.

Poule Verte is not prepared in a jiffy, but it can be put together ahead of time without pressure and with mostly unattended, foolproof cooking.

The stuffed chicken needs to be cut up at the last minute; the other pieces of chicken, the baby chicks, and the vegetables are slid from the pot to the serving platter. The sauces are ready to be passed around.

FOR *8* PEOPLE

UTENSILS

Double-decker steamer or 2 large soup kettles
Large soup kettle
Plenty of cheesecloth
1 or 2 large platters for serving

Trussing needle and string

BROTH

1 veal shank
5 quarts water
1 chicken gizzard and neck
A few chicken bones
Bouquet garni (page 231)
2 onions, peeled and studded with cloves
Salt
10 peppercorns (approximately)

VEGETABLES

8 carrots, peeled and cut in half lengthwise
8 turnips, peeled and halved or quartered
8 leeks (white part only), trimmed, split lengthwise, cut into 4-inch pieces, and tied into a bundle with string
4 onions, peeled and halved or quartered
5 fennel bulbs, cut in half lengthwise
8 celery stalks, cut into sticks
1 large cabbage; to yield at least 10 large cabbage leaves for the "baby chicks" bundles

SAUCES

Bowl of vinaigrette (page 302) with minced fresh herbs
Bowl of vinaigrette (page 302) with 2 tablespoons minced shallots, 2 hard-boiled eggs, chopped, and 1 tablespoon Dijon-style mustard

STUFFING

(Enough for 1 chicken and 8 cabbage-wrapped bundles)
2 tablespoons vegetable oil
2 medium onions, peeled and chopped
½ cup chopped chicken livers
2 pounds fresh spinach, trimmed, cooked, and drained; or one 10-ounce package frozen spinach, thawed, drained, and squeezed dry
3 pounds cured ham and/or lean salt pork, coarsely chopped
4 garlic cloves, peeled and sliced
4 cups chopped flat parsley
4 shallots, peeled and chopped
3 teaspoons dry thyme
Pinch of freshly grated nutmeg
2 slices of bread, moistened and squeezed

4 eggs, slightly beaten
Salt
Freshly ground pepper

CHICKEN

1 large chicken, ready for stuffing (about 4½ pounds)
1 tablespoon butter
1 tablespoon oil or more if needed
6 drumsticks
6 thighs

GARNISH

Bowl of minced parsley or chives

You can prepare the broth, vegetables, stuffing, chicken, and sauces one day ahead. Then you have only to reheat the chicken and cook the vegetables 1½ hours before the dinner.

Prepare the broth: Put the veal shank in a large soup kettle. Add about 5 quarts of water, the chicken gizzard and neck, bones, bouquet garni, onions, salt, and peppercorns. Bring to a boil and simmer for 1 hour, uncovered.

Wash and trim the raw vegetables, cover with plastic wrap, and refrigerate.

Prepare the sauces, cover, and refrigerate.

Prepare the stuffing (which should be very tasty and heavily spiced): Heat the oil in a skillet and sauté the onions for a few minutes. Add the chicken livers for 1 minute, stir with a wooden spoon, and then remove from the stove. Place in a large bowl and add the spinach, sautéed onions and chicken livers, chopped ham, garlic, parsley, shallots, thyme, nutmeg, soaked bread squeezed dry, eggs, salt, and freshly ground pepper. Chop the mixture coarsely with a knife or scissors, or in a food processor, pulsing a few times. The mixture should not be too fine. Stir the mixture carefully. Stuff the mixture into the chicken with a spoon, making sure it is not packed too tightly. Set aside the rest of the stuffing. Sew up the openings of the stuffed chicken and truss it so that it will keep its shape as it cooks.

In the butter and 1 tablespoon vegetable oil brown the chicken in a large skillet for a few minutes. Take off the flame and set aside. Add a little oil to the skillet and sauté the drumsticks and thighs until they are nicely browned all over. You may need to do this in 2 batches.

Add the stuffed chicken to the broth and bring gently to a boil. Simmer for 30 minutes, then add the chicken pieces to the broth.

Simmer 30 minutes more. Let the chicken cool in the broth. Cover with plastic wrap and refrigerate.

Meanwhile, blanch the cabbage for 15 minutes in a kettle of boiling water or steam it. Remove the cabbage from the water and separate the leaves, reserving about 10 large ones or 20 small ones. Discard the rest of the cabbage or use it puréed as an accompaniment.

Place a piece of cheesecloth on a work surface. Spread 1 large cabbage leaf or 2 small ones, overlapping slightly at the stem end. Sprinkle with salt and pepper, and place 1 tablespoon stuffing in the center. Tuck in the leaf so as to make a little bundle and fold the cheesecloth loosely around it. Proceed until you have 8 bundles. Place the bundles, folded side down, on the perforated tray of the steamer. Steam for 30 minutes. If you do not have a steamer, use a wide kettle. Let the bundles cool to room temperature, cover with plastic wrap, and refrigerate.

One and a half hours before your dinner take everything out of the refrigerator, including the trimmed raw vegetables and the sauces.

Remove all the fat from the broth and correct the seasoning. Bring the broth to a boil. Check every piece of poultry to make sure it has no gristle or fat. Remove the skin both from the stuffed chicken and from the thighs and drumsticks. Place the stuffed chicken and chicken pieces in the boiling stock, cover, and simmer for 30 minutes.

Bring the water in the bottom of the steamer to a boil. Place the vegetables on a tray and cook for 15 minutes. Add the 8 green bundles to the second tray and cook 20 minutes more. If you do not have such a steamer, cook the vegetables in a kettle of salty water and the bundles in another kettle of water.

Warm 2 large serving platters. When you are ready to serve, carve the stuffed chicken, remove its stuffing which should be in one compact piece, and slice it. Place the overlapping slices of the stuffing in the center of the platter and place the pieces of carved chicken around it. Add the thighs and drumsticks to the platter. Spoon a few tablespoons of hot stock over everything and sprinkle with salt, pepper, and chives. Cover tightly with foil to keep warm.

Place the little cabbage bundles on another platter, remove the pieces of cheesecloth, and discard them. Surround with the steamed vegetables, spoon a little hot broth over everything, and season with salt and pepper. Cover with a piece of foil.

When everybody is seated at the table remove the foil from the platters and bring them to the dining room on the rolling table along with the Poule Verte, warm plates, 2 bowls of sauce, chicken broth, and bowl of minced fresh parsley or chives.

Serve a piece of chicken, a slice of stuffing, a green cabbage bundle, and a few vegetables on each plate. Spoon a little hot broth and a pinch of minced herbs on top before handing the plate to each guest. Pass the bowls of sauce and warm broth around the table.

Note: If you are a good carver, you may prefer to show the Poule Verte surrounded by the little green chicklets and the lovely vegetable assortment. It is beautiful and an appetizing sight.

I tend to think that once you have more than 6 persons at a table the process of carving, slicing, and serving takes so long that by the time all guests are served the meal is lukewarm, at best, or cold, which is a great pity for such a delicious dish. However, if you have a good carver you can trust to help, you may serve the rest of the dish on each plate while he or she carves so that serving does not take too long and the theatrical aspect of the process remains.

WINE   A light red, a dry white wine, or a full-bodied red wine

WHAT TO SERVE BEFORE AND AFTER POULE VERTE

APPETIZERS TO BE SERVED WITH THE DRINKS:
1. Gougère, page 49
2. Pissaladière, page 63
3. Pissenlits aux Lardons, page 65

DESSERTS
1. Mousse au Chocolat Glacée, page 282
2. Grand Baba, page 273
3. Poires, Pruneaux, Oranges au Vin Rouge et aux Épices, page 289
4. Tarte Tatin aux Poires et aux Pommes, page 292

DECORATION OF THE TABLE

This is a fairly messy dish, although you will keep the platters themselves on a side table.

You may wish to use two short vases instead of a single centerpiece and fill them with a variety of tulips or peonies a few hours before your party. By the time you light the candles, the stems will have taken unpredictable curves.

Better not use a delicate light-colored tablecloth. A thick fabric, woven like a country rug, with many shades of brown, rust, and beige, or a piece of patchwork quilted fabric (not a valuable antique—you are interested only in a pretty print rendering) could be lovely, and you might like a few faded or dark green accessories for the crockery, shakers, butter pots, and napkins.

But even if you have the plainest setting, set a pile of raw eggs in a pretty basket in the center of the table and relax: Your royal platter with the mother hen and her green baby chicks is so overwhelming that it will steal the show.

STRATEGY FOR THE SUGGESTED MENU

- Guests invited for 7:30 P.M.
- Meal served at 8:30 P.M.

- One day before the Feast: Prepare the Mousse au Chocolat and freeze it. Cook the stuffed chicken, cabbage bundles, drumsticks, and thighs as indicated. Wash and trim the vegetables and garnish. Prepare the sauces. Prepare the orange salad for the Mousse.

- On the day of the Feast:
- 5:00—Take everything except mousse out of the refrigerator.
- 7:00—Make the Gougère and bake it as indicated.
- 7:30—Bring chicken broth and water to a boil in the steamer or kettle. First guests arrive.
- 8:00—Serve Gougère with the drinks. Cook the vegetables and stuffed cabbage bundles in water and reheat the stuffed chicken and cut-up thighs and drumsticks in the chicken broth.
- 8:30—Light the candles. Prepare platters as indicated and serve when all your guests are seated at the dining room table. Return all leftovers to the steamer or kettle to keep warm until second helpings are needed—about fifteen minutes.
- 9:00—Change plates and serve the Mousse au Chocolat with the orange sauce and a platter of thin cookies.

- Later: Coffees and teas.
- Later: Cold water, fruit juices, or Perrier.

1. Croquettes: Make with chopped leftover chicken, 2 eggs, and a little fresh parsley.

2. Omelette verte: Add chopped leftover chicken and stuffing to beaten eggs. Season with salt and pepper.

3. Chicken soup made from the broth, some chopped leftover chicken, and a little rice.

4. Gratin: Can be made with leftover stuffing thinned with a little broth, sprinkled with bread crumbs, dotted with butter, and baked for 30 minutes at 375°. You may also add chopped leftover meat and chopped leftover vegetables to the mixture.

5. You can freeze any leftover chicken stock and use it as a base for a sauce or a soup such as Gratinée Lyonnaise (page 182) later.

DESSERTS

CERVELLE DE CANUT

This herbed fresh cheese is whipped with cream and dry white wine.

A "canut" is a worker in the silk factories of Lyon, this dish was called a "worker's brain" because it is like a true canut: high spirited, demanding, passionate, and colorful.

One of the most invigorating and fresh ways of ending a heavy meal, Cervelle de Canut is made with a variety of herbs and must be beaten vigorously—"just as if it were your wife," as the appalling saying goes.

Mores have changed in Lyon as elsewhere, but this delicious dish prevails.

FOR *8* PEOPLE

INGREDIENTS

1 pound farmer or cottage cheese
4 tablespoons sour cream
3 tablespoons heavy cream
1 cup finely minced chives, tarragon, dill, or parsley
2 garlic cloves, peeled and finely minced
2 tablespoons dry white wine
1 tablespoon red wine vinegar
2 tablespoons olive or vegetable oil
Salt to taste
Freshly ground pepper to taste

ACCOMPANIMENT

Bread, toasted and cut into triangles

Whip all the ingredients by hand for a few minutes. It should be smooth but not frothy. Correct the seasoning. Cover with plastic wrap and refrigerate.

Serve with a large spoon along with a linen-lined basket of warm toast points.

Note: Or, with a basket of Crudités, serve it as an appetizer.

COMPOTE DE POIRES

These pears, simmered in butter and flavored with grated lemon peel and fresh ginger, are served with homemade crème fraîche.

A light, fresh family dessert to make ahead of time, this is wonderful after a heavy *plat de résistance*. You can serve the pears with thin cookies and pass a bowl of homemade crème fraîche. French crème fraîche is a cream that has been allowed to mature. Its distinctive nutty flavor is hard to reproduce, but you can make a very good homemade version. Bitter chocolate sherbet is also splendid with this—store-bought is fine.

FOR *8* PEOPLE

CRÈME FRAÎCHE
1 cup heavy or whipping cream
1 tablespoon buttermilk

PEARS
8 firm, ripe, preferably Anjou pears, cored, peeled, and quartered
½ cup (1 stick) unsalted butter
4 ounces fresh ginger (approximately), peeled and cut up into tiny thin sticks
1 lemon peel, thinly grated
½ cup sugar
1 tablespoon cold water

Mix the cream with the buttermilk in a pan. Heat the mixture gently to lukewarm, then pour it into a bowl. Cover and keep it in a warm place (60° to 80°) for a day. Stir to make sure the mixture has thickened, then place it in the refrigerator until ready to serve. It will keep a week.

To prepare the pears: Preheat the oven to 375°. Place the quartered pears in a pretty oven-proof dish. Dot with butter, sprinkle on the ginger sticks and grated lemon peel, and dot with butter again.

Pour the sugar in a thick skillet, add a tablespoon of cold water, and bring to a boil over high heat without stirring. As soon as it turns deep brown, pour this caramel over the pears.

Bake the pears for 10 minutes, then lower the temperature to 350°

and cook 10 minutes more. Remove from the oven when the pears are soft, but not mushy.

Serve the pears lukewarm in their oven-proof dish or cold in a pretty glass bowl. Pass the crème fraîche and, if you want, a dish of bitter chocolate sherbet.

CRÉMETS AUX FRUITS

A delicate mixture of whipped cream, whipped egg whites, lemon, and sugar, drained overnight and served with puréed and fresh berries.

They are no longer served in Normandy's country inns or along the Loire valley's little restaurants, but Crémets remain the proper dessert in well-run homes where the traditions of fine food have been carefully maintained.

It appears on the table for big occasions after a hearty *plat de résistance,* when their light and delicate texture, enhanced by the sharpness of a fruit purée and the crispness of fresh fruit, makes for the most delicious of combinations.

You can mold the Crémets in those little white heart-shaped molds with draining holes or in a colander lined with cheesecloth so that the liquid will easily seep from the Crémets and drain away.

They are served with raspberry (or strawberry) purée, fresh berries, and fresh cream, for "complete pleasure," as the farmers put it.

A rich cousin of Crémets is Coeur à la Crème which is generally made with cream cheese, cottage cheese, and cream.

FOR *8* PEOPLE

UTENSILS
1-quart mold, pierced for drainage, *or* several small porcelain molds or straw baskets in the shape of hearts and pierced for drainage (Coeur à la Crème molds), *or* a large colander lined with a dampened piece of cheesecloth.

CRÉMETS

4 cups whipping cream
1 tablespoon sour cream
5 egg whites
3 teaspoons finely grated lemon peel
2 teaspoons sugar

PURÉE

1 quart of fresh berries, trimmed and cleaned
1 cup of sugar (approximately)
Juice of 2 large lemons (approximately)
        or
2 frozen packages of berries (10 ounces)
Juice of 2 large lemons
Sugar to taste

ACCOMPANIMENTS

3 tablespoons light cream
Bowl of fresh raspberries or strawberries, cleaned and drained

One day and a night before the Feast prepare the Crémets and fruit purée.

Whip the cream until it makes soft peaks. Fold in the sour cream. In a separate bowl, whip the egg whites until firm, then fold them gently into the whipped cream until stiff.

Mix in the grated lemon peel and sugar. Gently pour into the pierced little molds or colander lined with cheesecloth and fold the piece of muslin over the top. Set the mold or colander into a bowl and let drain for a few hours in a cool place. Refrigerate overnight.

To make the purée: If you are using fresh fruit, whip the ingredients in a blender until smooth. Add more sugar or more lemon to taste. If you are using frozen fruit, first thaw the berries, preserving any juice that melts off. Put the berries in a blender with a little of the juice, add lemon juice, and whip until blended. Add sugar to taste. (Frozen fruits often have sugar added already, so read the package.)

Just before serving, unfold the cheesecloth and invert the contents onto a wide serving plate or platter. Pour some light cream on top and spoon a little fruit purée around. Make it as neat as possible.

Serve the rest of the purée in a bowl or pitcher and the fresh berries in a flat basket lined with a paper doily or a few fresh green leaves.

CRÊPES NORMANDES

Thin crêpes stuffed with diced apples, simmered in brown sugar, sprinkled with Calvados brandy, spread with a pungent red currant sauce, and reheated at the last moment.

The names evokes austere ladies in lace headdresses officiating over their open-air griddles in Brittany marketplaces and spreading salted butter on their large golden crepes in front of gasping children. But the name also brings to mind bad memories of fancy burning affairs prepared out of copper dishes by effete butlers in pretentious restaurants.

Even though crêpes are the simplest and cheapest of desserts, for all children and most adults they will always spell "the best."

Crêpes Normandes offers a spectacular finale for any family Feast, and it is an easy dessert to prepare and to serve. Done ahead of time, and reheated thirty minutes before serving, Crêpes Normandes will go straight from the oven to the table in its baking dish.

Once again I have given you too big a recipe for eight people, and you may have five or six crêpes left at the end of the meal. But the sight of so many plump crêpes under their red foamy sauce is truly exciting and festive. And any leftover crêpe will reheat beautifully the next day as long as you dot it with butter and cover it with foil. In this recipe I use beer and water instead of the usual cream and milk for a thinner crêpe batter, and I choose the tangiest and sharpest apples I can find on the market, adding more lemon if I find them too sweet. I have seen very good chunky apple purée for sale in some markets that could be used as filling for the Crêpes Normandes if time runs short.

FOR *8* PEOPLE   About seventeen 7-inch crêpes

UTENSILS   2 small crêpe pans, 6½ to 7 inches bottom diameter, for a quicker
   preparation
   2 china or earthenware dishes, 8 by 12 inches; or one oval gratin
   dish, 14 by 9 inches; or a round dish, 9 inches in diameter
   Piece of cheesecloth

CRÊPE BATTER   *2 cups flour*
2 eggs, lightly beaten
Pinch of salt
1 cup beer
1 cup water, or more if needed
2 tablespoons vegetable oil or 2 tablespoons butter, melted
1 tablespoon orange blossom water (optional)
2 tablespoons butter or vegetable oil or a small piece of pork fat

FILLING   *3 pounds tart cooking apples (approximately): Granny Smith, Russet,*
Winesap, and so forth
2 tablespoons butter
10 tablespoons brown sugar
1–2 tablespoons lemon juice
1 lemon peel, grated (yellow part only)

TOPPING   *8 tablespoons red currant jelly*
1 tablespoon water
2 tablespoons Calvados brandy (optional)

To make the batter: Put the flour in a bowl. Make a well in the center and place in it the lightly beaten eggs and salt. With a whisk or a fork stir the flour gradually into the eggs. Beat in the beer, water, and oil until the batter is smooth; also add orange blossom water if you wish. Let stand for 1 hour or so.

To make the filling: Peel, core, and dice the apples. Place them in a pan with the butter, brown sugar, lemon juice, and lemon peel. Cover and cook slowly about 30 minutes (depending on the apples), until soft. They should not turn into purée. Set aside.

When you are ready to prepare the crêpes check the consistency of the batter and add more water if it is too thick: It should feel like a thick cream or a light custard. Heat the 2 crêpe pans. Rub them either with butter, oil, or pork fat. (You can put the fat on a fork or use a piece of cheesecloth dipped in oil and put at the end of a fork. The main thing is to feel comfortable while you oil the pans and be ready to act quickly. Very little fat is needed in the pans after the third crêpe.)

When the first pan is warm, add 2 or 3 tablespoons of batter, turning the pan so the surface is evenly coated. Use as little batter as possible so the crêpes are truly thin. Cook over a high fire. Oil and fill the second pan. After a minute or less turn the first crêpe on the other side with a spatula. It should detach easily if it is cooked. Wait a minute longer and then slide the crêpe onto a plate. Turn the second crêpe. Stack all the cooked crêpes together and place a large plate over them so they keep moist while you continue to make the other crêpes.

Place a large tablespoon of cooked apples in the center of each crêpe. Roll the crêpe so it looks like a 2-inch-wide cigar. Butter 2 baking dishes and place the rolled crêpes in them side by side and slightly overlapping. Dot the surface with butter. Cover with a sheet of foil. Set aside in the refrigerator or a cool place.

Thirty minutes before you sit down to dinner, preheat the oven to 350°. Pour the red currant jelly and the water into a pan, and heat on a slow fire, stirring until it turns into a syrup. Cover and keep warm.

When you sit down to dinner, place the 2 covered gratin dishes with the crêpes in the oven to reheat. As you go to the kitchen to change plates for the dessert course, remove the foil from the crêpe dishes, pour half of the warm jelly over the crêpes, and put them back in the oven for a few minutes to lightly glaze the surface. Bring the liquid refreshments to the table (see Wine below). Remove the baking dishes from the oven, sprinkle on a little Calvados, then pour the rest of the warm red currant syrup on the surface. Wrap each dish with a large kitchen towel or napkin and bring the 2 dishes to the table. Use a spatula to slide each crêpe onto the plate and use a spoon for any juice left in the bottom of the baking dish.

WINES   Serve cider or a sweet white wine, perhaps a heady Muscat wine or a fortified wine in which alcohol was added during fermentation to seal the sweetness of the grape. Chilled sweet Champagne would also be lovely.

FLAN AU CARAMEL

An unmolded caramel custard.

An old favorite that is easy to prepare ahead, easy to serve, and loved by all, whether served in individual petits pots or as a spectacular unmolded amber dome. For a flamboyant finale you may want to serve it with an assortment, or a "Farandole" (the mad dance done hand in hand down the hills of Provence) of desserts, together with Mousse au Chocolat Glacée, and a basket of Frivolités since all can be prepared ahead of time.

Flan au Caramel is always best served at room temperature, and if you serve it in individual pots it is even better lukewarm.

FOR *8* PEOPLE

UTENSILS

2 charlotte molds, 1 quart each, or 2 scalloped custard molds, or 12 oven-proof porcelain ramekins, each $\frac{1}{2}$-cup capacity

An old "seasoned" mold, used mostly to prepare caramel, or a heavy skillet

CARAMEL

$\frac{1}{2}$ cup sugar
2 tablespoons water
Dot of butter

CUSTARD

2 cups sugar
5 cups milk
1 vanilla bean
6 eggs
6 yolks
1 tablespoon candied orange peel shavings or very finely grated fresh orange peel

The Flan must be prepared a few hours before you serve it. To prepare the caramel: Bring the sugar and water to a boil in the skillet. Lower the heat and let the caramel slowly develop a deep amber color; do not stir. Add the butter and quickly pour the amber-colored syrup into the 2 cooking molds or individual molds, turning in all directions so the caramel coats the bottom and sides before it hardens.

Preheat the oven to 350°. Make the custard by combining the sugar, milk, and vanilla bean in a thick-bottomed saucepan rinsed with cold water. Bring to a boil. Meanwhile, beat the eggs and egg yolks together until pale. Add the warm milk slowly, stirring constantly, then pour the custard mixture into the caramelized molds.

Place the molds in a large baking pan and pour enough hot water into it so the molds are immersed by half. Bake for 40 minutes for a large mold or 20 minutes for individual molds. Test by plunging a knife into the custard—if it comes out clean, the custard is finished.

Cool the custards to room temperature. To serve, run a knife around the edges of the molds and unmold in a decisive movement just before serving. Sprinkle the tops with candied orange peel or grated orange peel. Reheat the molds to soften any leftover caramel in the bottoms and pour it over the orange peel.

If you have china molds and do not want to unmold the custard, you can do the following: Make a little extra caramel, grate some orange peel on top of each pot, reheat the caramel, and pour it on top.

It is better to serve this at room temperature or even lukewarm than dead cold so leave in oven if prepared a few hours ahead.

WINE   A mellow white dessert wine, Sauternes, Barsac, or a demi-sec Champagne

GRAND BABA

A moist plump cake filled with fruit, flavored with syrup and brandy, and decorated with apricot glaze and candied fruit.

The small cylindrical Rum Baba, plumb golden, like a toy, with a touch of whipped cream and heavy dose of dark rum, is the traditional bistro dessert. But for a family extravaganza, for a big family Feast, the Baba grows. Made in a large ring mold its name changes to "Savarin," in memory of the grand gourmet Brillat-Savarin.

Of course for the true Baba lovers, and for children who don't care to master such differences, there are only two desserts worth mentioning: Petit Baba and Grand Baba. Savarin is too highbrow and does not ring right.

Where do babas come from: Apparently from a gourmet king. The story is that a Polish King Stanislaw Leszczyński who, on tasting a delicious briochelike little cake impregnated with Malaga wine, named it Ali Baba because the pastry was worth belonging to the cavern of treasures of this famous Thousand and One Nights' world of delights. Today the name has become plain Baba to us. For a memorable dessert, make two Grand Baba rings. Fill the center of one with diced apples sautéed in butter, brown sugar, and lemon, and impregnate the cake with a kirsch-flavored syrup. Fill the center of the other with fresh sliced oranges and Grand Marnier. Pass a bowl of whipped cream around.

Some cooks add Malaga raisins seeped in Malaga or port wine for an hour or diced candied fruit to the dough before baking the babas. I find the fruit garnish, glaze, and syrup enough to dress up the delicious babas.

Make the cakes a day or so ahead and freeze them. Prepare the syrup and jam glaze ahead of time. Cook the apples ahead. Slice the oranges and flavor them. Cover both dishes and leave in the refrigerator until a few minutes before serving the cake. Three hours before the dinner reheat the cakes, syrup, and glaze for a few minutes.

Grand baba should slowly soak up the syrup and be very moist but not soggy. Pour out excess syrup. It can be glazed with an apricot glaze and decorated with candied (glacée) fruits, or if you have tiny strawberries you may prefer, just before serving, to make tiny incisions on top and then insert the strawberries before pouring on the glaze.

This is one of the most relaxing yet spectacular and popular of family desserts.

FOR 8 PEOPLE

UTENSILS   2 ring molds, 9 inches in diameter and about 2 inches deep
                    2 large platters

PASTRY

8 tablespoons butter

2 packages fresh yeast ($\frac{1}{3}$ ounce each)

4 tablespoons sugar

1 teaspoon salt

4 eggs, slightly beaten

4 cups flour

2 tablespoons butter, softened (for the molds)

FILLINGS

FOR BABA #1:

2 tablespoons butter

3 large apples (Granny Smith, Greening, MacIntosh), peeled, cored, and cut into dice 1 by 1 inch

2 teaspoons brown sugar

Lemon juice (optional)

FOR BABA #2:

5 oranges

Juice of 1 lemon

3 tablespoons Grand Marnier

Sugar

CHANTILLY CREAM

1 cup chilled whipping cream

2 tablespoons confectioners' sugar

2 teaspoons vanilla extract (optional)

GLAZE

$\frac{1}{2}$ cup apricot preserves

3 tablespoons sugar

2 tablespoons rum

Lemon juice

SYRUPS

FOR BABA #1:

2 cups water

1 cup sugar

Juice of 1 lemon

$\frac{2}{3}$ cup dark Jamaican rum or kirsch

FOR BABA #2:

1 cup sugar

2 cups orange juice

3 tablespoons Grand Marnier

To make the pastry: Heat the butter over a low flame. Let it cool. In a bowl crumble the fresh yeast and add sugar, salt, and eggs. Beat until well blended. Pour the flour in a large bowl. Add the cooled butter and stir carefully. Add the yeast and egg mixture, and knead with your fingers, lifting the dough and pulling it for a few minutes. After 5 or 6 minutes it turns smooth and elastic. Pull it between your hands to make sure it is no longer too sticky and it can stretch.

Scrape the dough into a large ball and place it in the bottom of the bowl. Cut a cross on top of the dough and sprinkle it with 1 table-spoon of flour. Cover the bowl with 2 folded wet towels and place it in a *very* low oven, perhaps just a turned-off oven with the pilot light on.

After 2 hours punch the dough with your fingers and fold the outside back into the center.

Butter the 2 ring molds. Sprinkle 1 tablespoon of fine bread crumbs or a little flour in each, shaking and twisting the molds to coat the sides and bottom lightly. Pour the dough into the 2 molds. They will be about one-third full.

Let them rise in the lukewarm oven, uncovered, for 1 or 2 hours. Punch with a finger to deflate the dough once more.

Preheat the oven to 375° and bake both rings for about 20 minutes. The sides will shrink a little and the top will be golden.

Turn each cake upside down on a rack. After 5 minutes, remove the molds and cool to room temperature. You can freeze them as soon as they are cool.

To make the filling for Baba #1: Heat the butter and cook the prepared apples until soft but not brown. Cool to room temperature. Sprinkle with the brown sugar and a little lemon juice, if desired. Cover and refrigerate.

To make the filling for Baba #2: Peel and thinly slice the 5 oranges. Put the slices in a bowl with the lemon juice, Grand Marnier, and a little sugar. Cover and refrigerate.

To make the Chantilly Cream: Pour the chilled cream into a large chilled bowl and beat it, lifting the cream and turning the beater around as you go. It is ready when a bit of Chantilly retains its shape when you lift it. Fold in the sugar and vanilla. Cover and refrigerate.

To prepare the glaze: Press the apricot preserve through a sieve and then into a little saucepan over a medium flame. Stir for 3 minutes or so; it will become syrupy and sticky. Stir in sugar, rum, and lemon juice and cook for a few moments more. Keep in a jar or in the pan to use later.

Prepare the 2 syrups and, when they are at room temperature, add rum or Kirsch to one and Grand Marnier to the other.

When you are ready to assemble the cakes: Place the 2 frozen cakes in a 300° oven on the middle rack for about 30 minutes, until the insides are lukewarm. Prick the top and side of each cake with a fork delicately. Place the cakes on 2 wide platters, upside down, the brown flat side against the plate, the porous bottom side up.

Reheat the syrups and spoon half of each syrup slowly over each cake. Let it soak for about 30 minutes, then add the rest. The dough is very spongy so all the syrup should soak in after an hour. Pour off any excess syrup after 30 additional minutes. The babas should be moist, not soggy.

Sprinkle a little extra Kirsch, rum, or Grand Marnier on top of each cake. Reheat the glaze for a minute or so and apply lightly on the tops of the 2 rings. It will cool into a shiny glaze. You may want to apply a piece of "angelica," green candied fruit cut in little diamond shapes and glacéed cherries cut in half. Pass a bit of glaze over them too.

Spoon the cooked apples into the center of one of the babas, and the sliced oranges in the center of the other. Pour Chantilly into a pretty serving bowl and bring the 2 Grand Babas and Chantilly Cream along with the dessert plates to the dining room.

Pass the babas and the bowl of Chantilly Cream around the table. Each guest will have a piece of both babas with their respective garnish and a bit of Chantilly Cream.

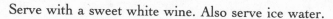

WINE   Serve with a sweet white wine. Also serve ice water.

GRANITÉ AU VIN

A red or white, sweet or dry wine sherbet served with chopped mint leaves.

This must be done with a good wine: a sweet Sauternes, a good port, or a heady Bordeaux. Taste the wine to make sure of its quality. Prepare the Granité a day ahead and then spoon into pretty glasses and decorate with a few mint leaves, if you have them, or a small cut flower or a tiny swirl of lemon peel.

This is clearly not nursery food, so keep it for the finale of a rich meal and serve a plain ice cream to children and timid souls.

You may like to serve the Granité in a large crystal bowl surrounded by poached peaches or pears. Their sweetness, texture, and color will be a pleasant counterpoint to the Granité. Scatter mint leaves on top.

FOR *8* PEOPLE

UTENSILS
Large ice cream mold or a tin mold and some aluminum foil
Large glass bowl or individual parfait, Champagne, or beer glasses

GRANITÉ
1½ cups sugar
¾ cup water
3 orange and 2 lemon peels, grated
Juice of 2 large oranges
Juice of 2 lemons
3 cups Bordeaux or Sauternes or port wine

GARNISH
Several mint leaves
Several tiny cut flowers or 8 little lemon twirls
4 poached peaches or pears

Bring the sugar, water, and grated lemon and orange peels to a boil. Turn off the heat after 5 minutes. Cool. Add the fruit juices and the wine. Stir thoroughly and then pour into a wide shallow dish. Cover with foil and put in the freezer. After 1 hour or so scrape with a fork all the solid icy parts on the bottom and sides of the dish, and stir well. Repeat after another hour. The Granité should be flaky and a little mushy. Cover with foil and leave in the freezer overnight.

Just before serving the Granité, remove the foil and stir once more with your fork so the ice is crisp and even. Spoon the Granité into either parfait, Champagne, or tall Pilsner-type glasses and shape the tops in pretty domes. Plant a twig of mint, a small cut flower, or a tiny swirl of lemon peel on top. Or place poached peaches or pears in the bottom of a shallow dish, put the Granité on top, and scatter mint leaves over both. You might also like to pass a platter of thin cookies.

WINE   The same you have used in the Granité, or Champagne

MADELEINES TIÈDES AUX FRUITS

Lukewarm Madeleine cakes served with an assortment of fruit preparations.

Even if they don't remind you of Proust, even if they don't evoke your grand visits with elderly relatives in nostalgic manors, Madeleines are inspired and inspiring. Composed in the spirit of yesteryear, they speak of lazy afternoons under a linden tree, deep wicker chairs, Chinese tea in fine china cups, mint and verbena infusions, and they are a wonderful response to stress, anguish, angst, or whatever it is you try to banish when you organize your Feast.

Madeleine cakes should always be served lukewarm, with their plump shell-like sides up, along with a tray of assorted preserves, compotes, honeys, or fruit preparations. They can be prepared ahead of time and reheated. If Madeleines are served with dessert, a sweet wine or Champagne is perfect.

FOR 8 PEOPLE

UTENSILS   1 or 2 large tin Madeleine molds (3 sizes are available in house-wares sections of most department stores or in gourmet shops;

the largest shell is best because the Madeleine cakes remain moist and pretty)

MADELEINES

½ cup (1 stick) butter
4 eggs, separated
1 cup sugar
Salt
1¾ cups flour
Peels of 2 small or 1 large lemon, grated

GARNISH

Choose 1 or more of the following
Bowl of sliced oranges marinated in lemon juice and Campari vermouth
then sprinkled with sugar
Bowl of cooked apples and pears sprinkled with a little lemon juice
Mousse au Chocolat Glacée, page 282
Bowl of raspberry and lemon purée, page 268
3 bowls of different preserves gathered on a round tray
Assortment of honey

Soften the butter. Beat the egg yolks and sugar until pale yellow. Add the butter, stirring until totally smooth and light yellow.

Whip the egg whites until firm, then add a little salt. Add the egg whites, spoonful by spoonful, to the yolk mixture, alternating with spoonfuls of flour and lifting with a spatula delicately. Add the lemon peel.

Preheat the oven to 300°. Butter the Madeleine mold thoroughly and pour the batter into the mold. Each Madeleine should be ¾ full.

Bake for 5 minutes, then raise the temperature to 350° and bake 10 minutes more. Unmold.

A few minutes before serving, place the Madeleine cakes on a cookie sheet. Cover them with a sheet of foil and reheat in a 350° oven for a few minutes.

Put the Madeleine cakes on a flat platter lined with a paper doily and serve along with the garnish you have chosen.

WINE

A sweet wine or Champagne

MÉLANGE DE FRUITS

A fresh fruit salad.

A lovely finale after a heavy meal, this can be prepared entirely ahead of time. Whether it is a simple mixture of fresh ripe fruits or a sophisticated dessert enhanced with a mixture of lemon, orange juice, and brandy or a purée of fruits, Mélange de Fruits is delicious. Served with a chilly Champagne it turns into a Mélange de Fruits Royal.

FOR *8* PEOPLE

UTENSILS   Citrus zester, the small flat type that finely grates only the orange part
Large glass bowl

FRUITS   *Choose 12 to 15 ripe fruits to make about 9–10 cups of cut-up fruit.*

In winter and fall:
Melons, oranges, kumquats, tangerines, pineapples, apples, bananas, nuts

In spring or summer:
Peaches, apricots, pears, plums, strawberries, raspberries, blueberries, black currants, red currants, grapes, figs
Mangoes (wonderful all year round)

DRESSINGS:

DRESSING *#1:*   *Juice of 1 lemon*
Juice of 2 oranges
4 tablespoons of cognac, rum, kirsch, or Grand Marnier
$\frac{2}{3}$ cup sugar (approximately; according to taste and to the sweetness of fruit selected)
Several pieces of candied or fresh ginger, thinly shaved
Mint leaves
Bottle of chilled Champagne (optional)

DRESSING *#2:*   *2 ripe mangoes, peeled*
2 very ripe peaches, peeled

Juice of 1 orange
Mint leaves

If you are going to use Dressing #1: Wash, peel, and slice the fresh fruits and place them in a large bowl. Pour the lemon and orange juice on top and add the liquor to taste. Cover the bowl and refrigerate.

Just before serving, sprinkle a little sugar and ginger shavings on top. Bring the bowl to the table, toss gently, add mint leaves, and serve. If you want to add Champagne, bring the cool bottle to the table, open, and pour it on the fruit salad. Don't toss. Serve at once.

If you are going to use Dressing #2: Blend the dressing ingredients in advance in a blender or food processor, then keep refrigerated. A few hours before the party, wash, peel, and slice the fresh fruits. Place all of them except the berries in a large bowl and pour the dressing on top. Dot with the berries and fresh mint leaves. Cover with plastic wrap and refrigerate until ready to serve.

Mélange de Fruits is served with either Panier de Frivolités (page 286) or a platter of cookies.

MOUSSE AU CHOCOLAT GLACÉE

A frozen chocolate mousse meringue with coffee and orange flavorings.

Everybody loves chocolate mousse, but there are two pitfalls to avoid: Some are so light and fluffy that they lack substance. You look forward to them but when they reach your mouth, there is nothing there. On the other hand, some chocolate mousses are rich and heady but so overwhelmingly buttery, chocolatey, or sugary that your liver cries for mercy after the third spoonful.

This frozen version is wonderful and seems to avoid the pitfalls; it is velvety, tasty, yet quite light. It should be prepared one day ahead, then placed in the freezer and taken out a few minutes before serving.

FOR *8* PEOPLE

UTENSILS	Charlotte mold

ORANGE SAUCE
Juice of 4 oranges
⅓ cup honey
5 large oranges, peeled and thinly sliced

MOUSSE
3 tablespoons water
3 tablespoons instant coffee powder
14 ounces German semi-sweet chocolate, cut in pieces
8 egg yolks
1 cup sugar
3 teaspoons grated orange peel
14 egg whites
Pinch of salt
10 tablespoons confectioners' sugar

GARNISH
Bowl of fine chocolate shavings
1 cup fruit purée (page 268), or ⅓ cup whipped cream or ½ cup sour cream
combined with ½ cup heavy cream and 4 tablespoons sugar gently
whipped together or ½ cup of Orange Sauce poured over 4 sliced oranges

To make the sauce: Bring the juice and honey to a boil and pour over the peeled orange slices. Place in the refrigerator until ready to serve.

To make the mousse: Heat the water and instant coffee powder in a thick-bottomed saucepan. Add the chocolate pieces and heat over a low flame, stirring until smooth. Turn off the heat and set aside. Beat the egg yolks with the sugar until the mixture turns a pale yellow. Add to the coffee and chocolate mixture, stirring for a few minutes. Grate the orange peel into the pan. Taste to see if you should add more orange peel or some salt.

Beat the egg whites with a pinch of salt. When they turn white and frothy, add the confectioners' sugar and keep beating until the egg whites are firm and solid white.

With a spatula fold the egg whites into the lukewarm chocolate and eggs mixture, lifting gently as you draw the bottom to the top.

Pour into a lightly oiled charlotte mold and cover tightly with waxed paper or pour into a tightly closed ice cream mold and place it in the freezer, where it should remain for at least 24 hours.

Just before you are ready to serve dessert, remove the Chocolate Mousse from the freezer and dip the bottom of the mold into a pan of hot water for a few seconds. Place a large serving plate over the mold and, holding tight to the sides of the charlotte mold and the edge of the plate, turn the plate and mold over in a decisive movement. The Mousse should slide out of its mold easily.

Sprinkle the surface of the dome with chocolate shavings and pour some fruit purée or lightly whipped cream or a mixture of slightly beaten sour cream and heavy cream or some peeled oranges covered with light honey sauce all around the Chocolate Mousse.

If your meal is delayed, cover the unmolded Mousse with a large bowl and return it to the freezer until ready to serve.

OEUFS À LA NEIGE ET AUX FRUITS

Poached pears, covered with a light custard, topped with soft meringues, and sprinkled with caramel and bitter chocolate shavings.

Some like to refer to Oeufs à la Neige as nursery food, but I always think of this dessert as *faux naïf,* a falsely naïve one. There is indeed nothing babyish or overly simple in this dessert as each guest goes from delight to delight, plunging his spoon into the beautiful snow bowl, the crunchy chocolate and caramel top, the fluffy meringue balls, the silky custard, and the mellow pear.

This can all be prepared ahead of time. You may prefer to flavor the custard with a little orange water and the pears with a little Calvados brandy, but if you would rather omit them, the flavor of a vanilla bean in the custard is also quite lovely.

FOR *8* PEOPLE

UTENSILS   Wide skillet or saucepan
Large glass or china bowl

MERINGUES	*8 egg whites*
	¾ cup sugar
CUSTARD	*2⅔ cups milk*
	8 egg yolks
	1 cup sugar
	1 tablespoon orange blossom water or *1 vanilla bean* or *1 tablespoon vanilla extract*
PEARS	*4 large pears, peeled and sliced,* or *4 large canned pears, drained*
	2 tablespoons butter
	1 tablespoon Calvados brandy (optional)
GARNISH	*Piece of semi-sweet German chocolate (to yield about 3 tablespoons of shavings)*
	½ cup sugar
	2 tablespoons water
	Several drops of vinegar or *lemon juice*
	½ teaspoon butter

To make the meringues: Bring a wide skillet or saucepan of salty water to a boil. Meanwhile, beat the egg whites until stiff. Add ¾ cup of sugar and continue to beat slowly for a few seconds. Lower the flame and keep the water simmering. Slide the egg whites spoonful by spoonful into the hot water, which should not reach the boiling point. After 5 minutes use a wide spoon to turn the meringues over. With a large slotted spoon or skimmer remove them from the water to a wide tray placed so that it will drain. You will have to make the meringues in several batches.

To make the custard: Rinse a saucepan with cold water, leaving a few drops of water at the bottom to avoid scorching. Add the milk and bring to a boil. In a bowl beat the egg yolks and cup of sugar until they become pale yellow. Add a little hot milk and keep stirring with a wooden spoon. Add more milk and then pour the whole mixture back into the saucepan, stirring—the mixture should not boil at any time. Stir with a wooden spoon on a low flame until the custard thickens and coats the spoon. Place this pan in a pan of cold water and stir for a few minutes to cool the custard. Add the orange blossom water, vanilla bean, or vanilla extract.

To make the pears: Cook them in the butter until soft or drain the canned pears and use them. Place the pears in the bottom of a wide and pretty bowl, sprinkle with a little Calvados if wanted, and pour the cooled custard over them. Place the meringues delicately in the center. Cover with plastic wrap and leave in the refrigerator.

Using a potato peeler shave the piece of softened chocolate. Place the shavings in a small bowl and cover with plastic wrap. Keep refrigerated. Place the sugar and water in a saucepan and heat slowly, stirring with a wooden spoon. When the mixture starts boiling, add the vinegar. When the sugar caramelizes and turns brown add the butter and turn off the heat. It will harden. Set aside for later.

About 5 minutes before serving the dessert, reheat the caramel on a medium flame. Take the dessert bowl out of the refrigerator. Sprinkle the meringue balls with the chocolate shavings and dribble the hot caramel over them. Serve at once.

WINE   A sweet white wine, a Banyuls wine, any commercial *vin cuit* in which cognac and a little sugar have been added, or a homemade orange wine.

A pitcher of cold water is also a good idea.

PANIER DE FRIVOLITÉS DE TANTE YVETTE

Crisp fritters.

These are *the* festive dessert par excellence. Traditionally served at carnival time and for Christmas, weddings, Christenings, Sunday meals, and all the family Feasts, they help celebrate the past as well as the ages to come. Frivolités is an exceptionally pretty dish, made for important occasions.

These may be called Merveilles (wonders) or Oreillettes (little ears) or Frivolités (little frivolous goodies) according to the region they come from. They can be fried in shortening, olive oil, corn oil, peanut oil, lard or goose fat. The dough may be prepared with flour, eggs — or yolks only or whipped egg whites — with an addition of oil, butter, or no fat at all, and flavored with lemon peel, cognac, Grand Marnier, or orange blossom water.

My Aunt Yvette is living proof of what an organized mind can deliver when she prepares this traditional dessert, and there is nothing frivolous in the way she deals with Frivolités. She goes about kneading the dough, heating the oil, and cutting strange geometric figures in record time. Then she demands total attention and total efficiency from her husband as he sprinkles sugar on both sides of each crisp, ethereal Frivolité, shakes them of their excess sugar, piles them into a wide flat blasket as soon as they have cooled, keeping up with her most extraordinary pace and even taking time — it isn't for fun but out of duty — to nibble on an occasional broken or twisted Frivolité and ponder briefly its texture and taste to make sure quality and traditions have once more been kept.

This is not an improvised dish. You must prepare the dough two hours or so ahead, own a good frying pan or a large skillet, and count on about one hour to fry. A child, a friend, a husband, a wife — two, even three people — are welcome to dry the Frivolités on paper towels and sprinkle them with sugar while you attend to the frying.

In France most country cooks have a special smooth, unmarked bottle instead of a wooden rolling pin for spreading the dough. They think the glass, its weight and coolness, makes for paper-thin Frivolités, but a regular pin is, of course, perfectly efficient. Frivolités are traditionally served in a big basket (generally a wide and flat linen basket) lined with big white napkins. Wide white ribbons are often gathered in bows on the basket handles for a truly festive touch. Make sure you prepare a huge stack of Frivolités. They are so light, so crunchy, so delicious that they are nibbled very quickly. For a grand finale, serve Frivolités with Oeufs à la Neige (page 284), Poires, Pruneaux, Oranges au Vin Rouge et aux Épices (page 289), or Mousse au Chocolat Glacée (page 282). But Frivolités by themselves are most delectable. The difficulty lies in knowing how to stop nibbling them.

FOR 8 PEOPLE

UTENSILS   Heavy skillet or electric fry pan (a wide surface to allow many
Frivolités to be fried at one time but not a deep fryer)

INGREDIENTS   *1 teaspoon yeast*
2 tablespoons lukewarm water
4 cups all-purpose white flour (hard wheat)
2 eggs
1 tablespoon orange blossom water
1 teaspoon finely grated lemon peel
Cooking oil or shortening
Crystallized sugar

You can prepare the dough on the morning of the Feast and leave it in a cool place, covered with a piece of cloth, or you can prepare it a day ahead if that is easier.

Stir the yeast in the lukewarm water and wait a few minutes, according to the directions on the package. Put the flour in a bowl. Make a well in the center and stir in the dissolved yeast and the eggs. Mix vigorously until smooth. Knead for a few minutes — the dough should be quite elastic. Cover with a wet towel and let it rest for about 2 hours. Then add the orange blossom water and lemon peel, kneading for a minute and adding a little flour or a little cold water so you have a supple dough. Let it rest, covered, for 1 hour more.

Sprinkle a little flour on a table top or counter and spread the dough paper-thin, or as thin as you possibly can, stretching as you roll the pin.

Cut the dough into uneven pieces, whichever comes easiest: triangles 3 by 3 inches, strips 3 by 2 inches, squares 3 by 3 inches. Then with a sharp knife make a 1-inch slit in the center of each Frivolité for "breathing" as it fries.

Heat the oil until it is very hot but do not let it reach the smoking point. Add a few Frivolités. After frying a batch, let the temperature return to the same level before frying the next batch. Do not crowd the pan. Keep skimming off the bits of dough or crumbs that appear on top of the fat. Have a large supply of paper towels to drain the crisp Frivolités. Since the dough has no butter, oil, or sugar, it will not absorb fat, unlike rich doughs.

Cook several small batches, remembering that they should not be too close together while they cook. Be careful at all times not to overheat the oil. The Frivolités must be "surprised" by the hot oil and turn crisp and golden in the process, but they do so very quickly, so remain very attentive. Turn them once, cook 1–2 seconds more, then place them on a tray lined with paper towels. Sprinkle on both sides with crystallized sugar. Shake off the excess sugar and place the Frivolités in a clean linen-lined basket.

When all are done, cover with a clean towel and keep in a dark place or tightly closed container until ready to serve. These are best eaten the same day they are made, but they will keep for 4 or 5 days in a container.

Note: Sometimes a small decanter of good brandy, Calvados, cognac, or grappa, is passed around the table so each guest may sprinkle a drop as he bites into the crisp Frivolité. Timing and a good hand are essential here so the Frivolité will have no time to turn soggy.

WINE

Serve with a good sparkling wine, a Champagne, or a sweet and mellow dessert wine

POIRES, PRUNEAUX, ORANGES AU VIN ROUGE ET AUX ÉPICES

Pears, prunes, and oranges cooked in red wine with fresh oranges and spices.

This is a racy, pungent, spirited dessert, perfect to conclude a rich meal.

Prepared a day ahead, the fruit will cool in its own juices and be served in its pretty glass, porcelain, or earthenware bowl with a platter of thin cookies or a basket of Frivolités.

FOR 8 PEOPLE

UTENSIL

Large glass, porcelain, or earthenware bowl

INGREDIENTS

1 cup raisins, preferably large black Spanish or California type, washed
20 large pitted prunes (approximately)
9–10 small thick-skinned pears, peeled but not cored, with stem on

1 quart full-bodied red wine
2 cups sugar
1 teaspoon black peppercorns
Pinch of grated nutmeg
Pinch of cinnamon
1 teaspoon coriander
2 cloves
4 bay leaves
Juice of 2 lemons
Juice of 1 orange
3 large pieces of orange and lemon peels
Oranges, peeled and thinly sliced
5 tablespoons red currant jelly
2 orange peels, finely grated
1 tablespoon grated fresh or ground ginger

Place the raisins and prunes in lukewarm water for 1–2 hours. Place the peeled pears, stem up, in a saucepan. Pour in the red wine and add the sugar, spices, lemon and orange juices, and peels. Cook on a low flame for 10 minutes. Drain the prunes and raisins, add to the saucepan, and simmer 15 minutes more. Add the peeled, thinly sliced oranges and red currant jelly and turn off the heat. Let the fruits cool in their poaching liquid.

Place the prunes and raisins in the bottom of a pretty glass bowl. Place the pears, stem up, on top. Add the orange slices around the edges and set aside at room temperature.

Bring the poaching liquid to a boil and reduce for a few minutes on a high flame. Add the 2 orange peels, finely grated, and the grated ginger. The juices should become a little syrupy. Check the taste and add more ginger if needed.

Remove the large pieces of orange and lemon peels and pour the syrup with the bay leaves over the cooked fruit. Cover and refrigerate.

Remove the bowl of fruit from the refrigerator just before serving. You may pass warm Madeleines (page 279), a basket of Frivolités (page 286), or a plate of cookies along with the bowl of cooked fruit.

WINE   A sweet white dessert wine, or, of course, Champagne

TARTE AU CITRON ET AUX AMANDES

A tart and delicate lemon and almond pie.

This gourmand dessert is so delicate yet so tart that it is a perfect way to end a "serious" festive meal. You must not be shy about the large quantity of lemon juice; it will make all the difference.

The mixture of lemons and almonds is traditional in Provence and along the Riviera. The two ingredients have grown there for centuries and are used in a variety of refreshing and pungent regional desserts.

I like to serve this tart with a brilliant raspberry purée; both are as pleasing to the eye as they are to the palate.

FOR ABOUT *10* PEOPLE

UTENSILS
12-inch tart ring with removable base
Lemon peeler
Several dry beans or pebbles

PASTRY
2 cups all-purpose flour, sifted
¼ cup ground almonds
½ cup sugar
¼ teaspoon salt
1–2 teaspoons finely grated lemon rind
½ cup unsalted butter, cut into small cubes
1 egg yolk
3–4 tablespoons ice cold water

FILLING
4 eggs
½ cup sugar
2 tablespoons finely grated lemon rind (about 2 lemons) — retain the juice
1 cup unsalted butter, melted and cooled
1 cup coarsely ground unpeeled toasted almonds

GARNISH
2 tablespoons confectioners' sugar
2–3 cups raspberry purée, page 268

To prepare the pastry: Combine the flour, almonds, sugar, salt, and lemon rind in a large bowl. Lightly rub the butter into the flour, using your fingertips, until the mixture resembles coarse cornmeal. Mix the egg yolk with 3 tablespoons of the ice water and stir into the crumbled mixture. The dough should form a soft ball. Add the remaining tablespoon of water if all the ingredients are not well combined. Wrap the dough in plastic wrap and refrigerate for at least 2 hours or overnight.

Preheat the oven to 425°. Roll the dough out to form a circle large enough for the tart ring. Line the buttered tart ring with the dough and refrigerate for 30 minutes. (*Note:* It is essential to butter the tart ring.) Prick the dough with the tines of a fork. Line the dough with waxed paper and beans or pebbles and cook for 5 minutes. Set aside to cool.

To prepare the filling. Preheat the oven to 350°.

Beat the eggs, sugar, and lemon rind together until pale in color and very fluffy. Slowly beat in the lemon juice and then the melted butter. Gently fold in the almonds with a spatula and transfer the filling to the prepared tart ring. Set the tart ring on a baking sheet and cook for 30 minutes, or until the filling is firm. Set aside to cool.

Prepare the raspberry purée according to the directions in the recipe.

When you are ready to serve: Sprinkle the cooled tart with the confectioners' sugar and cut into wedges. Spread a little raspberry purée on the bottom of each plate. Place a slice of tart on top and pour a little purée all around before handing it to each guest.

You may prefer to cut the Tarte au Citron into wedges and pass the platter around the table along with a bowl of raspberry purée.

WINE   A sweet white wine or Champagne

TARTE TATIN AUX POIRES ET AUX POMMES

Warm caramelized apple and pear upside-down tart served with a bowl of whipped cream and ginger.

This is a sumptuous dessert with a long history. It was apparently invented by three old maids who ran the Hotel Tatin et Terminus's little restaurant in Lamotte-Beuvron, a tiny village not far from Paris. They were ambitious and resourceful, and since they did not have a proper oven, they had to improvise and cook their tart upside down on top of the stove.

Their Tarte Tatin, a true creation, became so famous that Maxim's restaurant quickly decided to obtain the recipe. A cook-spy disguised as a gardener was sent to the premises. He came back with the secret, and it has been on Maxim's menu ever since.

The recipe that follows is a variation on the famous Tarte Tatin, but I use pears along with apples for a more delicate texture. Because these fruits truly enhance each other, I also add quince whenever I can find it.

The problem is that one tart is not quite enough for eight people, so I suggest baking two. If any leftovers are found, who will complain?

Since the fruit is caramelized in a skillet, no special mold is needed to bake this tart. Any Pyrex, copper, earthenware, or aluminum mold will do, although there is a special copper mold for Tarte Tatin. If you own one, you can use it (whenever you are not preparing Tarte Tatin) in the center of your dining table filled with anemones or fruits.

You can prepare both tarts and the whipped cream ahead of time and gently reheat the tart for a few minutes before serving it.

FOR *8* PEOPLE

UTENSILS   Two 9-inch round tart pans

PASTRY
2 cups all-purpose flour, sifted
2 tablespoons sugar
1 teaspoon salt
8 tablespoons chilled butter
3 tablespoons vegetable oil
6 tablespoons cold water

FILLING
2½ pounds pears
2½ pounds apples: Russet or Granny Smith
½ cup plus 4 tablespoons butter

3 cups sugar
Juice of 3 lemons
1 lemon peel, finely grated

GARNISH   *3 cups chilled whipping cream*
6 tablespoons powdered sugar
3 tablespoons finely chopped candied ginger

The dough must rest about 1 hour, so prepare it first. Place the flour, sugar, salt, and butter in a large bowl. Rub flour and butter together between the palms of your dry hands until it feels crumbly, like coarse sand. Add the oil and cold water rapidly and press into a ball. The dough must not be sticky. Place on a floured work surface. Pressing the pastry with the heel of your hand, push it bit by bit away from you in a quick motion. When the flour and oil are well blended, gather into a ball and knead it for a second. Sprinkle with flour, wrap in plastic wrap, and place in the freezer for about 40 minutes to firm while the fruit is cooking.

Peel, core, and quarter the pears and apples. Heat the butter in the skillet and add the fruit. (You may have to cook them in 2 or 3 batches.) Sprinkle with sugar, lemon juice, and grated lemon peel. Cook on a high flame, uncovered, for 15 minutes. Butter the tart pans. Remove the fruit with a slotted spoon and place in the tart pans. Bring the leftover juice in the skillet to a boil and cook until the liquid is brown and syrupy—about 5 minutes. Pour it on the cooked fruit. If the apples are watery, this process will be slower.

Meanwhile, whip the whipping cream with the sugar and stir the ginger into it very delicately.

Preheat the oven to 370°. Take the pastry out of the refrigerator. Roll the dough quickly. Place it on a floured work surface and beat it with a rolling pin if it is too hard to handle. Knead it for a few minutes, then cut it into 2 balls.

Place the rolling pin in the center of the first ball and roll back and forth firmly. Lift the dough, turn it once, and continue rolling. Sprinkle a little flour as you go. When you have a circle about 14 inches in diameter and $\frac{1}{8}$ inch thick, reverse the dough on the rolling pin and unroll it over the tart pan with the cooked apples and pears. Take the edge of the dough and slide it inside the dish, between the fruit and the side of the dish. With the tip of a knife cut a few holes in the dough so the steam can escape. Proceed with the second tart.

Place the 2 tart pans in the lower third of your oven and bake for about 30 minutes, until the pastry turns brown.

If you are ready for dinner, unmold on a serving dish. If not, take out of the oven, cover with a piece of oiled foil, and set aside.

Thirty minutes before serving dessert, preheat the oven to 350°. Take the prepared Tarte Tatin out of the refrigerator. Place the tarts on the middle shelf of the oven for a few minutes. Remove from the oven; they should be lukewarm. Place a wide platter on top of a tart and in a decisive movement, holding the edges of the mold and the platter firmly, turn each tart upside down. The tops should be caramelized and brown, and the fruit should have a moist but consistent texture. It should not be runny. Take the ginger-flavored whipped cream from the refrigerator and bring it to the table along with the 2 warm tarts. Use both a spatula and a deep spoon to serve.

WINE   A sweet white wine or Champagne

ACCOMPANIMENTS

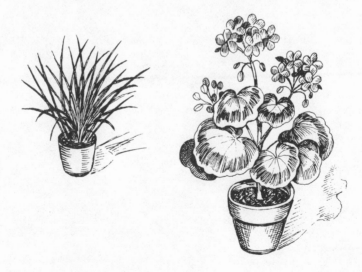

BROCCOLI PURÉE

2 pounds broccoli
4 tablespoons cream
Salt
Freshly ground pepper

Boil the broccoli for 10 minutes. Drain. Purée in a food processor. Stir in the cream, salt, and pepper (to taste). Blend until smooth.

CABBAGE PURÉE

2 heads of cabbage, core removed, quartered
2 tablespoons butter
Salt
Freshly ground pepper

Blanch the cabbage until tender, about 20 minutes. Drain. Purée the cabbage in a food processor, then add the butter, salt and pepper (to taste). Blend until butter is well mixed in.

CELERIAC PURÉE

2 large celeriac, peeled and quartered
3 large potatoes, peeled
3 tablespoons heavy cream or *2 tablespoons butter*
Salt
Freshly ground pepper
Milk (optional)

Prepare the potatoes and the celeriac and cook them for about 30 minutes in a pan of salty water until tender. Drain. Pass through a blender or a food processor. Stir in the cream or the butter. Add salt and pepper to taste. Reheat on a low flame, stirring, and add a little milk if mixture is too dry.

FENNEL PURÉE

5 fennel bulbs
2 potatoes, peeled
3 tablespoons heavy cream or *2 tablespoons butter*
Salt
Freshly ground pepper
1 tablespoon fennel feathery leaves, cut with scissors

Wash then trim the bulbs of any tough fibrous parts. Quarter them. Cook bulbs and potatoes in salted water for 20 minutes. Drain. Pass through blender or food processor. Stir in cream (or butter), salt, pepper. Sprinkle fennel leaves over dish just before serving.

GREEN SALADS

Whether served as a first course (Pissenlits aux Lardons, page 65) or as a refreshing accompaniment, tossed green salads are always welcome at festive meals.

Prepared ahead of time—washed, trimmed, and kept in the refrigerator—they are seasoned and tossed at the last minute. Remember that you should be "generous with oil, a miser with vinegar, and a wise man with salt" when you prepare a green salad but you may definitely be bolder when you add shallots, mustard, or herbs.

GREENS   You need about four cups of trimmed greens for eight people. The variety offered in most U.S. markets is immense: Bibb lettuce, loose leaf lettuce, red leaf lettuce, Boston lettuce, escarole, watercress (making sure there are no yellow leaves), endive, romaine, young chard, young spinach, young dandelion greens, arugula, and young chicory.

Greens should be trimmed of rough stems and tougher outer or discolored leaves. Separate the endive leaves and rinse carefully several times under very cold water. Tear them by hand into bite-size pieces, wrap in a thick kitchen towel or paper towel or turn in a salad spinner to dry. Keep salad greens in the lower part of the refrigerator until ready to use.

You can mix several types of greens in one tossed salad. Chicory, arugula, young dandelions, watercress, tender spinach, and young chard are wonderful with a dressing of bacon and warm vinegar (page 65) or a vinaigrette dressing with mustard. They can be served with garlicky bread crusts—cut lengthwise from a French loaf, preferably in two-inch-long pieces—or thin rounds of bread, oven-dried or stale and then rubbed with garlic.

Escarole cut in small bite-size pieces can be seasoned with a vinegar and oil dressing, a few fork-mashed anchovy fillets, and a little garlic for an invigorating salad.

Chicory and Bibb lettuce or watercress and endives will be delicious with a dressing of olive oil, fresh lemon juice, and Dijon-style mustard sprinkled with fresh herbs.

Watercress, arugula, and endives also will make a refreshing accompaniment to a hearty dish when it is seasoned with vinaigrette flavored with some mustard.

Endives and escarole, seasoned with a very mustardy vinaigrette and garnished with halved walnuts or quartered hard-boiled eggs, makes a lively accompaniment or a good first-course salad.

Boston and romaine lettuce can be seasoned with vinaigrette and fresh chervil and parsley or a small amount of tarragon.

Field lettuce, also known as lamb's tongues, corn lettuce, and mâche, is still somewhat rare in the markets although it is easy to find growing wild, and many gardeners find it easy to grow. It is a delicate fall green that must be washed several times and trimmed carefully. This very fragile green should have a light dressing and be tossed very gently.

Green salads are best served in a very large glass bowl or in a long shallow dish so you can toss without bruising the greens or spilling the dressing. Whenever you serve endives place them like the spokes of a wheel around the dish or your bowl, then add the watercress or other greens in the center. Sprinkle with herbs, such as mint and basil, crumble hard-boiled egg yolks on top, cover with plastic wrap, and keep refrigerated until used. Or you may wish to cut each endive leaf crosswise before adding it to other greens.

An hour or so before you serve dinner take the greens and dressings out of the refrigerator. Pour dressing in the bottom of the salad bowl, cross the serving fork and spoon on top, and arrange the greens above so they do not come in contact with the dressing. Sprinkle herbs, walnuts, or croutons on top. The salad will be tossed just before you are ready to bring it to the dining table. There is no such thing as usable leftover tossed salad, so discard whatever remains after the meal.

DRESSING	For eight people you need about ten tablespoons of dressing.
VINAIGRETTE	This is the freshest and easiest of dressings, and it may also be the best with most of the dishes in this book.
INGREDIENTS	*4 tablespoons red wine vinegar* or *fresh lemon juice* *1 cup first-pressed, extra-vierge olive oil (available in supermarkets throughout the country)*

1 tablespoon salt
½–1 teaspoon freshly ground pepper

Stir well to blend and keep in a closed jar.

You may like to toss one or more of the following ingredients into vinaigrette dressing at the last moment:

2 tablespoons chopped fresh herbs: flat parsley, dill, coriander, basil, mint, savory, chives, chervil, or tarragon (in small quantity)
2–3 tablespoons Dijon-style mustard
2 garlic cloves, peeled and crushed
3 tablespoons Roquefort, mashed with a little cream and a drop of cognac, pepper, and sherry vinegar (use with escarole or any tough leaf greens)
3 tablespoons finely minced shallots
Anchovy fillets mashed with a fork
Croutons (bread rounds or pieces of crust, 2 by 1 inch, fried or oven-dried), sprinkled with olive oil and Parmesan or rubbed with a garlic clove
Walnut halves or coarsely chopped walnuts
Crumbled hard-boiled egg yolks
Hard-boiled egg whites and egg yolks, finely diced

RICE

1½ cups raw long grain rice
2 quarts water
3 bay leaves
2 twigs of fresh thyme or 2 teaspoons dry thyme
2 tablespoons butter
2 teaspoons salt
Freshly ground pepper

Pour the rice in a large pan of boiling salted water, stirring with a fork. Add the herbs and boil uncovered for 15 to 20 minutes. Rinse under lukewarm water. Discard herbs. Stir in butter, fluffing the rice lightly with a fork. Season with salt and pepper and serve.

To reheat, dot top with butter, cover loosely with foil, and place in a lukewarm oven.

Note: About ¼ cup of raw rice per person is enough.

INDEX

A

About the Author

Mireille Johnston was born in Nice, educated in France and America, and now divides her time between the two countries. She is the author of *The Cuisine of the Rose: Classical French Cooking from Burgundy and Lyonnais*, *Cuisine of the Sun: Classical Recipes from Nice and Provence*, *Central Park Country: A Tune Within Us*, and various articles in France and America. She is the translator of the film script for *The Sorrow and the Pity* by Marcel Ophuls and Henri Lefèvre's book, *Criticism of Everyday Life*. She is married and has two daughters, Margaret-Brooke and Elizabeth.